Seers, Witches
and Psychics on Screen

Seers, Witches and Psychics on Screen

*An Analysis of Women
Visionary Characters in
Recent Television and Film*

KARIN BEELER

McFarland & Company, Inc., Publishers
Jefferson, North Carolina, and London

LIBRARY OF CONGRESS CATALOGUING-IN-PUBLICATION DATA

Beeler, Karin, 1963–
    Seers, witches and psychics on screen : an analysis of women
visionary characters in recent television and film / Karin Beeler.
    p.   cm.
    Includes bibliographical references and index.

    ISBN 978-0-7864-3346-9
    softcover : 50# alkaline paper ∞

    1. Women prophets on television.   2. Witches on television.
3. Women psychics on television.   I. Title.
PN1992.8.W65B44   2008
791.45'675 — dc22   2008036567
British Library cataloguing data are available

On the cover: Patricia Arquette as Allison Dubois in *Medium*
(NBC) Season 2 ©NBC/Photofest; Doorway ©2008 Shutterstock.

Manufactured in the United States of America

*McFarland & Company, Inc., Publishers
  Box 611, Jefferson, North Carolina 28640
  www.mcfarlandpub.com*

To my daughter Amelia
and her girl power

Acknowledgments

My research for this book began a few years ago as several television series about mediums, psychics and women with visions first aired in the United States and in the United Kingdom. Shortly thereafter, I presented papers on the topic at a number of conferences and am grateful for having had the opportunity to do so.

Substantial work on this book was completed during my research leave from the University of Northern British Columbia. I would like to thank the university for conference travel support and for seed grant funding which allowed me to travel to the British Film Institute in London to research British television programs and other material for this project. The staff at the BFI research viewing service was incredibly helpful.

I appreciate the invaluable research assistance provided by Lisa Emmerton, an English M.A. student at the University of Northern British Columbia, whose own work in the field of television studies will undoubtedly make a positive contribution to research.

I want to thank Michael Lamport, co-producer of *Rescue Mediums*, and his staff for helping me to acquire DVD copies of *Rescue Mediums* episodes as well as transcripts of the programs. He also supplied the publicity photos of Jackie Dennison and Christine Hamlett, the "rescue mediums," for inclusion in this book.

Kathy Plett at the College of New Caledonia in Prince George worked on the index, and I appreciate her assistance with this facet. Stan Beeler, my husband, deserves a huge thank you for his ability to locate and retrieve the most recent television series — his technological know-how never ceases to amaze me. I continue to remain grateful to my colleague Dr. Dee Horne and her family for their support throughout the years.

A special thank you goes to my mother, Elisabeth Kondratzky, for many hours of childcare, which freed up time for me to work long hours on this book. Finally, thank you Amelia, for visiting the British Museum in London with Daddy while I did research at the BFI.

Table of Contents

Table of Contents

Part 3. Investigating the Dead: Mediums and Psychic Detectives

Introduction

*Seers, Witches and Psychics on Screen: An Analysis of Women Vision-
ary Characters in Recent Television and Film* addresses the pervasive representation of women with unique visionary abilities in postfeminist
television and film from the 1990s to the present. Television series such
as *Joan of Arcadia, Wonderfalls, Firefly, Angel, Charmed, Hex, Tru Calling, Afterlife, Medium, Ghost Whisperer, Rescue Mediums* and *Psychic
Investigators* and films like *Ghost, The Gift, Serenity* and *Premonition* attest
to the prominence of the seer and the psychic in visual culture. This book
examines how these television shows and films reflect third wave feminist or postfeminist (and postmodern) ideas including an emphasis on
negotiation or mediation of the female visionary who is the protagonist
of these works in many cases. These women experience shifting or hybrid
identities and also serve as a means of advocating cultural, sexual, or
social diversity, thus challenging a narrow definition of what it means to
be "normal." In addition to their special psychic or visionary abilities,
this diversity can take the form of alternative family structures or relationships that do not resemble the "nuclear" family. Women of vision in
television and film articulate resistance to patriarchal attitudes, but also
suggest the need to subvert the polarization of men and women and the
polarization of science or reason with the inner world of visionary, mystical experience.

Whether they take the form of seer figures, witches, mediums or
women with the ability to see or know the future, these "women of
vision" suggest unique ways of constructing female heroes as saviors in
a postfeminist era. While visionary power is ordinarily perceived as a
"passive" power, these women demonstrate agency with their abilities.
This book also examines these women and their visionary power in the

context of a "third space" or alternate space. The concept was originally developed by cultural theorist Homi Bhabha to discuss cultural hybridity or the kind of alternate space that post-colonial cultures inhabit (*The Location of Culture*). However, it is an effective term to apply to women with visionary powers, since they often live in a hybrid world, acting as mediators between different worlds of experience (e.g., the world of the living and the world of the dead). I analyze their abilities in relation to ideas expressed by third wave feminist criticism, sometimes also called postfeminism.

The main corpus of this study consists of American, Canadian and British television programs and selected films from the 1990s to the present. The primary "genre" comprising this study is that of telefantasy (or fantasy television) and fantasy film, although the latest international fashion of reality television series that incorporate supernatural phenomena (e.g., *Psychic Investigators* and *Rescue Mediums*) also receives some consideration. What this book does not claim to do is provide an exhaustive survey of all kinds of reality-based or documentary-style television about psychic phenomena, nor does it mention examples of brief psychic moments experienced by characters in a particular series. The book addresses selected fan responses to several television series in order to provide views of the heroines in postfeminist television series, but concentrates more on the television and film narratives themselves than on television fan culture, as this could easily form a separate study. The television series that comprise the core of this examination include women of vision as their primary characters or heroines at the "center" of the series, and this is one of the reasons that this phenomenon is so significant. The female psychic is not merely a clichéd spectacle; she forms an integral part of the narratives of these programs or films.

While there are television shows and films that depict men with psychic abilities (*Seeing Things* [1981]; *The Sixth Sense* [1999]; *The Dead Zone* [2002–2007][1]), the phenomenon is not as pervasive as for women-centered series. Perhaps this is because even in recent series, male heroes often follow the trajectory of the traditional warrior figure or action hero who is "out there in the world" (Campbell, *The Power of Myth*, 153), relying on physical strength or skills in his encounters with the unknown. (Even the recent series *Heroes* sustains the image of the male warrior-action

2

hero through the figure of Hiro.) Historically and in myth, women have often been linked to "the home" (Campbell, *The Power of Myth*, 153) environment and to inner strength or intuition (e.g., women's intuition). The knowledge systems of men and women have also been articulated differently. The knowledge perpetuated by men has been articulated in the context of reason or the rational mind while women, as Mary Wollstonecraft pointed out in *A Vindication of the Rights of Woman* (1975), were not treated "like rational creatures" but treated "as if they were in a state of perpetual childhood, unable to stand alone" (141). Women with unique knowledge in the form of mystical visions were viewed as witches or as "mad." For example, Katharine Hodgkin indicates that "the witch, the female prophet, and the madwoman" may be related (219). All three see or experience "something that is neither seen nor experienced by others, that puts [their] perceptions at odds with those of others around [them]" (Hodgkin, 222). The ancient binary opposition between the visionary realm and the rational mind, however, is subverted in many postfeminist television series or films that depict visionary women, especially in the psychic investigation programs where the scientific skills of crime investigation interface with the spiritual realm of the mediums, thus creating a hybrid third space for these women of vision to create a new vision of a heroine who is no longer simply relegated to the space of the "irrational." Consequently, what is considered "normal" varies according to one's situation or particular context.

While this study recognizes the prominence of women of vision as depicted in television and selected films since the rise of third wave feminism, the chapter discussions do not idealize these women as heroines. These psychics, seers and women with the gift of special sight still face challenges and share some of the limitations of their mythic or historical prototypes, Cassandra and Joan of Arc: they may be viewed as mad or their legitimacy as women who have access to the supernatural may be questioned. However, the erosion of the binary opposition between intuition and reason or spirituality and science that takes place in these recent television shows and films, reveals how these heroines who negotiate or cross between worlds of experience offer a diversity of models for women as friends, helpers or savior figures. These women use what has been traditionally conceived of as a passive power in an active way.

Published Works on Women of Vision

Other studies have considered women with supernatural abilities. For example, Ruffles' *Ghost Images: Cinema of the Afterlife* focuses on the ghost in film and includes a few pages that discuss the "medium" in film. Robin Blaetz's *Visions of the Maid: Joan of Arc in American Film and Culture* addresses the importance of Joan of Arc, but does not cover two recent television series on this important phenomenon. Studies of visual culture have contributed to the discussion of a specific telefantasy series. Rhonda Wilcox (*Why Buffy Matters*) and Early and Kennedy (*Athena's Daughters*) have examined the topic of women warriors on television. Schofield Clark has considered the general topic of teen audiences and popular culture (*From Angels to Aliens: Teenagers, the Media, and the Supernatural*). However, none of the above studies emphasizes the significance of women as visionary figures or women who occupy a kind of "third space" or alternate space in the context of postfeminism or third wave feminism, and what this might suggest for a range of women (young women, mothers, single women). Why has this image of the "woman of vision" become so pervasive in recent television series? Some of the emphasis may be the result of Western culture's search for different models of heroism for women to serve as an alternative to the more limited image of the male warrior (Taylor, 133). While some of the female characters in these series (River in *Firefly*, Phoebe in *Charmed*) still engage in warrior-like activities (*Buffy* the slayer-visionary in *Buffy the Vampire Slayer* is a key postfeminist example), the use of visions serves as an important mythic or fantastic alternative.

These series also search for ways of reconfiguring "old" ideas in a new fashion, often in the context of third wave feminism (Baumgardner and Richards; Heywood and Drake; Henry). This is especially true in the depiction of the seer as a mother figure and through portrayals of the seer as mad. My study illustrates the liberating aspect of telefantasy programs and films with fantasy content that depict the "woman of vision" while also pointing out some of the social limitations experienced by female visionaries. Seers from a range of different social groups including mothers, teenagers and members of groups traditionally marginalized because of sexual orientation, race, class, or (dis)ability, are analyzed in this study. This book also provides some consideration of the role of the national context for these television works and films (American, British, Canadian) while recognizing that visionary women in television and film have become a transnational phenomenon. Analyzing brief fan responses to several television series (*Charmed, Angel, Firefly*) will also contribute to an understanding of how viewers respond to these new heroines in postfeminist television.

A component of the study which receives some consideration is how these women with extraordinary visionary abilities are represented in different national contexts (British television, American television and film, and Canadian television series) while also reflecting a transnational interest in the phenomenon of visionary or psychic abilities. These series and films reflect cultural, gender and social anxieties pertinent to each nation. The American series *Ghost Whisperer* reflects the fear of air travel in the age of 9/11 (*Ghost Whisperer* 1.21; 1.22). *Afterlife*, a U.K. series, addresses the impact of train disasters on the British consciousness and also depicts the fears of the childless, single woman in a postfeminist era. *Medium*, another American series, portrays the challenges experienced by a "working" mother. *Wonderfalls*, an American-Canadian joint venture set in Niagara Falls, USA, but filmed in Niagara Falls, Canada (Bredin), crosses national boundaries and incorporates depictions of the seer and North American Indian culture in the context of cultural diversity and women's experiences (Warn). American series such as *Angel* and *Firefly* and British series such as *Hex* and *Afterlife* share an awareness of the need to create new models of family life and new kinds of female heroes.

Research

Earlier versions of several chapters in this book were presented as conference papers at popular culture, cinema studies and comparative literature conferences in Canada and the United States. Research for this project was conducted in a number of different locations and through a variety of means. I visited libraries in Vancouver and Edmonton, Canada, as well as London, England, before and during my sabbatical leave to research the secondary sources related to the topic, including articles on third wave feminism or postfeminist readings of television and film. Many of the "primary sources" or television series and films were acquired in DVD format but others, like U.K. television series and documentaries, were viewed at the BFI (British Film Institute) in London. I was also able to analyze DVD versions of the Canadian program *Rescue Mediums* thanks to Michael Lamport, the producer, who supplied DVDs and transcripts for some of the episodes. Seed grant funding from the University of Northern British Columbia permitted me to hire a graduate research assistant (Lisa Emmerton), who helped locate articles on third wave feminism or postfeminism and assisted in the examination of various television series fan sites.

Women of Vision

The "visionary" powers of female "seers" and "psychics" in contemporary television and film include the gift of premonition, the ability to see or "hear" (e.g., Oda Mae, the medium, in the film *Ghost*) the dead, and the ability to see or hear God or animated "inanimate" objects. All of these powers would generally be perceived as supernatural. While there have been male seer figures in myth and history (e.g., Tiresias), women have generally been associated with intuition more frequently than men, perhaps because of their more limited roles in the physical world of male activity. According to Joseph Campbell, "The male usually has the more conspicuous role, just because of the conditions of life. He is out there in the world, and the woman is in the home" (153). Postfeminist spaces for women have changed to depict women "out there in the world" as well as "in the home," thus highlighting the hybrid lives that women live and allowing for a seer figure with elements of the passive power that she "receives" along with the agency to go out in the world to help others with this power. The women of vision depicted in television shows and films have a range of abilities and a variety of terms may be used to describe their powers. Each of these terms has its own historical and mythical associations and sometimes the expressions may be used interchangeably; however, in other cases, a different concept is more appropriate to describe the specific ability of a female character or woman who has a unique form of knowledge.

Terminology

The term "psychic" resonates in a contemporary context largely because of the number of psychic reality television shows that provide an alternative outlet to people who may not be interested in traditional religions for spiritual comfort (Sancho, 4–52). A "psychic" is someone thought to be influenced by a "non-physical force assumed to explain spiritualistic phenomena" (*The Concise Oxford Dictionary of Current English*) and is therefore closely linked to the concept of a medium. It is a term that may also suggest some clairvoyant ability or an ability to know what others might be thinking. Some psychics may not necessarily have an ability to communicate with the dead, although some psychics may also be mediums. Allison Dubois, the woman on whom Patricia Arquette's character in the NBC series *Medium* is based, says that a medium can "predict future events ... get into a person's mind ... and communicate with the dead" (*Don't Kiss Them Good-bye*, xx). She prefers not to use the word "psychic" to describe someone like herself since the word has been tainted "between all the con artists out there and the gypsy and witch stereotypes" (xxi).

Historically, the role of the medium became prominent during the nineteenth century when interest in psychic phenomena developed (partially as an extension of mesmerism[2]), but more so through the emergence of the Spiritualist movement consisting of individuals who claimed to have contact with the spirits of the dead. By the early 1850s, Spiritualism "had begun to spread quite widely through the Eastern United States" (Gauld, 304) and by the mid–1850s, mediums and "home-circles" were to be found throughout Europe.

The term "seer" may be applied to a person who has a vision of future events and has often been equated with the figure of a prophet. A seer is usually defined as a person who has visions or as an individual with preternatural insight regarding the future (*Concise Oxford Dictionary of Current English*). The seer (*mantis*) was a prominent figure in ancient Greek society (Michael Flower, *The Seer in Ancient Greece*) and played a key role in Greek mythology. According to Flower and John Marincola, "the most respected and sought after seers belonged to families that had practiced seercraft for many generations, reaching back to an eponymous ancestor who had acquired prophetic power either as the gift of a god ... or by some other supernatural means" (166). Historically and mythically, the Delphic Oracle in Greece was the source of prophecies: "The oracle itself was a cleft in the ground which emitted cold vapours, inducing ecstasy. Over the chasm the seer sat on a gilded tripod inhaling the vapours and uttering enigmatic words which were recorded by a priest and interpreted as the revelations of Apollo" (Cotterrell and Storm, *The Ultimate Encyclopedia of Mythology*, 43). Prominent seer figures in Greek mythology are Tiresias, who confirms Oedipus' doom that he will slay his father and bed his mother, and Cassandra, who received the gift of sight from Apollo, the god of prophecy. Seer figures in contemporary television appear as individuals who are actually referred to as seers (like Cordelia in *Angel*), or they may take the form of individuals like Phoebe in *Charmed* and Cassie, a Cassandra figure in *Hex*, who have visions without actually being called seers. They acquire knowledge of the future, even though this "knowledge" may only be partial. Jaye Tyler in *Wonderfalls* does not consider herself to be a seer; however, many signs in the episode "Totem Mole" suggest that she is. In the film *Serenity*, River is called a "reader" rather than a seer, which may be a way of suggesting that her ability is not so much about predicting the future as it is about interpreting the signs of the world and the behavior of the people around her.

Like the term "seer," the expression "visionary" has been applied to women and men who have had access to a divine force or the ability to see the future (Tierney, 364). Women during the medieval period wrote visionary or spiritual autobiographies that described their experiences of the divine and in some cases were widely respected. Some of these women visionaries, however, like Marguerite Porete, Na Prous Boneta and the famous Joan of Arc, were not so fortunate, and were burned at the stake and declared heretics or "witches."

Witch is an expression that has a rich history of usage that exceeds the scope of what can be discussed in this book. In folklore and fairy tales, a witch is a sorceress. The word witch is derived from the Old English word *wicce* ("female magician, sorceress"). Witches in myth and history are women who practiced sorcery, but they have also been recognized for their special knowledge or the ability to see the future, and the term "witch" has a plethora of historical and cultural associations. For example, it was applied to Joan of Arc and other women who were declared heretics because of their visions of the divine. Thus the term has been applied to women whose beliefs or practices fall outside "normal" human understanding or whose behavior and views transgress what was deemed to be socially or institutionally acceptable by religious authorities. Witches in literature were often invested with knowledge of the future; the witches or "weird sisters" in Shakespeare's *Macbeth* predict his fate, for example. A postfeminist television series like *Charmed* subverts the ancient image of the witch as a hag, presenting witches as young, beautiful "kick-ass" women who inherited their abilities from a long line of witches.[3] In *Charmed*, Phoebe's premonitions of the future extend the mythical associations of the witch with special knowledge. Her premonitions often suggest fatal events which make her both a witch and a seer figure.

All of these terms for women who experience visions (seer, psychic, medium, witch) are in some way connected to a special form of knowledge which has traditionally been associated with a more passive kind of ability than the scientific, male-dominated line of inquiry. Women of vision who are depicted in contemporary television and film use their abilities in various ways; most of the time these characters resist the traditional image of the seer or visionary woman as victim or as a passive vessel with little agency, and manage to serve as savior figures and mediators who initiate change in the lives of others.

Cassandra and Joan of Arc: Two Women of Vision in Myth and History

History and myth mention many visionaries, but two female figures, Cassandra and Joan of Arc, stand out largely because they serve as icons of the woman of vision. They are key prototypes or points of departure for many of the postfeminist television series and films about women who have visions (Cassie in the U.K. series *Hex* even has the name Cassandra). The story of the Trojan seer Cassandra is relevant in the analysis of contemporary seer figures and aspects of her character are discussed in relation to female characters in television and film who have visions or knowledge of the future. Cassandra was the daughter of Priam, the king of Troy. She acquired the "gift" of prophecy from the god Apollo but because "she refused his advances" (Cotterrell and Storm, 30), he ensured that her prophecies would never be believed. In Aeschylus' tragedy *Agamemnon*, Cassandra relates how Apollo "came like a wrestler/magnificent, took [her] down and breathed his fire" (1211). Her ability to foretell the future is demonstrated through her foreknowledge of King Agamemnon's murder and knowledge of her own murder at the hands of his wife Clytemnestra. She is generally portrayed in Aeschylus' play as a woman who sees the truth, but who is cursed because she cannot prevent her fate or the fate of others. Many of the postfeminist women of vision in contemporary television occasionally share Cassandra's view that the "gift" of second sight is a curse or a form of madness; however, they also try to subvert the powerlessness associated with being a Cassandra-seer figure by either attempting to change the fates of others or by engaging in "active" transformations of their own lives.

Like Cassandra, Joan of Arc has resonated with the creators of postfeminist television series. Joan of Arc is the teen warrior who has been used as an icon to suggest courage, leadership, resistance, liberty and sacrifice. Joan of Arc, the fifteenth-century French heroine who successfully led a French army against the English, and who was originally declared a witch and a heretic (for her claims that she had divine visions and received instructions from God), has achieved mythic and iconic significance over time for a number of reasons. Not only was she named a saint by the Catholic Church in 1920 (when her powers were recognized as God-inspired), but she has become an example of a woman warrior figure who crossed gender boundaries through her role as a female soldier. Joan of Arc's popularity in American culture has been discussed by Robin Blaetz in *Visions of the Maid: Joan of Arc in American Film and Culture* and she continues to have an influence on the creators of North American television series. The heroines in two postfeminist television series, *Joan of Arcadia* and *Wonderfalls*, are based on Joan of Arc but each is a very different reconstruction of this heroine. Joan Girardi in *Joan of Arcadia* sees and talks to God while Jaye Tyler in *Wonderfalls* hears and sees inanimate objects speak to her as a way of shaking her out of her state of indifference to help others.

Psychic Investigators

While seer figures and mediums have often been portrayed as "empty vessels" that receive communication from divine or supernatural sources, this representation of the passive aspect of the psychic has changed in recent years. Television shows and films since the 1990s reflect a renewed interest in psychic abilities, thus investing the psychic with a new kind of agency. The medium of television has become a popular way of reaching audiences for both male and female psychics who practice their abilities through reality television shows like *Most Haunted, Psychic Investigators* or *Rescue Mediums*. Female psychics are represented in *Psychic Investigators* and are the central figures in *Rescue Mediums*. Examples of television drama like *Ghost Whisperer, Medium* and *Afterlife* highlight the psychic abilities of female protagonists as well as the investigative quality of their work, thus breaking down the opposition between intuition or psychic ability and reason. In many of these examples of psychic television and in several films, the psychic's ability is legitimized through the complementary use of technology or the police-style investigative techniques that these women use to delve into the mysteries of the afterlife.

Genre

While a number of the television series examined in this book belong to genres such as dramedy (*Wonderfalls*), family drama or teen drama (e.g., *Joan of Arcadia*), they may also be classified as telefantasy, which is a term that embraces what many viewers know as "fantasy, science-fiction and horror television programmes" (Catherine Johnson, 2). Johnson, who incorporates Steve Neale's discussion of generic and socio-cultural verisimilitude (*Hollywood and Genre*, 32), explains how telefantasy is a "non-verisimilitudinous genre" (Neale, 37). She elaborates on this short definition and suggests that telefantasy is dependent on maintaining some kind of generic similitude as well as departing from socio-cultural verisimilitude or "culturally accepted notions of what is believed to be real" (4). Johnson mentions that generic verisimilitude "is constructed through the relationship between producer, text and viewer, and between texts that employ conventions of that genre" (4) and that socio-cultural verisimilitude "does not equate directly with truth or reality, but with broader culturally constructed and generally accepted notions of what is believed to be true" (4). Such a way of approaching the fantastic offers some flexibility for how we view women with visionary powers in television and film because of the conventions associated with a particular television genre, but the issue of socio-cultural verisimilitude still causes some problems with the categorization of certain programs with supernatural content. While most television viewers would probably classify series like *Charmed*, *Angel*, or *Hex* as telefantasy because of the inclusion of vampires, demons and witches with supernatural powers (that are culturally accepted as unreal), another program like *Joan of Arcadia* may not be perceived in the same way if the broader cultural consensus is that God does exist. One would have to determine how this "broader cultural consensus" is determined in order to provide a more definitive classification of this particular program. Does one consider "belief" in God at a national level, or does one survey the viewership of a particular series to determine what constitutes broader cultural consensus? One might have to be more specific and actually examine how "God" is represented in the show. Even if the audience of *Joan of Arcadia* were to agree that God does exist and that the show does not depart from this kind of verisimilitude, viewers might still agree that the show departs from the usual expectation of how people experience God, since most do not see God in many different manifestations as Joan does, including the form of a cute teenage boy. Thus *Joan of Arcadia* could still meet the criteria for telefantasy.

Reality television shows with supernatural content present another challenge when using the term telefantasy. They occupy a more ambiguous space, but they could still be accommodated within the definition under certain conditions. Reality television shows that depict supernatural events like *Psychic Investigators* and *Rescue Mediums* try to convince their audiences that the psychic powers of the "actors" (who are real-life psychics) are real. Here again we need to examine the conventions of a genre; reality television is now an established genre, but psychic reality television is a relatively new creation and introduces supernatural elements like psychics who communicate with the dead, a feat which many people would regard as impossible. While many viewers of reality television are undoubtedly under the impression that this genre is closer to reality than other television genres, critics of television point out the "constructed" aspects of the genre: "Some apparently real events in television programmes become performances" (Bignell, *An Introduction to Television Studies*, 184). Critics of reality television are bound to be even more skeptical of the purported reality in psychic reality television. Whether one categorizes "psychic" reality television as telefantasy would depend on whether there is a broad enough cultural consensus to determine that the powers represented in psychic television shows are not "real." If believers in psychic phenomena make up the majority of the viewers, then psychic reality television might not fit the definition of telefantasy. If skeptics of psychic phenomena make up the broader cultural consensus in the assessment of the show, then the term telefantasy could apply. A third possibility would be to simply recognize that psychic reality television constitutes a new, hybrid genre and that existing ways of discussing fantasy and reality do not account for the way such a genre incorporates a blend of "real" people, "real" locations and supernatural elements; however, for the purposes of this study of "telefantasy" television and "fantasy" film, I will consider psychic reality television as a special kind of telefantasy.

Fantasy as a literary genre has been equated with escapism but also with the capacity to reflect contemporary social issues in an unconventional way. Rosemary Jackson argues that "like any other texts, a literary fantasy is produced within and determined by, its social context" (3). It is therefore not surprising that telefantasy or fantasy film would be popular genres for postfeminist ideas and for the presentation of alternative models of heroism through the representation of visionary women.

Postfeminism, Third Wave Feminism and a Third Space

Third wave feminism emerged in the late 1980s as a new generation's response to some of the ideas of second wave feminism. As Merri Lisa Johnson acknowledges in the introduction of her collection *Third Wave Feminism and Television: Jane Puts in a Box* (2007), "'Third Wave' feminism is a term that has been used by a number of women, as well as popular media, to describe contemporary versions of feminisms that evolved over the past decades" (ix). The same statement applies to the term "postfeminism." Both are contested terms and are used synonymously by some critics and quite differently by others. Johnson indicates that the term "has been used to describe a number of diverse feminist and anti-feminist theories and practices" (*Third Wave Feminism and Television: Jane Puts It in a Box*, ix). In this book, I do not use the term postfeminist in the sense of anti-feminist, which has been one of the ways the term has been used or is still used in the discussion of popular culture (Hollows and Moseley, 8). Often postfeminists or third wave feminists have defined themselves against second wave feminists, in order to distinguish themselves from a previous generation. Sites or moments of empowerment and resistance may not be recognized as such by second wave feminists (Garrison, 147). It is the goal of this study to offer a more inclusive recognition of the variety of feminine experiences available in visual culture which foregrounds women with visionary abilities.

In this book I use the terms "third wave feminism" and "postfeminism" interchangeably since third wave feminism "appears to emerge in the same period as debates about post feminism" (Hollows and Moseley, 13). Third wave feminists have embraced the contradictions and diversity among feminists instead of focusing on feminist solidarity. In this book I examine the tendency of visionary women as depicted in television and film to embrace the contradictions and hybridity in their lives through their experience of supernatural phenomena while interacting with others who do not have their "gift." I opt for the more compact adjective postfeminist (rather than third wave feminist) to describe both the time period of the television shows and films examined here as well as some of the characteristics of these women who occupy a hybrid, alternate space.

More specifically, I read women with visionary abilities in television and film as women who occupy a gendered "third space" (see *Thirdspace: a journal of feminist theory and culture*). In adopting the term "third space," I am consciously interweaving third wave feminist ideas with the concept of the "third space" or in-between space (38) proposed by cultural critic Homi Bhabha (36–37). Bhabha uses the term "third space" to discuss a hybrid space that may be applied to cultural rather than gender difference; however, the term has also been embraced by a variety of critics to discuss a space where mediation or subversive activities may take place for marginalized groups (Arts Education Partnership). I adapt Homi Bhabha's concept of the "third space" to discuss these female characters who negotiate (Kinser) between the worlds of the living and the dead, and who subvert the binary concepts of "normal" vs. "mad," reason vs. intuition through their unusual powers. These women are creations of a third wave feminist era, and demonstrate how the body of the seer/psychic/witch/medium functions as a site of third wave feminist contradictions: it is a site of individuality and difference and mystery but also serves as a locus of revelation and social connection to others.

In the case of some of the younger female characters in television and film, their psychic or visionary ability is a demonstration of the "girl power" that has become associated with third wave feminism or postfeminism even though the term "is neither coherent or fixed" (Gonick, 6). The term is often traced back to the Riot Grrrls, a group of women who had their foundation in punk rock music and who wanted to reclaim the word "girl" (Hesford 1999, 45) to celebrate "the fierce and aggressive potential of girls" (Gonick, 7). Other examples of girl power include the popular U.K. band, the Spice Girls, whose catchy songs and lyrics about sisterhood appealed to pre-teen girls, and the leading female characters in shows like *Xena: Warrior Princess* and *Buffy the Vampire Slayer*, who subvert stereotypes about women.

Third wave feminism has re-articulated women's roles as heroines, mothers, family members, and spouses. Critics of television and film have demonstrated how many of these postfeminist programs and films not only depict the third wave feminist concept of girl power but also include a persistent focus on "difference," which may include alternative lifestyles such as "non-nuclear" family arrangements and the ability to negotiate between different worlds of experience. Thus, third wave feminism serves as a relevant theoretical framework and historical context for examining the visual or narrative images of visionary women in television and film. The image of the female visionary has become a metaphor for a generation of women who may see the world differently than others, whether these "others" include the patriarchal establishment or second wave feminists. The female psychic or woman of vision in recent visual media represents a new kind of woman warrior who occupies a unique alternate space (a "third space") that allows her to serve as a cultural and feminine mediator between different worlds of experience (e.g., the living and the dead) while also acting as a subversive force that resists the limitation of the ordinary or the status quo. Her particular form of knowledge — obtained through visions or psychic ability — reflects the third wave feminist or postfeminist appreciation and reconfiguration of contradictions; seemingly incompatible concepts such as intellect, intuition, and corporeal responses to phenomena can co-exist within the female visionary.

Female Hero/Heroine

Why has this image of the "woman of vision" become so pervasive in recent television series? Some of the emphasis may be the result of Western culture's search for different models of heroism for women as an alternative to the more limited image of the male hero, who is often a warrior figure. They also serve as alternatives to the prominent image of the physically-oriented woman warrior. While several women of vision still engage in warrior-like activities (similar to those of Buffy the Vampire Slayer), the use of visions serves as an important mythic alternative or complement to any martial arts skills they might possess (e.g., Phoebe in *Charmed*, River in *Firefly* and *Serenity*).

Some existing theories of the hero and heroine (Campbell; Frye; Powers; Helford) can be applied to the various heroines presented in these television series and films. Several aspects of Joseph Campbell's theory are relevant. For example, the reluctant seer figure echoes Campbell's concept of the reluctant male hero who does not initially respond to "the call" to adventure and the definition of a hero or heroine as someone "who has found or done something beyond the normal range of achievement and experience" (*The Power of Myth*, 150) certainly applies to many of the women of vision discussed in this book. The feminist critique of the patriarchal marginalization of women in myth (Daly; Purkiss; Powers) has included an awareness of the limited options for women with special powers: "If the goddess is crazy or chronically misunderstood, as was Cassandra, her power is dismissible" (Powers 130). I argue that because of their unique role as postfeminist women who occupy a third space between worlds, the seers, psychics and visionary women in recent television and film necessitate a new way of viewing the role of a female hero in a complex postfeminist world. While the postfeminist heroine may still encounter patriarchal opposition and may also "suffer," she is not just a victim who must accept her fate. She can actively transform or save the lives of others with her powers. Her role is not necessarily to imitate the role of the traditional male warrior figure, but to act as a mediator-facilitator who must negotiate between spaces, since she occupies an unusual third space of hybridity where contradictions abound (reason and madness co-exist or the lines are sometimes blurred). For this reason, she may even take on the role of anti-hero (e.g., River in *Firefly* and *Serenity*) simply because of her unconventional or unpredictable way of dealing with others. Critical discussions of different expressions of motherhood including the "monstrous" female body (Hills and Williams), family (Feasey), like the re-definition of family in a postfeminist age, and lesbian experience (McKenna), form part of my analysis of the postfeminist seer, psychic and visionary as heroine who becomes synonymous with difference. I generally use the terms "female hero" and "heroine" interchangeably throughout this book, although I am cognizant of how traditionally "heroines" in narrative forms like novels or films have played a secondary role to their male counterparts. With the exception perhaps of Cordelia in *Angel* and River in *Firefly* (she has a more fully developed role in the film *Serenity*), most of the female visionaries in television and film are the main focus.

Chapter Divisions

This book is divided into three main parts: (1) "Postfeminist Cassandras: Seers, 'Witches' and Women Who Know the Future," (2) "Joan of Arc in Contemporary Television: Images of a Reluctant Seer," and (3) "Investigating the Dead: Mediums and Psychic Detectives." Each chapter highlights the female visionary or gifted woman in one or more works. The first two parts of the book offer an examination of women with visionary powers in television and film and relates the representation of contemporary female characters to a mythic or legendary prototype. Part 1 includes discussion of the figure of Cassandra, and Part 2 addresses the modern reworking of Joan of Arc in two television series. While some of the characters in the third part of this book could also be compared to Cassandra or Joan of Arc because of their visionary abilities, this part develops the role of women in the context of criminal or personal investigations. The psychic or medium attempts to navigate between different realities and contradictory kinds of information to arrive at some kind of truth.

"Postfeminist Cassandras: Seers, 'Witches' and Women Who Know the Future" addresses the mythic figure of the famous seer Cassandra, who may be compared to the women in the five chapters that comprise this part. These chapters cover a range of popular television series like *Firefly, Angel, Charmed* and *Hex.* The first chapter in this part, "Cheerleader/Seer: The Hybrid Visions of Cordelia Chase in *Buffy the Vampire Slayer* and *Angel*," analyzes Cordelia's role as the "suffering seer," mirroring that of the mythic Cassandra, yet she moves beyond the limitations of this particular mythic prototype by actually being able to help others; she accomplishes this in part by crossing boundaries and identities, a key phenomenon in the genre of telefantasy and an important form of postfeminist expression. Chapter Two, "The Transformation of River Tam: Psychic Warrior, Female Prodigy and Anti-Hero in *Firefly* and *Serenity*" discusses how the actions of the psychic and psychologically disturbed River Tam sometimes border on the heroic. However, her psychic ability combined with her unpredictability, the result of mysterious scientific experiments performed on her mind, make the term "anti-heroine" a more appropriate category for describing this unusual character who resides in her own unique "third space." Phoebe Halliwell, one of the three witch sisters in *Charmed*, is the focus of Chapter Three, "Phoebe and the Power of Sight: The Witch as Seer in *Charmed*." Phoebe, a young witch whose primary power consists of receiving or calling up premonitions, has a number of different identities throughout the series. Her visionary power has been identified in the series as a "passive" power, but this concept is re-examined in light of the development of Phoebe's visionary abilities and her many transformations as a character, especially in the early part of the series. Chapter Four examines the U.K. series *Hex*. "Visions of the 'Mad' Outsider in *Hex*: Cassandra, Witches and Lesbian Appetite" reveals how the series not only uses the device of "the vision" to evoke the figure of Cassandra and the image of the witch, but also develops the concept of the "vision" to suggest that Cassie's friend Thelma (who has become a ghost) is Cassie's vision. Thelma also becomes a visually powerful illustration of appetite and lesbian desire and reinforces the postfeminist emphasis on diversity and alternative sexuality. In "Postfeminist Savior: Seeing the Future and Reliving the Day in *Tru Calling*," the fifth chapter of Part 1, I argue that Tru Davies, the heroine of the series, is a unique postfeminist reconstruction of the Cassandra figure; she knows the fate of individuals not because she is a seer in the traditional sense of a person who has "visions" but because she relives the same day. She subverts the powerlessness of Cassandra by trying to save the lives of people who seem destined to die.

The second part, "Joan of Arc in Contemporary Television: Images of a Reluctant Seer," addresses two television series that incorporate characters based on medieval visionary Joan of Arc. Chapter Six, "Teen Visions of God: Postfeminist Heroism and Genre Crossing in *Joan of Arcadia*," depicts American teenager Joan Girardi as God's "chosen one." She hears God and sees God in many different guises. By incorporating elements from various genres, *Joan of Arcadia* offers a unique form of postfeminist, postmodern, hybrid television to a contemporary teen audience while still sending some "traditional" messages about altruistic behavior, sacrifice and leadership. In "Joan of Arc in Niagara Falls: Signs of a Seer and Cross-Cultural Contact in *Wonderfalls*," the seventh chapter, I discuss how the mythic pervades the life of Jaye Tyler, a reluctant seer and cynical heroine. Her new ability changes her from an ordinary, disengaged twenty-four-year-old woman into a postfeminist hero who is more of a mediator figure than a conventional leader.

Part 3 of this book is called "Investigating the Dead: Mediums and Psychic Detectives." This part addresses the psychic as investigator or as an individual who helps others investigate a crime. "Professional" psychics and the fascination with the paranormal have entered the realm of popular culture through psychic readings, infomercials and reality television programs such as *Rescue Mediums* and *Psychic Investigators*. Television dramas such as *Medium, Ghost Whisperer* and *Afterlife* as well as films like *Ghost, The Gift* and *Premonition* attest to the interest in depicting individuals who cross the boundaries between the world of the living and the world of the dead. In Chapter Eight, "Psychic Women, 'Dead' Men and the Search for Truth: Cross-Gender Communication in *Ghost, The Gift* and *Premonition*," I discuss how three films offer three very different images of women with special kinds of knowledge and generate new ways of talking about women, agency, their use of "passive" powers and how they negotiate between either the absence or the overpowering presence of men in their lives. Chapter Nine, "*Rescue Mediums* and *Psychic Investigators*: Television for Women and Paranormal Programming," explores two programs on W Network, a Canadian specialty channel for women. *Psychic Investigators* and *Rescue Mediums* are psychic reality shows which include the point of view of female psychics. The hybrid aspect of this television creates a "third space" in which women with visionary powers establish their presence. Both shows provide the "conclusions of rescue and relief" (Corner, 98) that are common in "reality tv" (98). Chapter Ten, "Resisting the Myth of the Bad Mother: Psychic Visions and Maternal Anxiety in NBC's *Medium*," addresses concerns in the series surrounding "bad" mothering and a medium's attempts to resist this image. The series suggests that even in a postfeminist age, inflexible attitudes towards mothers (not to mention mediums) can still be a reality. Chapter Eleven, "Looking for Closure: Investigating Mothers, Daughters and Disease in *Ghost Whisperer*," analyzes the communication or lack thereof between mothers and daughters, as well as the role of technology as a means of communication and as an investigative tool in a postfeminist, post–9/11 world. The final chapter of the book, "A Medium's Visions of a Third Space: Finding Family in the

U.K. Series *Afterlife*," focuses on that British series. The concept of family in this show reflects a postfeminist, postmodern and supernatural transformation of the traditionally stable family consisting of a husband, a wife and two living children into an alternative family structure.

The book's conclusion emphasizes how television programs and films about women with special ways of "seeing" and knowing reveal diverse ways of defining the female hero in a postfeminist age as savior, healer, mediator or anti-heroine. These women occupy a unique "third space" or "in-between space" because of their powers, and represent a range of age groups and identities. However, the primary expression of difference in these telefantasies and fantasy films is the visionary ability itself.

PART 1

Postfeminist Cassandras

Seers, "Witches" and
Women Who Know the Future

ONE

Cheerleader/Seer

The Hybrid Visions of Cordelia Chase in Buffy the Vampire Slayer *and* Angel

In her article "Walking the Fine Line Between Angel and Angelus," Stacey Abbott describes the vampire Angel from Joss Whedon's television series *Angel* (1999–2004) as a hybrid character who inhabits a world of "moral ambiguity" (par.22, *Slayage*). Abbott also indicates that Cordelia is unsure of Angel's identity in "Reprise" when she says, "I don't even know what you are anymore." A similar statement about changing identities, however, may be made about the character of Cordelia Chase (Charisma Carpenter), a seer figure who occupies a kind of hybrid "third space" in the series because of her experience as a seer who becomes part-demon. She accepts the hybridization of her identity to carry on as a seer figure or visionary for Angel Investigations and to avoid suffering excruciating pain from her visions (a point of departure from the mythic Cassandra, a seer who suffers). Moral ambiguity also informs Cordelia's role in *Buffy the Vampire Slayer* and *Angel* and suggests the changing notion of heroes in a postmodern, postfeminist world. If one examines Cordelia's transformations or hybridization of the self in *Buffy the Vampire Slayer*, some transformations already predate *Angel*, the spin-off series. In *Buffy*, Cordelia experiences a hybridization of the self. Her reinvention of the self is consistent with postfeminist and postmodern plurality and the crossing of boundaries. She also reflects the play with contradictions and irony that are a part of postfeminist and postmodern culture.[1] These identity shifts which occur in *Buffy* and then continue in *Angel* once she acquires her primary role as seer, are related to Cordelia's changing relationship to the importance of the inner world of experience vs. the outer world of appearance. In *Angel*, shifting notions of what it means to be a "demon" also contribute to the depiction of Cordelia as someone who occupies an alternate space or "third space." However, her changing identity is already evident in the television series *Buffy the Vampire Slayer*. Cordelia's ability to move between different groups in *Buffy* anticipates her movement between different states of being in *Angel*. In the course of the series, she is an actress, a princess, a suffering seer, a seer who is part-demon, a mother, a woman in a coma and a woman with an out-of-body experience. While her role as a suffering seer parallels that of the mythic Cassandra, she moves beyond the limitations of this particular mythic prototype by actually

Charisma Carpenter plays Cordelia Chase in two series, ***Buffy the Vampire Slayer*** (1997–2003) and ***Angel*** (1999–2004). In ***Buffy the Vampire Slayer*** she is a popular girl and a cheerleader who becomes one of Buffy's allies. In ***Angel*** she acquires the ability to have visions and agrees to become a demon in order to receive visions without suffering incredible pain.

being able to help others; she accomplishes this in part by crossing boundaries and identities, a common phenomenon in the genre of telefantasy and a key aspect of postfeminist expression. This crossing of boundaries, however, combined with the moral ambiguity and ironic remarks uttered by her character, prevent her from being either a victim with no agency or a triumphant savior figure. She is a postfeminist heroine who remains in a kind of "third space" or in-between space.

Homi Bhabha's concept of a "third space" provides a useful way of analyzing a seer figure or visionary like Cordelia. For Bhabha the term is linked to cultural hybridity or the "in-between space" (38) that individuals in post-colonial societies occupy as a result of contradictory forces: They "negotiate and translate their cultural identities in a discontinuous intertextual temporality of cultural difference" (38). This existence in a third space or in-between space which includes identity transformation applies to Cordelia in a number of ways in both *Buffy the Vampire Slayer* and in *Angel*. In the *Buffy* series she reveals her preoccupation with appearances but also becomes a supporter of Buffy's group of friends who engage in a more serious pursuit: the fight against evil. In *Angel* she enters a third space or in-between space as a woman who receives visions and becomes part-demon. Cordelia's crossing over from one television series to another and the changes she undergoes in the second series are a kind of "intertextual temporality of cultural difference" (38), since the audience is familiar with her former identities in *Buffy* and some of these aspects (like her former ability as a cheerleader) continue into the spin-off series *Angel* when she is able to use the mental and physical skills of cheerleading to remember some fighting techniques that Angel taught her ("Billy," 6.3). At the same time, the audience must also acknowledge the different "culture" of the world of *Angel* and the new kinds of transformations that occur in Cordelia's character. According to some fans, she is the most memorable character in the series because she experienced more than other characters ("Angelus Arcanum").

Like post-colonial theorist Homi Bhabha, postfeminists and postmodernists also recognize the importance of contradictions, difference, and changing identities. According to Linda Hutcheon, the postmodern shares with post-colonial and feminist theory "their positive valuing of the different, the 'other'" (Makaryk, 612). For postfeminists or third wave feminists, the focus on the expression of the individual and the recognition of diversity among feminists has been important: "Related to emphasis on the differences among women, be it in their subjectivity or perspectives, postfeminism also critiques oppression or discrimination based on other aspects of one's identity" (Lotz, 115). The capacity to constantly reinvent oneself has been an expression of many postfeminist pop music icons like Madonna, Pink, and Gwen Stefani. While Cordelia's changes in *Angel* are often not of her own making, the transformations reflect the unpredictability of the fantastic universe in which she is a character. These transformations must also be viewed in the context of seer figures and the nature of their abilities. They are conventionally the recipient of visions[2] so they are often constructed as "passive." Therefore, examples of agency will be more difficult to find in such a character than in the more active, "kick-ass" heroine like Buffy the Vampire Slayer or Xena the Warrior Princess.

The genre of telefantasy also contributes to the concept of identity renewal or shifts; while the genre usually sets up these shifts in relation to the polarization of good and evil forces, postmodern and postfeminist telefantasies often indicate the difficulty of ascertaining the differences between good and evil. Life consists of gray areas and the concept of the "right" choice is relative, depending upon the perspective in question. Myth critic Joseph Campbell mentions how one person's hero might be another person's "monster": "Whether you call someone a hero or a monster is all relative to where the focus of your consciousness may be" (Campbell, *The Power of Myth*, 156). Even though he is not considered a postmodernist, as a myth critic from the structuralist, Jungian school, Campbell actually reflects the sentiment of postmodernists on relativism: "Postmodernism ... is premised instead on the understanding that all knowledge is relative and multiple; it is thus characterized by paradox and inconsistency" (Shugart et al., 196). His view, like the views of postfeminists, legitimizes subjectivity or the perspective of an individual.

Cordelia Chase appears as a character in two related series, *Buffy the Vampire Slayer* and the spin-off *Angel*. Her role is more extensive in the latter when she acquires her ability as a seer figure; however, the fact that she crosses over from one series to another suggests her in-between, hybrid state. From a telefantasy perspective, she is a character who experiences a variety of identities.

Charisma Carpenter has actually played the role of a character by the name of Cordelia in two series, *Buffy the Vampire Slayer* and *Angel*. In *Buffy* she experiences an identity shift. At the beginning of the series she is little more than a mean-spirited cheerleader who marginalizes those who are unpopular; however, over the course of the series she becomes a supporter of the Scoobies (Buffy's gang). While her role as seer is not developed until her cross-over into the series *Angel*, her character in Buffy already lays the foundation for unexpected transformations of character and demonstrates that Cordelia does occupy a kind of hybrid, in-between space that allows her to take on multiple identities. In *Buffy* she appears as a popular high school cheerleader who heads a group known as the "Cordettes." She is initially presented as a wealthy, superficial girl concerned with the world of visual display in general or fashion in particular: She tells Buffy, the new girl at Sunnydale High, "You wanna fit in here, the first rule is: know your losers. Once you can identify them all by sight, they're a lot easier to avoid" (*Buffy*, "Welcome to the Hellmouth," 1.1) Her disparaging comment about Willow Rosenberg's fashion sense in episode 1 of season 1 ("So glad you've discovered the softer side of Sears") also reveals her focus on the world of appearances. These are two early indications of how Cordelia's "vision" serves as one of the defining aspects of her character. She uses her "sight" to separate people into winners and losers, but it is clear that this ability focuses on superficial appearances and not on the inner self of an individual. However, in *Buffy* a significant transformation occurs in Cordelia's own life when her father's financial troubles affect her ability to afford her former life of luxury. In order to maintain the appearance that she is wealthy, she must transform herself by "lowering" or humiliating herself to work at an expensive boutique in order to pay for a prom dress on a payment plan and to preserve the all-important image of herself as a well-to-do young woman.

Furthermore, during various episodes of *Buffy* Cordelia helps Buffy's gang and joins the crowd of "losers" without entirely losing her connection to the "in" crowd of cheerleaders. Cordelia makes the transition from her earlier space of privilege to an indeterminate space since she helps the Scoobies battle evil but still holds onto her earlier image of herself and makes comments that are critical of Buffy ("Put yourself in Buffy's shoes for just a minute, okay? I'm Buffy, freak of nature, right? Naturally, I pick a freak for a boyfriend..." ("Dead Man's Party," 3.2). Yael Sherman states that "Cordelia is both a popularity queen and Scooby member." In other words, she embraces the kinds of contradictions that some critics have identified with postfeminism or third wave feminism. In this particular example, Cordelia goes against the "either it is or it isn't" (Gonick, 10) mentality, a departure from the binary opposition she creates between "losers" and those who are not losers when she is first introduced as a character in *Buffy*. It is worth noting that as Cordelia becomes more involved in the Scoobies' battle against unknown forces and a demonic serial murderer, she regards her earlier position of privilege as a cheerleader as a marginalized position. After she reads a suicide note a boy called Jonathan sent to the school paper, she asks: "Doesn't anyone write in to praise the Cheerleaders? We are so unsung" ("Earshot," 3. 18). She pleads for acknowledgment of the underappreciated cheerleaders who are rendered invisible because they are "unsung." Because her plea is unlikely to generate much sympathy from the Scooby gang or her television fans, she is a morally ambiguous character.

In *Buffy*, Cordelia appears to be part of a new group (the Scoobies) without entirely abandoning her allegiance to another (popular girls). If Buffy is clearly the postfeminist "kick-ass" heroine of the series, what does this make Cordelia? Her role seems to change depending on the situation. Homi Bhabha talks about "the moment of transit where space and time cross to produce complex figures of difference and identity, past and present, inside and outside, inclusion and exclusion" (1) and Cordelia is an example of a character who occupies this kind of "third space." She is both an insider and an outsider. For example, she helps Buffy and the Scoobies in "Graduation Day — Part 2" by using a flamethrower against evil forces; however, in the same episode she still makes comments like, "This is just *such* a Buffy thing to do... She is *always* thinking of herself."

The crossing over of Cordelia from *Buffy* to *Angel* reflects the popular transportability of telefantasy characters.[3] It has become a common practice to take characters from one series and place them in another — perhaps as a way to ensure crossover fans for a new series — but also as a way of ensuring that fans of the newer series revisit the show that generated the spin-off. The placement of a particular character in a spin-off series generates a new set of dynamics with different characters and enhances the hybrid aspects of the spin-off series. *Stargate: Atlantis* includes the appearance of characters from *Stargate SG-1*, Buffy makes a special appearance in *Angel*, and the character Faith from *Buffy the Vampire Slayer* also reappears in *Angel*. In Cordelia's case, the re-invention involves the acquisition of a new fantastic ability: receiving visions. This new power also enhances her role as an integral part of the series.

She is part of the team of Angel Investigations, a detective agency, and is the personification of AI's motto "We help the helpless."

It is impossible to discuss Cordelia's visionary powers without considering the role of the demon in *Angel* and Cassandra's gift or curse. Cassandra acquires her visions from Apollo, but they form part of her cursed existence in the sense that no one believes the veracity of her visions. In addition, the visions she experiences are generally linked to the unhappy fates of individuals (e.g., King Agamemnon's murder and Cassandra's death at the hands of Clytemnestra) or the defeat of an entire culture (the destruction of Troy as described in the *Aeneid*). Her visions are also painful: "his *fire!*—sears me, sweeps me again—the torture! Apollo Lord of the Light, you burn" (Aeschylus 162). Cordelia's new-found "gift" of inner sight is acquired when Doyle, a half-demon, kisses her and transfers this ability to her just before he dies. Doyle's "gift" to Cordelia is framed in an interesting way; it is a trick, or an act of violation that echoes Apollo's gift or curse of visionary ability for Cassandra. In *Angel*, the transmission of the vision is sexualized: "I thought our kiss meant something, and instead he [Doyle]—he used that moment to pass it on to me! Why couldn't it have been mono or herpes!"

The pain that Cordelia experiences and the sores that she develops before turning part-demon echo the kind of madness and physical pain the mythic Cassandra experiences when she has visions. Cordelia refers ironically to the visions as gifts, the kind of "having-my-head-torn-open-and-hot-lava-poured-into-my-skull gifts" ("That Vision Thing," 3.2).[4] In Cassandra's case, the supernatural intervention is almost always perceived in exclusively negative terms—not as a gift—since her visions generate suffering. Cordelia's visions, on the other hand, help Angel Investigations. Cordelia's ability as a seer is also mediated by the shifting concept of the demon in *Angel*. While demons do have negative associations in *Angel*, this is not always the case. As the series evolves, it becomes evident that the lines between good and evil blur, and the affiliation of demons with either good or evil is not always clear. In other words, the relationship between the outer world of appearances and the inner self is not always consistent and it is this instability that characterizes the universe of *Angel* and Cordelia's experiences of human-demon hybridity.

Lorne

The television series *Angel* actually featured several characters with visionary abilities: Lorne, Doyle and Cordelia. Lorne is the benevolent "male" demon Host, or Krevlorneswath of the Deathwok Clan, a green-skinned[5] lounge singer whose psychic abilities are triggered by people who sing karaoke. Lorne may be compared to the male seer Tiresias from Greek mythology who lived life as a woman for a period of several years. Lorne's character also suggests an alternative kind of sexuality and perhaps even hybridity because of his indeterminate sexuality; while he is never explicitly identified as homosexual, he uses "flamboyant indicators of homosexuality" (Stan Beeler, 93). Although he serves as an important symbol of the margins (as a green demon who works with Angel), Lorne seems to come by his visions "legitimately"; in the *Angel* universe, demons are able to have visions without experiencing physical pain. While one episode did foreground Lorne's visions and pain, the suffering was primarily experienced by humans when Lorne's visionary ability was exploited by humans to read the futures of Las Vegas casino patrons to steal their luck ("The House Always Wins," 4.3). Cordelia's interaction with Lorne is particularly important when he restores her memory with a spell ("Spin the Bottle," 4.6) after she lost her memories when she returned to Earth from another dimension.

Doyle and Cordelia

Another character in *Angel* with the power of second sight is Doyle, a half-human, half-demon character (a half-blood). His visions assist Angel, the vampire and his crew of detectives in solving cases. Just before his death, Doyle passes his gift of vision on to Cordelia ("Parting Gifts," 1.10). For Cordelia, the transmission of visionary powers is analogous to the transmission of a "disease"; thus she demonizes the "demon" and denies any sense of hybridity in her body or consciousness. In this sense, her response to receiving visions is initially one of rejection like Cassandra's view of Apollo's violation of her mind: "Apollo Lord of the Light, you burn, / you blind me" (Aeschylus, 1270–1271). However, since she was already a hybrid character in *Buffy* it is in a sense no surprise that she would be a hybrid character in *Angel*. She experiences incredible pain while having the visions, and the only way to alleviate this pain is for her to accept the idea of becoming part-demon. One could argue that this acceptance is only an affirmation of what was already the case. She had already inherited a demon-like ability from Doyle: the power to receive visions courtesy of "The Powers That Be."[6] Cordelia makes the choice to keep her visionary power and the state of hybridity, or at least to recognize hybridity by becoming part-demon. She tells the demon Skip, "So, demonize me already" ("Birthday," 3.11), thus demonstrating agency and a keen sense of humor.

Angel presents the concept of hybrid demon identity in a more positive light when Cordelia chooses to becomes part-demon in "Birthday." Her suffering prior to this decision may represent the conflicts she experienced between her earlier image of herself as an actress and her work for Angel Investigations, a conflict that is brought to the forefront in this episode. A demon by the name of Skip gives her the option of living her life as "an incredibly famous and wealthy actress" with her own show called *Cordy* or becoming part-demon in order to hold onto her visions in a pain-free fashion. The episode therefore highlights the hybrid aspects of Cordelia in a number of different ways. She exists in two different possible realities: She is Cordelia the actress in one reality, and Cordelia the seer in another.[7] Cordelia chooses to become part-demon to keep her visions because the visions are part of her purpose in life. Her choice is also a heroic act of sacrifice so that Angel would not have to experience the pain of being a seer.[8]

Another reminder of Cordelia's hybrid identity as a human who acquired the power of sight from a half-demon (Doyle) is paradoxically presented through the external "third eye" that she acquires in the episode "Epiphany" (2.16). She is attacked by a Skilosh demon whose forked tongue creates an eye on the back of her head. While this demon is presented as sinister, unlike Doyle a half-demon who worked with Angel and Cordelia, the act of "violation" is reminiscent of Doyle's transfer of visions to Cordelia without her consent. The visual representation of this eye on Cordelia's head functions in two different and apparently contradictory ways. The eye on the back of the head has a hybrid significance; it suggests both the monstrous through an association with a figure like the one-eyed Cyclops and Cordelia's clairvoyant ability. If one interprets the third eye as a cyclops eye, it "signifies a personal absorption in the external world and watchfulness permanently directed towards the outside" (Chevalier and Gheerbrant, *The Penguin Dictionary of Symbols*, 363). The foreign eye would therefore reinforce Cordelia's interest in the world of external appearances (e.g., her desire to be an actress and perhaps even her earlier *Buffy* roles as cheerleader and popular girl). When read as an indicator of "inner vision," the third eye "is indicative of a superhuman state" (Chevalier and Gheerbrant, 363). The removal of Cordelia's extra eye in "Epiphany" may suggest that Cordelia has evolved from an individual preoccupied with the world of appearances as suggested by her character in *Buffy* to a character whose inner life of vision is more important. It may also imply that her "inner" vision will become integrated into the inner self and therefore not require outer expression. Eric S. Rabkin has argued that in fantastic literature, the metamorphosis of an individual is a literalization of a quality that person already possessed. Rabkin says that metamorphosis is "a fantastic device used for making dramatic a quality which had previously been only a part of a character's psychology" (*Fantastic Worlds: Myths, Tales and Stories*, 24). In other words, the third eye is an external representation of Cordelia's inner sight. Its removal does not necessarily suggest her rejection of the demon sphere; in fact, it anticipates her own decision to become part-demon ("Birthday") as a way of avoiding the pain associated with her visions. Thus the external representation of the eye is no longer necessary in order to demonstrate that she is part-demon. And unlike the mythical Cassandra, she is in a position to choose whether she should keep or not keep receiving visions, thus demonstrating a postfeminist form of agency not evident in Cassandra's case.

Cordelia's position as a hybrid character and her placement in between two men in her life is developed during her stay in the demonic world of Pylea, which happens to be the birthplace of the demon Lorne. While there, she becomes a princess and falls in love with the Groosalugg, a part-human, part-demon character. However, she is informed that once they consummate their relationship ("comshuk"), her visions will be transferred to him. Despite her feelings for "Groo," she does not wish to lose her visions because they define her and she feels that she has a responsibility to Angel Investigations to maintain her role as seer. Yet this loyalty to Angel does not mean that Cordelia wishes to avoid having sex with Groo, and so she discovers the existence of a "mystical prophylactic" ("Couplet," 3.14) to still have sex without losing her visionary powers. One of the more humorous moments in this episode is when Cordelia asks Angel to procure the prophylactic for her even though she and Angel have romantic feelings for one another. When read in the context of the myth of the seer Cassandra, she engages in an interesting postfeminist subversion of the Cassandra myth which showed how Cassandra was "cursed" with the gift of prophecy by Apollo for refusing to have sexual relations with the god. Unlike Cassandra, Cordelia keeps her visions and satisfies her sexual appetite, thus demonstrating a kind of hybridity and postfeminist agency that allows her to negotiate between the men in her life.

Cordelia enters even more morally ambiguous territory when her character changes as a result of Jasmine's possession of Cordelia. Jasmine is a demonic entity that apparently orchestrated many of the events in the first few seasons of *Angel.* While Matt Hills and Rebecca Williams suggest that Jasmine's possession of Cordelia is a key example of Cordelia's lack of agency, one could argue that this change may be viewed as the creative re-invention of a character through another feminine entity. The possession of Cordelia can also be read as a postfeminist reconfiguration of the Cassandra myth. For example, the mythical Cassandra experienced birth pangs that were associated with visions: "the pain, the terror! The birth-pang of the seer/who tells the truth" (Agamemnon 160). Unlike Cassandra, Cordelia does not only "give birth" to visions, she gives birth to a full-grown woman or feminine entity (Jasmine). Here we have another example of the literalization or manifestation of Cordelia's visionary ability. After Jasmine is born (or gives birth to herself!), Cordelia lapses into a coma. While Matt Hills and Rebecca Williams read Cordelia as the victim of assaults (206), in the telefantasy worlds of *Angel* and *Buffy the Vampire Slayer* the moral universe is not always black and white. Because of the kind of postmodern relativism (Shugart) at work in these series, one needs to reevaluate the possession of Cordelia by Jasmine in the context of the myth of Cassandra to see if one can re-read Cordelia outside the dominant discourse of victimization that has dominated much of the discussion surrounding this character.

If Cordelia's experience is read in the context of the Cassandra myth, the "birth" may be viewed as a postfeminist rewriting of the Appollonian "rape" of Cassandra. Jasmine's orchestration of her own birth is an interesting example of a pregnancy that is possible through a feminine force, and in this sense it is a rewriting of the possession experience of a seer figure; instead of being possessed by a male god, Cordelia is possessed by a feminine entity, thus suggesting an alternative third space of woman-mediated possession. Since Jasmine orchestrated Doyle's passing of visions to Cordelia, this re-reading of how Cordelia received her visionary power actually displaces Doyle as the demon who transmitted this power. Some might argue that Jasmine's possession of Cordelia still constitutes a form of violation, but one needs to recognize powerful female forces when they occur in telefantasy or fantastic film for the postfeminist "third spaces" and alternative narratives that they create. In their analysis of Jasmine's possession of Cordelia, Matt Hills and Rebecca Williams comment on the lack of birth fluids (207) present when Cordelia gives birth, but Jasmine's "clean, spectral" (207) emergence as a form of light could represent the kinds of alternatives available to women in a postfeminist reproductive era, when women have children through the process of adoption or through surrogate mothers. Jasmine's birth as a "supernatural light" (207) may also foreshadow Cordelia's own reappearance during her final appearance in season five of *Angel*, after she emerges from a coma.

Jane Stadler argues that "hybridization" can be "represented as empowering"; Cordelia's final appearance occurs in the episode "You're Welcome" when Angel sees her in the hospital after she has apparently woken up from her coma. Some critics (Rambo and Cruisie) have criticized the series for not allowing Cordelia to respond to her own needs and desires and for showing too much concern for Angel. However, instead of suggesting that Whedon has somehow failed his heroine, one must acknowledge the innovative and important role of hybridity in the construction of Cordelia and other characters in the series. Reading her against her mythical prototype, Cassandra, also offers a way of seeing how the character allows for a postfeminist rewriting of an ancient seer figure who unlike Cordelia cannot use her visions to help others. The depiction of Cordelia in *Buffy the Vampire Slayer* and *Angel* suggests a postfeminist recognition of the female hero as a multi-dimensional hybrid figure. She serves as a fantastic extension of the unpredictability of a postmodern world of plurality where changing circumstances demand rapid changes, and people must reinvent themselves. In "You're Welcome," Cordelia is a self-described "vision of hotliness" interacting with Angel and her friends courtesy of the Powers That Be. One of Cordelia's statements in this episode reminds both Angel and the television audience of her transformations over the course of the series: "I'm just on a different road."

While some might argue that Cordelia is disempowered in certain ways, viewers must also remember that she does demonstrate one more kind of agency or control and that is through her famous sense of irony, which fans laud as her signature trait. Her wry and witty remarks are an important part of her character that is maintained throughout the series, thus reflecting one of the major qualities of telefantasy in a postfeminist and postmodern age. Yvonne Tasker and Diane Negra refer to the "irony and self-reflexivity that characterize so much of postfeminist and postmodern culture" ("Postfeminism and the Archive for the Future," 171) and Cordelia's words in "You're Welcome" certainly capture her sense of self-irony: "Mystical comas. You know, if you can stand the horror of a higher power hijacking your mind and body so that it can give birth to itself, I really recommend 'em." While Cordelia could have focused on her suffering, she chooses instead to treat the experience of "possession" in an ironic or humorous fashion. The use of humor is a strategy employed by members of minority groups or by those who have suffered from an illness as a way of healing themselves.[9] The result for the person who has suffered is a renewed self—a state of mind that Cordelia would probably recommend.

Two

The Transformation
of River Tam
Psychic Warrior, Female Prodigy
and Anti-Hero in Firefly and Serenity

Joss Whedon's incorporation of third wave feminist "girl power" is evident in his construction of the "kick-ass" heroine Buffy Summers, the vampire slayer; his slayer also experienced visions and she achieves a mythic kind of importance as one slayer from a line of slayers. However, Whedon's interest in the postfeminist warrior woman coupled with a visionary/mythic dimension did not end with his *Buffy* series. He introduced a unique female character by the name of River Tam (Summer Glau) in the short-lived series *Firefly* (2002). *Firefly* has been described as an "sf western" (Wright, 157); it is set in the 26th century and depicts the adventures of a crew of renegades led by Captain Malcolm "Mal" Reynolds (Nathan Fillion). The crew on the ship *Serenity* often find themselves in conflict with the government entity known as the Alliance. River Tam, a young, vulnerable-looking woman with psychic abilities, is a far cry from the heroic, yet down-to-earth Buffy. River Tam is a very "girl-like" woman who was the victim of brain experiments conducted by the Alliance, who intended to create a human weapon.

While River's character and physical powers lie dormant throughout much of *Firefly*, she becomes more integral to the narrative in Whedon's companion film, *Serenity*. One could argue that River's identity as an outsider contributes to her status as anti-hero or anti-heroine, both within the series *Firefly* and within the series *Serenity*.[1] The term anti-hero has often been used to describe a character who is unlucky or naïve like Voltaire's character Candide or "the converse of most of the traditional attributes of the hero" (Holman and Harmon, 28). One of the ways of defining the qualities of the anti-hero may be linked to the responses of uncertainty this character elicits from others. River's anti-hero(ine) status is dependent in part on her psychic ability which generates ambivalent reactions (ranging from admiration to fear) from other individuals. Her knowledge of future events suggests her gifted Cassandra-like qualities, but at the same time her knowledge of past events in the lives of strangers earns her the title of "witch" ("Safe," 1.7). Despite her child-like and innocent demeanor, she is "dangerous" because of her erratic outbreaks which include destructive episodes, her use of weapons, and her proven ability to injure a member of Mal's crew (Jayne, played by Adam Baldwin). Her psychic ability allows her to assist the crew of *Serenity* on a number of occasions, but the eerie nature of this form of knowledge coupled with her instability places her outside the framework of other crew members, including Zoe (Gina Torres), Kaylee (Jewel Straite), and Inara (Morena Baccarin). These three women are strong in their own way without posing the risk of danger to the "crew" and without possessing the fragility of mental instability that characterizes River. Thus River occupies an ambiguous space, a "third space" that puts her in the position of an anti-heroine since "she's not quite right" ("Safe"); she is dangerous "cargo" for the crew of *Serenity* to transport.

While some might argue that this categorization of River as dangerous and abnormal devalues her, it actually enables her in a paradoxical way and she becomes a unique illustration of postfeminist "girl power." Her unusual abilities, especially her psychic warrior abilities, are exactly what make her such a unique, multi-valent character; she is a psychic, a witch, a warrior, a genius, yet she also possesses the qualities of a child-like woman. She even becomes equated with an "inanimate object" (the ship *Serenity*) and occupies a clearly distinct space that reinforces the importance of individuality and difference for third wave feminists. River's actions sometimes border on the heroic (some fans on the *Firefly* section of the "Television Without Pity" website identify her as a very strong character since she is a survivor ["Crazy"]) but her psychic ability and the mystery surrounding the nature of the experiments on her mind make the term "anti-heroine" a more appropriate category for describing this unusual character who resides in a feminine "third space."

River, the Smart Girl

River's genius is one of the key qualities that distinguishes her from the average person and even from her intelligent brother Simon (Sean Maher), a physician. The representation of "brainy" girls on television may be viewed as proof that women do not necessarily play second fiddle to men as characters in postfeminist TV.[2] *The Gilmore Girls, Veronica Mars*, and *Buffy the Vampire Slayer* (the character Willow in particular) suggest the rise in this kind of representation of the intelligent "girl" whose intellectual powers help redefine the heroine in Western culture. As a child, River reveals her analytical abilities when she tells Simon (who is studying), "The book is wrong. This whole conclusion is fallacious" ("Safe"). River's intelligence enables her to fly the ship *Serenity* in Whedon's film; according to Mal, the ship's captain, she clearly shows "some aptitude." A humorous yet somewhat disturbing expression of River's braininess is evident in a comment she makes to the morally questionable Jayne: "Also, I can kill you with my brain" ("Trash," 1.14).

However, it is important to note that intelligence and the ability to calculate numbers are not the only measure of a female character's ability to serve as a potential hero. At times "numbers" and logic cannot answer the bigger questions concerning faith and religion. For example, in "Jaynestown" (1.4) when River examines Shepherd Book's (Ron Glass) Bible (Book is the preacher figure in *Firefly* and *Serenity*), she tears out pages, pointing out that she is trying to fix his Bible because "it's broken. It doesn't make sense." Book replies, "You don't fix faith, River. It fixes you," thus indicating that using logic or intellect to assess the Bible is not necessarily the best way to approach all kinds of situations. Mal also tells River, "It ain't all buttons, and charts" (*Serenity*), and suggests that love is also important when flying a ship, and presumably in life.

River: Psychic or Psycho?

While River's intelligence in the purely scientific sense may be one of her most obvious abilities, she has an even more remarkable talent as a psychic: "She's a reader. Sees into the truth of things," Mal says in *Serenity*. His response to River helps shape her status as an anti-hero who occupies a "third space" of uncertainty. In "Safe" he makes the wry comment that River has added "cussing and hurling about of things to her repertoire. She really is a prodigy." He is aware of the risks associated with harboring her on the ship (the Alliance wishes to capture her) but he also thinks that this kind of ability could be useful so he allows her to stay on board.

River has a Cassandra-like ability to see the truth, yet the problem with this kind of special knowledge is that it is often perceived as madness by others, as was the case in the mythic character Cassandra, whose visions of the future were discounted since she was destined never to be believed. River's instability and spontaneous fits "makes things not be smooth" ("Safe") according to Mal, whose main mission is to transport goods (e.g., cattle) with as few incidents as possible. Yet Mal defends River on more than one occasion, including when Jayne tries to turn River over to the Alliance in exchange for money. He tells Jayne that if Jayne turns on his crew, then he considers this an attack against Mal ("Ariel," 1.8), thus establishing that he views River and Simon as part of his crew.

The status of River in *Firefly* and through much of *Serenity* suggests that she occupies a kind of indeterminate space, a space of postfeminist contradictions that also position her as an anti-heroine. River becomes a dangerous woman, thus acquiring the aggressive qualities reminiscent of the chaos associated with a postfeminist, punk character like Tank Girl or the punk feminist Riot Grrrl culture, both examples of "girl power."[3] She could be cast as an enemy of the crew because she cuts Jayne with a knife in "Ariel," yet because the audience knows that Jayne is not exactly an ethical character (he tried to hand her over to the Alliance, the villainous government in *Firefly* and *Serenity*), her actions are not entirely unjustified. River's dangerous qualities cause more alarm for the viewer and for the rest of the crew when they are emphasized by Kaylee, the ship's mechanic. Kaylee is a charming and likable character, so her assessment of River should be taken more seriously than Jayne's. One day, Kaylee reveals that River killed some men with her eyes closed and comments, "Nobody can shoot like that that's a person" ("Objects in Space," 1.10), thereby categorizing River as alien or non-human. River seems to be using some kind of inner "vision" to accomplish this act. In this example, River killed men trying to harm the crew of *Serenity*, and should in theory acquire a heroic dimension as a result of this act. Yet Kaylee provides this information and seems like a trustworthy source, so the crew worries about their safety. This combined with the mystery surrounding River's violent outbursts, and the impossibility of explaining how she can shoot with her eyes closed, may make River more of an anti-heroine than a potential heroine; thus the possibility of River becoming a hero in the traditional sense of a hero whose values and actions are consistent[4] remains unlikely.

Another demonstration of River's intellect (contributing to her identity as a psychic warrior) is demonstrated in "Trash," when River tells Jayne that she can kill him with her brain and the audience may wonder whether this is possible or whether this statement is simply a reflection of River's odd sense of humor. In an earlier scene she told Simon that Jayne is afraid that she and Simon will "know." She may be suggesting that since their trip to Ariel (in the episode with the same name), Jayne is afraid that they will know that he played a part in handing over River and Simon to the authorities. The initial part of River's conversation is communicated in fragments without a subject pronoun or accompanying verb. She simply says "afraid" and even her brother misunderstands her and thinks she is referring to someone else. She responds, "Not her. Jayne." River's comment about Jayne's fear leads the viewer to think that perhaps Jayne is afraid of River because she slashed him with a knife, but when she mentions knowledge ("afraid we'll know") it becomes clear that he may be more afraid of her mind. He could fear that the rest of the crew will find out that he tried to hand over River to the authorities ("Ariel"), thereby betraying Simon and River who have become part of the crew. River's emasculation of Jayne when she says "Jayne is a girl's name" ("Trash") makes her power over him quite obvious and suggests that despite her "dangerous" qualities, she has the moral high ground over Jayne and should not simply be dismissed as a mad-woman or as untrustworthy "girlfolk" ("Trash").

Even though River possesses an ability to see the truth, her role as a seer or as a woman with psychic ability continues to be related to the realm of madness, whether this madness is equated with her statement that she can kill someone with her brain or because she has some affili-ation with the dreaded cannibalistic Reavers. Her own name is eerily similar to the word Reaver, the violent, mad creatures depicted in *Seren-ity* as another example of an Alliance experiment. When Mal says, "She's a reader" (*Serenity*), viewers of the film might well hear "Reaver." In the film's narrative, the Reavers were humans who were given the drug "Pax" to remove aggressive tendencies; however, as a result they became fren-zied cannibalistic monsters.[5] The link between being a "reader" or a woman of vision, and a "Reaver," a mad creature, is not unusual in the context of how women with visionary and psychic abilities have been constructed in literature and culture. Cassandra was presented as a mad seer because people did not believe her prophecies and because the impact of the visions was so strong that it affected her psyche and her body: "the pain, the terror!" (Aeschylus 1220). Interestingly, witches in western cul-ture were also cast as madwomen (Hodgkin), and River is called a witch in "Safe," and in "Objects in Space." In "Safe" Simon's sister displays her knowledge of the past when she comments on events in the lives of strangers. The people on this planet react by trying to burn her at the stake. When Mal and the rest of the *Serenity* crew are told that River is a witch, Mal responds, "Yeah, but she's our witch" ("Safe"). Mal sub-verts the negative associations with witches by turning the tables on the people who view River in a limited fashion. As one of the "heroes" in *Serenity*, Mal also reverses the notion that the hero kills the witch; instead he is her advocate. This multiple coding or revaluation of the word witch is repeated in "Objects in Space" when Jayne asks, "Are you saying she's a witch?" and Wash answers, "Yes. A witch." Wash may be implying that Jayne's question is a ridiculous idea or he may be simply agreeing with Jayne but at the same time suggesting that this is not a problem. In the same episode, River self-identifies with the witch image, perhaps in an ironic fashion, when she says, "River's not on the ship. So, she melted. She melted away." The words echo the melting of the Wicked Witch of the West in the novel and film versions of *The Wizard of Oz*[6]; however, what is also worth noting about River's statement is that she refers to herself in the third person, thus placing herself in a kind of alternative or "third space" of detachment.

The fact that River is a witch, but isn't a witch, the fact that she is neither completely healthy nor completely mad and immoral, puts her in the postfeminist third space of an anti-heroine. Her in-between state is explained by her similarity to the Reavers, the enemy, on the one hand, and by her affiliation with the crew of *Serenity* on the other. Like the Reavers, she has been the subject of experiments at the hands of the Alliance, and the mystery surrounding these experiments, in addition to the violent outbursts that are characterized by Simon as "paranoid schizophrenia" ("Safe"). He tries to understand his sister, but at some level, he must admit that he has no idea what sets her off. Scientifically he can comprehend that most of the amygdala in River's brain has been stripped ("Ariel"), so that she "feels everything"; in other words, she lives without the benefit of an emotional filter.

The depiction of River as an individual who may feel too much is developed even further in the film *Serenity*. River harbors the secret about the origin of the Reavers, which is revealed to Mal through a message recorded by the Alliance. In the film, River risks her own life by fighting the Reavers who have attacked the crew and killed Wash, Zoe's husband. She thus demonstrates the "kick-ass" heroine quality that postfeminist viewers have come to expect of female characters like Buffy and Xena. Here her ability as a physical warrior is confirmed and her battle against the Reavers may be viewed as her desire to defeat the uncontrollable violent outbursts that she experiences as a result of the Alliance experiments on her brain. She effectively purges herself of the kind of negative influence associated with the violence of the Reavers. Her noble desire to try to save the crew of *Serenity* by fighting the Reavers would seem to be the stuff of postfeminist heroism, yet it is difficult to apply the term hero to River without qualification. She has saved others, but there is something terrifying and almost supernatural about her at the same time — the idea that a mere waif of a girl would pit herself against an entire group of Reavers. Perhaps she is only able to do so because she still has something in common with them.

While River has some affiliation with the Reavers, it is important to distinguish her from these creatures in one important way. The Reavers seem completely beyond hope or salvation. River on the other hand is integrated into the family of the *Serenity* crew. In one sense, she represents the sense of exile and the outsider status that all members of Mal's crew must feel as renegades choosing to eke out a living outside the control of the Alliance. Her hybrid identity as human psychic and female fighting machine suggest the kind of partial identity presented in Donna Haraway's postfeminist "A Cyborg Manifesto": "lived social and bodily realities in which people are not afraid of their joint kinship with animals and machines, not afraid of permanently partial identities and contradictory standpoints" (154).

River: Psychic Warrior

While River's physical prowess is certainly impressive, both *Firefly* and *Serenity* highlight her status as a psychic warrior who uses her "second sight" or extrasensory powers to outwit her enemies. Fans of the series *Firefly* indicate that it is not clear whether River can see the future or read minds or whether she is merely sensitive to the emotions of others ("Crazy").[7] In *Serenity*, she warns the crew of the arrival of the Reavers, and Mal suggests that if it had not been for River's prescient ability ("She felt them coming") they would not have survived. In "Ariel," River uses her psychic knowledge to find an exit in a building. Even when it appears that she has a physical skill, it is a skill that is really a form of psychic knowledge. For example, in the *Firefly* episode "Objects in Space," River saves a human life and shoots three men with her eyes closed; this action cannot be explained, at least not by Kaylee, the ship's mechanic who is firmly ensconced within the world of tools and machines. Her incomprehension of River's skill suggests that River truly is otherworldly or that she belongs to the realm of the supernatural, which not only reinforces River's identity as psychic warrior but as an anti-heroine since she is a savior figure, but not a savior who can always be trusted.

Perhaps the most interesting insight into River's character as anti-heroine and psychic warrior is provided in "Objects in Space," the final

Firefly episode, where River uses psychic powers on the character of Early (Chiwetel Ejiofor), a bounty hunter out to capture River. This episode reveals River's postfeminist hybrid identity as a psychic warrior. Here again River demonstrates her in-between state when she identifies in part with Early, her enemy even as she tries to protect the crew from him and avoid being captured: "Don't belong. Dangerous like you. Can't be controlled. Can't be trusted." It would appear that Early is clearly the enemy or the villain in this episode; in a traditional narrative where heroes are juxtaposed against villains, this would make River a heroine. And yet she is not a hero in the conventional sense, since she identifies with Early even as she tries to defeat him to protect herself and to protect the crew. This identification echoes her affiliation with the Reavers as outlined earlier in this chapter.

In "Objects in Space," River's disappearance could echo the mythic hero's quest as outlined by Northrop Frye (*Anatomy of Criticism*, 192) which includes the disappearance of the hero followed by the reappearance and recognition of the hero. Yet the disappearance or "death" is unique as far as disappearing heroes are concerned, and should more appropriately be called the disappearance of the "anti-heroine" in River's case. Mythic heroes often "disappear" or die and are then transformed into gods. River is transformed in an even more unusual way from River, former witch, into *Serenity*, the ship. River's voice proclaims: "River's not on the ship. So, she melted. She melted away. I'm not on the ship. I'm in the ship. I am the ship. You're talking to *Serenity*" (*Serenity*). The reference to River melting away is an intertextual reference to the melting of the Wicked Witch of the West from *The Wizard of Oz*. This "witch" is then supposedly transformed into the ship, a powerful image. Her disembodied voice functions as a psychic weapon as she plays with Early's mind and seems to know the secrets of his past: "Your mother knew ... saw a darkness in you. You're not well..."

Although River does not "magically merge with the ship" (Robert B. Taylor, 136), she convinces others that she becomes the ship and more importantly uses her psychic ability as a strategic weapon against Early. Even her brother begins to accept her changed state as a fact: "Well, my sister's a ship."[8] While this transformation from human to inanimate object may seem unusual, it is not all that surprising for the genre of telefantasy which includes science fiction. If spaceships like the *Enterprise* (*Star Trek*) or the Tardis (*Doctor Who*) can be personified, why can't people be turned into spaceships in fantasy television or fantasy films? River's subversion of distinct categories is a postfeminist challenge to the concept of the "complete" and may also be viewed as another example of the "partial," which is an important component of Donna Haraway's postfeminist essay on the cyborg. As River moves from human to machine and from machine to machine (she relocates from *Serenity* to Early's ship), she engages in the act of "boundary" transgression (Haraway, 152). In a paradoxical way, River confirms Kaylee's earlier conclusion that River may not be "a person." Of course, if she is not a person, she must be a ship, and she uses this "transformation" strategically as a psychic weapon against Early, her patriarchal bounty hunter.[9]

River: Heroine at Last?

In "Objects in Space," River achieves the literalization of her psychic potential; she turns the tables on the Alliance by playing with Early's mind (they had operated on her mind) and becomes a savior figure. Her status as a hero is still questionable, however, since one could argue that if she had not been on the ship, then the crew would not have been in peril in the first place. Mal says to her, "You know — you ain't quite right." While tragic heroes are far from perfect, River's imperfection is of an unusual, unpredictable order, and in many ways, the term antiheroine is still more appropriate for her character.[10]

In *Serenity*, Zoe, the second-in-command, says that the definition of the hero is "someone who gets other people killed." With this kind of definition, most people would probably prefer to be anti-heroes or anti-heroines. In *Serenity*, River, the anti-heroine, embodies the contradictions of postfeminist "girl power" and the "partial" as advocated by Donna Haraway in "The Cyborg Manifesto." She is part heroine-savior figure, part unpredictable human weapon and partially an image of vulnerability as the victim of scientific experiments. It is so tempting to cast River as a heroine in *Serenity* when she co-pilots the ship with Mal and when she resists Early, the bounty hunter in *Firefly*'s "Objects in Space."

Yet Joss Whedon resists this identification of River with the concept of the heroine in both the television series and the accompanying film. In *Firefly*, the meaningful conversation between River and Kaylee during a game of jacks in "Objects in Space" (written by Whedon) casts some doubt on River's "recovery." When River says, "I can win this," she is perhaps unconsciously referring to her battle with her disease or mental state. Kaylee replies "Oh, I'm hearing a lot of talk there, 'Genius.'" Through Kaylee's words, Whedon may be questioning whether River will be all right. Like the indeterminacy surrounding River's health in "Objects in Space," *Serenity* maintains the uncertainty surrounding River's future. While the film *Serenity* suggests that River may have achieved a form of catharsis after her battle with the Reavers, it is not clear what the future state of her health will be just as the crew of *Serenity* is uncertain about their future. In a sense, her instability reflects the social structure or fractured relationships that characterize the crew of *Serenity*. Furthermore, through her self-identification with Early, the bounty hunter, she serves as a reminder of how human beings can be "broken" whether they are River, Early or the aggressive, cannibalistic Reavers. While the audience may wonder whether River's personal "storm" or life will get better or worse, River's ability as a psychic girl warrior who "knows things" ("Objects in Space") cannot be disputed.

THREE

Phoebe and the
Power of Sight
The Witch as Seer in Charmed

Charmed is a television series that focuses on the lives of three modern witches, each of whom has a special power. The series ran a remarkable eight seasons on the American WB network (1998–2006) and built an international following.[1] While the series evolved with changes in cast members (the eldest sister Prue [Shannen Doherty] died in Season 3 and was replaced with a long-lost half-sister Paige [Rose McGowan]), what prevailed over the years was the emphasis on the characters' special powers. Prue had an ability to move objects and developed the power of astral projection, Piper (Holly Marie Combs) was able to freeze objects and blast them apart, Phoebe (Alyssa Milano) received premonitions and had an assortment of other more active powers, and Paige (the sister who "replaced" Prue) had the power of telekinesis as well as the power to magically transport herself ("orb") to other places because of her partial "whitelighter" (non-human) heritage.

Of all of the sisters, Phoebe Halliwell may well have the distinction of undergoing the greatest number of transformations, many of which were linked to her (passive) power as a seer. An etymological study of the word "witch" reveals that it is derived from the Old English word "wicce," meaning "female magician, sorceress." The ability to see or tell the future is clearly one of the dimensions of witchcraft that the series has highlighted through the character of Phoebe. Her very name suggests brilliance and light,[2] and her visionary powers prove particularly interesting given the popularity of other series such as *Angel* and *Firefly* that emphasize the visions of certain female characters.[3] In *Charmed*, Phoebe has the traditional ability of historical and mythological seer[4] figures to view the future. Like Cassandra, the famous Trojan seer and Agamemnon's "slave" (Aeschylus, 1235), Phoebe perceives herself as an outsider or as a peripheral figure. This is apparent when she characterizes her visionary power as a passive power that contrasts with her sisters' more desirable, active powers. The first three seasons of the series demonstrate Phoebe's struggle to validate her existing passive power of premonition while coveting more active abilities.[5] This development contributes to her increasingly dynamic role in the series. She thus serves as an emblem of feminine power and transformation, both within the series and for its target audience (primarily young women in their late teens or early twenties). Phoebe's visionary powers and the character's experience of alternative identities reveal how the "third space" or alternate space occupied by the female seer can be used as a means of questioning an oversimplified division of supernatural/fantastic powers into active (=effective) and passive (=ineffective). Phoebe's role as a seer not only allows her to embody traditional, mythic constructs of the "woman of vision" but to also go beyond some of the constraints placed on the visionary figure in historical or mythical contexts. In *Charmed*, Phoebe's various identities as unemployed single girl, youngest sister (until the arrival of the new sister Paige), scapegoat, vamp, Queen of the Underworld, and mother, add a variety to her character that is not experienced by the other sisters. Pauline Bartel describes her as the sister with "free-spirited eccentricities" (243). These different identities and their social contexts help reveal that what may initially be perceived as a simplified opposition of active (= good or effective) vs. passive (= bad and ineffective) powers needs to be re-examined in light of the development of Phoebe's visionary abilities and her transformations as a character, especially in the early part of the series.

The development of Phoebe's gift of "second sight" in *Charmed* is a postfeminist reworking or representation of the traditional seer figure whose "passive power" has been firmly established in myth and in history. The gift of prophecy may be viewed as a passive power, since the prophet or seer could normally not control the outcome of events. For example, in the context of Greek mythology, a seer like Tiresias had the gift of vision but could not change the course of fate.[6] Even though there are male seers in Greek mythology (Tiresias,[7] Calchas), it is the woman who has often been cast in this role both historically and artistically, partially because of the link between this gift and the concept of a passive rather than an "active" power. The figure of the Trojan seer Cassandra in Greek mythology is presented in tragic terms as Agamemnon's prize, "the gift of the armies, / flower and pride of all the wealth" (Aeschylus, 952–53) and as a figure of isolation, pain and madness. In Aeschylus' play *Agamemnon*, Cassandra foresaw the murder of King Agamemnon among other events (the destruction of Troy), and like other seers could not control the outcome of his fate; however, her passive power was made even more "passive" or disabling by the fact that no one would believe her prophecies, thereby eroding what was already a passive power.[8] Robert Fagles and W.B. Stanford indicate that first Apollo exploits Cassandra "as his medium, then he destroys her, 'treads [her] down'—his service is a rape" (29). The historical figure Joan of Arc would appear to be a more "empowered" figure than Cassandra since she was the recipient of a divine vision and used this passive power to achieve an active victory against the English. However, she too was demonized as a witch for her privileged access to the divine through her passive power.

The image of the visionary in the context of feminine passivity is also discussed by Katharine Hodgkin ("Reasoning with Unreason"). In her study of witchcraft in early modern England, she highlights the "construction of the visionary woman as channel, as passive voice" (225). In the early part of the series *Charmed*, Phoebe is struck by visions over which she has no control. In some ways, Phoebe's visions share the images of doom which are conveyed through Cassandra's visions, yet Phoebe's frustration is not linked to whether anyone believes her visions. Instead, Phoebe's primary frustration lies in the nature of her power, which she perceives as passive—hence her decision to take kickboxing or martial arts lessons as a way of compensating: "I got tired of being the one in the family with the passive power, so I started taking up self-defense classes which I've been putting on my new credit card" ("Which Prue Is It Anyway?" 1.16). Unlike her sisters Prue and Piper in the early part of the series, Phoebe cannot normally engage in an active use of her ability, except when she touches objects that may spontaneously convey visions. Thus she can use her passive ability to become a good detective, but she is far less effective as a fighter. Yet Phoebe's active abilities (unlike Prue's and Piper's active supernatural powers) are limited by her "natural" physical strength.

As fans of *Charmed* have noted, Phoebe's ability to turn her passive power into a more active one occurs in the course of Season 1 when she is able to call up and sustain a premonition (http://www.thepowerof charmed.com/PhoebesPowers.htm, December 30, 2005). For example, in "The Power of Two" (1.20) she holds onto a plane ticket to call up a future event: "I've been practicing how to call a premonition and I did it. I saw a future event." The series also makes clear that Phoebe's visions assist the Charmed Ones in their quest to solve the supernatural mysteries they encounter in each episode. In fact, her premonitions often allow the trio to prevent certain events from transpiring, thus suggesting that they are not to be dismissed because of Phoebe's pervasive view of them as passive. In "Déjà Vu All Over Again" (1.22) Prue tells a man by the name of Andy Trudeau that Phoebe's premonitions have allowed the Charmed Ones "to affect the outcome" (1.22) and that they may be able to prevent a death.[9]

Phoebe's ability to exercise some control over what is normally constructed as a passive power reveals how this Halliwell sister develops or changes in a more complex way that is not evident in the depiction of Prue and Piper (and even the new sister Paige), who have the kind of active powers more commonly associated with conventional male superheroes (the ability to move objects, to freeze, to move through space). In some ways, the term "active" may appear to serve as a code word for "masculine" since Prue and Piper's powers resemble those of active male warrior figures who have an ability to affect the actions of others through aggressive acts or physical intervention. Phoebe thus suffers from a form of "power envy." As the younger sister she feels deficient in a number of ways, and her passive power only highlights her sense of inferiority. The series writers and creators may have decided that unlike Prue and Piper, the two older sisters who often take on parental roles, Phoebe's character allowed for a more complex exploration of the doubts that *Charmed*'s target audience of young women in their late teens or early twenties might be experiencing.

Phoebe's dissatisfaction[10] with her passive visionary power (in the early part of the series) serves as the basis for exploring the tension between desires of the self and concern for others that for many young people marks the transition from being a teenager to becoming a socially responsible adult. Phoebe's youth and her immaturity as the unemployed sister in the first part of the series, contribute to her ongoing desire to have a more active or warrior-like power. Yet her desire for a better or more warrior-like power actually results in an undesirable outcome. For example, in "Morality Bites" (2.2), Phoebe is given the opportunity to step outside the parameters of her more limited "present self": She is transported into her own future and actually experiences a form of wish fulfillment[11] through a future self who has an active power. However, in this episode, the Phoebe of the future is on trial for having used her enhanced powers in an unacceptable way (to zap or electrocute a killer called Cal Greene, a baseball player). In "Morality Bites" Phoebe's premonitions and insight allow her to see the consequences of misusing an active power, thereby indirectly demonstrating the usefulness of having a passive power. Phoebe has the courage and the wisdom to commit an act of self-sacrifice by allowing herself to be "burned at the stake." Here she achieves the kind of mythic hero status that echoes that of other scapegoats in myth or history (Joan of Arc, Cassandra, Jesus Christ). She sees the bigger picture instead of simply reacting to her unpleasant situation by trying to stop the future from happening (which describes her earlier use of premonitions in the series): "Prue, we were sent here for a reason. Maybe not to stop this like we thought. But maybe to understand why this has to happen. Why you have to let this happen. I don't want to die. But I don't want you to die because of me."

Phoebe's use of her visions is a key example of how a simple binary opposition between passive powers as inadequate and active powers as enviable is an inadequate way of addressing Phoebe's powers in the series since her "passive" power of vision facilitates her intellectual growth and maturation. One of the most important lines in this episode solidifies the code which all the sisters must follow. They are not to use their powers to benefit themselves in an ethically or morally questionable fashion. Phoebe articulates this code perfectly in "Morality Bites": "The wrong thing done for the right reasons is still the wrong thing." While they periodically forget this law (as part of the dramatic necessity of the series), it is a law that resonates in a particularly strong way when the youngest sister, Phoebe, recognizes its importance.

The transplantation of Phoebe into her own future is just one of the ways that the writers of *Charmed* have developed the figure of the seer in contemporary television. "Morality Bites" reveals the intricate relationship between passive and active in the context of Phoebe's visions by challenging an oversimplified binary opposition between active and passive realms. What also distinguishes Phoebe from the typical representation of the seer figure in myth and history is that she is able to view past events, whereas most seer figures have been cast in the image of fortune tellers or prophets of future doom. Phoebe's ability to access a past unknown to the three sisters is first conveyed in "The Witch is Back" (1. 9), an episode where the Charmed Ones encounter one of their ancestors, Melinda Warren. After her initial surprise over Phoebe's ability to see "the past," Prue admits that they "always knew that [their] powers would grow." Phoebe adds, "Yes, but somehow I thought I was gonna get to fly."

Phoebe's desire to fly is actually realized in Season 3, but this ability to levitate was rather short-lived due to the expense associated with this special effect (according to various *Charmed* fan sites). However, her ability to see into the past is further artistically transformed or developed even further in the episode "Pardon My Past" (2.14) in which Phoebe actually becomes her former self. In "Pardon My Past," she uses her active power to cast spells to cross into the past where she plays the role of a vamp who is confident and ruthless, a far cry from the "boy-friendless" Phoebe in modern-day San Francisco, a city known for its large gay population. This "past Phoebe" also has the power to throw fireballs. Here is yet another episode that conveys the wish fulfillment of Phoebe who perceives herself as uninteresting and incapable of finding the right man. Her string of boyfriends attests to her inability to find a "keeper." In "Pardon My Past" Phoebe is depicted in her past life as a vamp who was morally questionable due to her "evil" ways. Even though this former Phoebe is presented in a critical light, the episode does allow for the transformation of a character by adding an alternate dimension to what would otherwise be a more static, predictable seer figure. Thus

Phoebe learns that active powers are not necessarily "good" or better than her power of premonition.

Some feminist critics might view this curtailing of Phoebe's active powers through negative representation as a way of limiting the kinds of powers that are acceptable for women. They could argue that her passive visionary ability is an extension of her passive lifestyle: her unemployed status in the early part of the series, her infantilized role as the youngest, least responsible of the Halliwell sisters (until Season 4 when sister Paige arrives). Yet this would be difficult to argue in the larger context of the series since the other sisters have been granted active powers that are not criticized or curtailed in the same manner. Thus, instead of functioning as a passive victim, Phoebe may well serve as an example of the variety of the powers or perspectives that women may have, a notion that resembles the desire of third wave feminists or postfeminists to recognize a range of identities. *Charmed* is a series that was born out of 1990s postfeminism or third wave feminism, which sought to articulate a new kind of feminism for a generation of young women referred to as the "'daughters,' both real and metaphorical, of the Second Wave" (Baumgardner and Richards, 402). This newer generation of women has found the feminism of the second wave feminists rather limiting, often because of the historical tendency of second wave feminists to critique women and their place in the home while championing women in the workplace.[12] Phoebe's passive power of vision can therefore be "read" as a validation of an alternative power that has its own remarkable qualities of introspection even though Phoebe may not perceive it to be as "effective" as the warrior-like powers of her sisters, which have been the hallmark of other women in telefantasy or fantasy television series (e.g., Buffy the Vampire Slayer and Xena, Warrior Princess).

From a purely technical standpoint, Phoebe's passive power of vision lends itself to fewer action-packed sequences than those involving her sisters who have active powers. From a narrative standpoint, her second sight serves primarily as a means of foreshadowing events in each episode or as a way of allowing the sisters to know information about the past. It is therefore not surprising that the series incorporated other ways of developing Phoebe's character through additional visual means. The role of the visual takes on a new dimension in "The Painted World" (2.3) when Phoebe casts a spell to make herself smart; this stems from her feelings of inadequacy (perhaps an extension of her dissatisfaction with her power as a seer.) It is in this episode that she develops a new degree of independence (in "Morality Bites" she was more of an archetypal victim figure) through her realization that she must use her own intelligence, an inner power, rather than relying only on active magic to help her sisters who are trapped inside a painting. The painting serves as an interesting metaphor for the mind or the imagination. In "The Painted World," Phoebe is transformed from a lazy, self-absorbed little sister to a resourceful woman who needs to rely on her cunning and imagination in her battle against a warlock who is determined to leave all three witches trapped in the painting. In the episode, her earlier search in the series for a more active physical power is again redirected into an effective intellectual ability that allows her to help her sisters, thus subverting the simplistic binary opposition of active=effective and passive=ineffective powers.

Phoebe: Season 4 and Beyond

Phoebe's role as a seer figure in *Charmed* develops in a new direction when she leaves behind her "unemployed single girl" image to become a mother and wife. This is a significant transformation since historically and mythically, witches have been single or childless (usually crones). As Debra Kaye argues, "At some points in history, childless women have been accused of being witches." In her book *Childless by Choice*, Marian Faux says that the witch has become a metaphor for the childless woman. Margaret Mead gives this descriptive image of the witch as anti-mother:

> The figure of the witch who kills living things, who strokes the throat of children until they die, whose very glance causes cows to lose their calves, and fresh milk to curdle as it stands, is a statement of human fear of what can be done to mankind by a woman who denies or is forced to deny childbearing and child-cherishing [2].

During Season 4, Phoebe shatters the myth of the childless witch and becomes pregnant with the child of her demon husband Cole. She becomes linked to another female figure who has visions; this entity is known as the Seer,[13] and Phoebe eventually discovers that the baby she is carrying is really the child of the Seer.[14] The pairing of the two seers appears to facilitate the demonization of Phoebe, since she becomes an evil Queen of the Underworld. Like the mythical character Persephone, who was abducted by Hades, the Lord of Darkness, Phoebe leaves the world of light and enters the world of darkness. Even though the series indicates that Phoebe's choice to follow Cole to the Underworld was morally wrong, the story arc of Phoebe's relationship with Cole allows her to experience the kind of cosmic and mythic transformation that is not duplicated by her other sisters.[15]

The entry into a world of darkness also functions as an interesting although not an entirely unproblematic way of describing Phoebe's state of motherhood, and acts as an extension of the struggle that characterized Phoebe's earlier anxiety about passive (visionary ability) vs. active powers. The passive/active distinction is re-articulated in a different way through the relationship between involuntary and voluntary acts and the experiences of the pregnant woman. *Charmed* presents the conflicting feelings a pregnant woman may experience about her baby in the face of her own body's transformation. For example, Phoebe's baby is a child of evil (whether the child is represented as the child of the Seer or as the child of Cole, the new Source of all evil) and has the power to change Phoebe into a woman who experiences intense hot flashes in the form of flames of fire shooting out of her head: "That wasn't me, it was the baby, I couldn't control him" ("Womb Raider," 4.21). Phoebe struggles to separate her body from the baby's. Thus, the lines between self and other, voluntary and involuntary, active and passive become blurred as they do for many expectant mothers. While most mothers would not dream of perceiving their babies as evil, Phoebe's evil baby serves as a metaphor for the discomfort of pregnancy and the hormonal fluctuations associated with this "alien" state. However, Phoebe's motherhood experience is relatively brief since the Seer, the person who tries to take over as the Source, reclaims her progeny ("Womb Raider," 4.21).

Phoebe returns to the world of light and re-embraces the role of the more conventional kind of seer or witch figure without the apparatus of either a husband or child.[16] Yet unlike Cassandra, the solitary seer figure from Greek myth, and unlike the solitary witch of European fairy tales, she is not alone. She rejoins her sisters in their battle against demonic forces and seems to benefit from her otherworldly experiences in the romance department by honing her skills as an advice columnist for a local newspaper, *The Bay Mirror*. This profession seems like a logical extension of her role as a seer figure in *Charmed* since her column is called "Ask Phoebe" and presents her as a contemporary representation of the archetypal seer figure, the source of knowledge.

Charmed *Fans and Phoebe*

Since *Charmed* has had such a dedicated following, it is important to see how fans of the series have responded to the various powers and transformations of this postfeminist seer figure. This response is an important indicator of how a contemporary television audience perceives the role of the seer and her effectiveness as one of three heroic witch sisters. Some discussions suggest that fans view Phoebe as a marginalized figure in relation to her sisters (including her half-sister Paige, who was equipped with the active power of telekinesis, the ability to call objects to her). Perhaps, because these fans have become accustomed to seeing other postfeminist "kick-ass" heroines like Buffy or Xena, they argue that Phoebe should have been allowed to develop additional, ongoing active powers (Charmed-net.com, 2003).

Various fan posts on http://www.thesistersthree.com/forums indicate that many viewers of *Charmed* do enjoy the series' "girl power" or woman-centered elements and do not believe that the show would be as popular with men in the leading roles. Other fans appreciate Phoebe's unique power of vision. A discussion on Charmed-net.com in 2003 reflects fans' profound dismay with the decreased frequency of premonitions in *Charmed*.[17] Fans lamented that since Season 4, Phoebe rarely had a premonition.

A post on Charmed.net (December 2005) bemoans the fact that Phoebe's premonitions used to be about demons and that the more recent ones only involve glimpses of her own future (her husband and children), including her bizarre ability to talk to herself in the future while she is having a premonition ("Vaya Con Leos," 8.10)! It appears that while some *Charmed* fans are enthusiastic about the usefulness of Phoebe's visions in bringing about the destruction of demons, they are less enthusiastic about the way the premonitions have evolved (instead of remaining more of the same thing). Her ability to use her premonitions to talk to herself in the future indicates a kind of empowerment of the self; Phoebe redirects her power to foreground herself as an individual instead of merely serving as a channel for other events or people, which was the case in the first season. Yet this use of premonitions to discover the self should not be interpreted as a lack of concern for others. It is possible that some *Charmed* fans may not have been able to appreciate the more subtle ways that Phoebe develops intellectually through her premonitions and how she redefines her earlier limited notion of what it meant to have a passive power. One possibility for the writers' ongoing development of Phoebe's passive power could have been linked to economic factors. Many fans were disappointed when economics or budget cuts played a role in the abandonment of special effects involving Phoebe's ability to levitate in Season 3. This economic reality may help explain the inventiveness of the series writers in finding creative ways of extending the boundaries of Phoebe's passive power. Regardless of how this development of Phoebe's visionary powers came about, it helped create a more complex character, especially during the series' first few seasons.

Phoebe's character as a seer figure resembles that of mythic and historical visionary figures. Like Cassandra, the mad seer figure from Greek mythology, and Joan of Arc who was tried as a witch for her visions, she feels marginalized, even among other witches. As a way of compensating for her passive power of premonition, she covets active powers. However, Phoebe's complexity as a character appears to be intimately connected to her visionary abilities instead of to her possession of any active powers such as levitation or throwing fireballs. She uses her intellect, not any active power, to save her sisters in "The Painted World" and her vision of her future self in "Morality Bites" makes her realize that active powers can be dangerous if used unwisely. Her connection to the demon Seer figure whose progeny she carries in her own womb, allows her to enter the realm of the mythic mother and spouse. She is also a Persephone figure, the Queen of Darkness, and her descent into the world of darkness allows her to acquire the kind of mythic knowledge that enhances her image as a seer. While some viewers and fans may focus on Phoebe's immoral abandonment of the realm of "light" in order to join the "dark side," Phoebe's statement in "Long Live the Queen" (4.20) suggests a more subtle postfeminist perspective that recognizes the contradictions in life.[18] This Halliwell sister argues the difficulty of conceding that everything is black and white: "Things are not as black and white as they used to be." Leo replies, "Phoebe, you can't be the Queen of the Underworld and a Charmed One. You can't have it both ways." And Phoebe resists: "Why not? Just because it's different doesn't mean that it can't work."

Eventually, Phoebe does choose to return to the side of "good" and rejoins her sisters, the Charmed Ones, because the fantasy format and formula of the series seem to demand this choice. However, Phoebe's immersion in the world of darkness through love, marriage and temporary motherhood, combined with her visions of the past and the future, place her in an "in-between space" where she can see the ambiguities of life and death. These colossal experiences depicted in the first few seasons of *Charmed* serve as a valuable foundation for the many other transformations that she will undergo in subsequent episodes of this long-running series.

FOUR

Visions of the
"Mad" Outsider in *Hex*
Cassandra, Witches and Lesbian Appetite

The Sky 1 postfeminist telefantasy series *Hex* (2004–2005), which premiered in the U.S. on Sci-Fi in June 2006, depicts a modern-day Cassandra figure who experiences visions of a fallen angel. *Hex* has been compared to *Buffy the Vampire Slayer* and, despite director Brian Grant's claim that it does not take itself "too seriously" ("Making of *Hex*"), the series does have a darker, more adult sensibility for an audience of twenty-year olds.[1] In *Hex*, the Cassandra myth is retold in the neo-gothic setting of a private school, Medenham Hall; the manor functions as a contemporary gothic castle. Parallels between the mythic seer figure and Cassie are established through visions, through the character of Azazeal, an Apollo figure who "possesses" Cassie, and through images of madness or excess. However, what distinguishes this series from other representations of the Cassandra myth is its postfeminist association of this myth with the knowledge and power of witches, the sexual desires of teenagers, and lesbian appetite. Cassie's visions connect her to a female ancestor who was a witch, and Cassie develops supernatural powers of her own. As Katharine Hodgkin indicates, witches in popular culture have often been presented with visionary abilities; they have also been linked to unusual appetites. (The cannibalistic witch in "Hansel and Gretel" is a well-known example.) *Hex* not only uses the device of "the vision" to evoke the figure of Cassandra and the image of the witch, but develops this device in an intriguing way by introducing the character of Thelma, Cassie's lesbian friend who dies near the end of the pilot and becomes a ghost. As one of Cassie's visions (in the sense that only Cassie and others with special abilities can actually see Thelma) and as a lesbian, Thelma occupies the most obvious "third space" or "in-between space" in the series. She becomes a visually powerful illustration of appetite; she is always eating food, and she has a sexual interest in women. Her eccentric fashion sense, her constant consumption of food and her desire for Cassie also serve as an exaggerated display of some of the appetites of other characters in the series, thus suggesting a new, postfeminist reconstruction of the "mad" outsider.

In classical mythology, Cassandra's visionary ability is coupled with the fact that she was doomed never to be believed. This frustration, combined with the painful nature of her visions, contributes to the seer's madness and to her status as an outsider.[2] The link between visions and madness is presented in the pilot episode, when Cassie (Christina Cole) receives strange visions of a historical past in which she plays a role. The obvious implication is that Cassie has been reincarnated. She hears voices and has various visions. For example, she sees a bloody woman in a mirror, a woman drowning and a male figure who is later revealed to be Azazeal (Michel Fassbender), a fallen angel or demon lover figure. Confiding in her friend Thelma (Jemima Rooper), Cassie worries that others may think that she is mad: "You think I'm crazy" ("Pilot").[3] She fears that no one will believe what she has seen, yet unlike Cassandra who had no one to believe her, Thelma (an outsider herself since she is a lesbian) assures Cassie that she does believe her friend.

Because Cassie's name and visions suggest the mythical Cassandra and the Trojan woman's sexual association with the god Apollo who "came like a wrestler/magnificent, took [her] down and breathed his fire" (Aeschylus, 1211) through her, it is not surprising that *Hex* also highlights the idea of sexual appetite. Azazeal, the demon lover / fallen angel who wants to possess Cassie in order to have a child, is an Apollo figure. In Greek myth, Apollo punished Cassandra for not completely yielding to him. Even though she acquired the gift of prophesy, she could not be believed, and she is possessed by Apollo over and over again when she sees a vision.[4] The correspondence with Apollo occurs in the pilot episode where one of Azazeal's first appearances presents him in front of a building with pillars reminiscent of Apollo's temples in Greece. The parallel between Azazeal and Apollo is also developed throughout *Hex* as Cassie is "possessed" by Azazeal. Along with the phallic images of the Apollonian pillars used as a backdrop for male power, the series foregrounds an old vessel or vase that Cassie has found in the school. The vessel symbolizes the female body. Cassie sees Azazeal through this vessel and cuts her finger[5] while touching it, thereby foreshadowing their future sexual union. As the series develops, Cassie cannot resist Azazeal, partially because he "possesses" her with some kind of supernatural power. She eventually becomes pregnant with his male child[6] who will apparently destroy the world. Like her prototype (the mythic Cassandra who foresaw the Trojan War and the destruction of her people), Cassie and her "mad" vision of Azazeal and her liaison with him create an atmosphere of doom.

Cassie not only resembles her mythical namesake (Cassandra) but also has strong associations with witches. While the term "witch" has been used in folklore to describe women with sorcery skills, it has also been applied to women with visionary abilities. Joan of Arc, a medieval visionary, was condemned as a witch because her claim that she had direct access to divine visions was deemed unacceptable (Blaetz, 1). Robin Blaetz argues that for those who called Joan of Arc a heretic, her visions "reconfirmed the hysteria of what was thought to be the womb-ruled sex" (184).[7] *Hex* also addresses the concept of madness through the well-known association of "madness" with visions and witches. Katharine Hodgkin, for example, indicates that "the witch, the female prophet, and the madwoman" may be related (219). All three see or experience "something that is neither seen nor experienced by others, that puts [their] perceptions at odds with those of others around [them]" (222). While madness in history and literature has not been restricted to women's experiences, there is a gendered component as is evident in the concept of female hysteria and through a literary image like Charlotte Brontë's "madwoman in the attic" in *Jane Eyre*. In *Hex*, madness also appears to be gendered for Cassie, the witch-like Cassandra figure. Cassie is a spiritual if not a biological descendent of witches who were associated with Medenham Manor. She has visions of a woman called Rachel McBain, who was declared a witch and who went insane. Cassie's own mother appears to have gone mad as well. She is mentally unstable and requires medical care.

However, it is important to note that Cassie's madness as well as the mental instability of Cassie's mother and Rachel McBain appear to be attributable to the powerful, patriarchal influence of Azazeal. He apparently possessed all of these women. Identifying this masculine link to madness is important since it does not totally ascribe madness to woman alone. The suggestion that Azazeal may have had a relationship with Cassie's mother displaces a biological explanation and suggests an environmental influence rather than a female, genetic predisposition. In any case, a masculine cause of madness can still be unsettling since Cassandra the Trojan seer was also the victim of male possession every time she had a vision.

Despite the masculine intervention in *Hex*— the series suggests that Azazeal may be the source of Cassie's powers — this postfeminist show is still very much concerned with feminine sexuality and different illustrations of "girl power." As Cassie continues to have visions of Azazeal and a past life linked to witches, and as she develops her own powers, she becomes more sexually powerful, changing from dowdy schoolgirl to one of the more popular girls (from outsider to insider status) with the power to protect herself from unwanted sexual advances. While many witches in literature have been cast as hags and therefore devoid of sexual appeal, others like Circe, the sorceress in Greek myth who turned men into pigs, are clearly sexually desirable and powerful at the same time.[8]

Cassie's new identity as a witch not only allows her to use her powers, but seems to enhance her sexual presence. She can fend off uninvited sexual advances from a young man called Leon. In one scene ("Pilot"), she sets him on fire, thereby reversing the stock image of the witch who is burned for her crimes. This moment of resistance also serves as a supernatural exaggeration of heterosexual relationships for young adults and a powerful fantastic/telefantasy representation of a young girl's message that *no* means *no*. This scene functions as a postfeminist reversal of the fairy tale, mythic image of woman/witch as predator of young men to an image of the modern witch as empowered figure of resistance. Finally, the scene can also be read as a postfeminist adaptation of the Cassandra myth. Cassandra resisted Apollo's complete sexual possession of her, but her punishment for resisting the god was to experience madness. She was psychologically burned by his "fire" whenever she received a vision ("Apollo Lord of the Light, you burn, / you blind me" (Aeschylus, lines 1271–1272). In this scene, it is the male who is burned by Cassie, the Cassandra figure.

Another important subversion that takes place in *Hex* is the overturning of the negative image of madness. Cassie's fear of her "mad" visions is subverted through Cassie's friend Thelma, who happens to be a lesbian and who becomes a ghost and primary ally. Cassie's ability to see her dead friend Thelma as a ghost is one of the woman-centered aspects of the show. While *Hex* initially appears to focus on Cassie and her fate and her role in Azazeal's master-narrative of trying to take over her body and mind, Thelma functions as a key counterpoint to this narrative. Thelma's role complicates the narrative of sexual appetite and the visions experienced by Cassie, the Cassandra/witch figure. Thelma is Cassie's lesbian platonic friend and her presence in the series actually eclipses that of Cassie in Season 2, leaving Thelma to soldier on against Azazeal's son Malachi. Thelma's link to appetite, both sexual and food-related, is established early on in the series. She is madly in love with Cassie and continues to remain so even though Cassie says "I'm not into it" and would prefer a heterosexual relationship; she is attracted to a young man by the name of Troy.[9] Thelma the lesbian outsider thus becomes the postfeminist manifestation of "mad" appetite in a curiously liberating way that goes beyond what Cassie can experience on her own. While Cassie's desire initially follows the pattern of the mythological Cassandra and Apollo's heterosexual possession of her, Thelma's desire is of a different order. She therefore serves as an interesting postfeminist reconceptualization of possession. Unlike Azazeal who violently possesses Cassie, Thelma remains by Cassie's side as her ghostly partner-in-arms. Cassie and Thelma share a bond that transcends the need to obtain the object of sexual desire through the act of "violent" possession. Together they unite as women against Azazeal and his plan to destroy the world. Thelma's very existence or "fate" appears to be linked to Cassie, and this link is even more clear when Thelma contemplates trying to save the world from Cassie and Azazeal's unborn son. Cassie also wants to terminate her pregnancy to prevent Azazeal's followers from returning to the world, but Thelma discovers that the consequence of this act would be that all ghosts, including Thelma, would vanish. Thelma is prepared to sacrifice herself to facilitate the destruction of the child and does not tell Cassie, thus demonstrating her qualities as a heroine: the willingness to give "her life to something bigger" than herself (Campbell *The Power of Myth*, 151). She is willing to sacrifice her love for Cassie to eradicate a more powerful, patriarchal force.

The images of sexual appetite and food are continued in the series in many ways, but Cassie's heightened sexual awareness and her friend Thelma's constant consumption of food provide key examples related to the figure of the "witch" and to the re-construction of the mad outsider. In addition to her sexual appetite for women, Thelma is also cast as someone with an extraordinary appetite for food (usually junk food). While Thelma is not a witch in the sense that Cassie is a "witch" with her powers of vision and her ability to set someone on fire, Thelma's appetite is suggestive of women who have lived on the borders of patriarchal society, and Thelma's lesbian desire certainly places her on the margins. Witches have also been depicted as having unusual or "mad" appetites, often linked to food or sexuality. For example, in fairy tales and folktales, the cannibalistic witch in "Hansel and Gretel" and Baba Yaga, the witch who lives in a house on chicken feet, have a taste for young boys or men. *Hex* revises this myth of heterosexual appetite by focusing on the relationship between two women as well as the concepts of appetite and the "mad" woman as outsider.

Before her own death, Thelma was always eating; the first classroom setting in *Hex* shows Thelma sucking on a green lollipop[10] and other scenes focus on her ongoing consumption of junk food. Even as a ghost, her interest in food continues; however, as a ghost she can eat all she wants without running the risk of gaining weight. Through her excessive appetite she reverses the idea that women's appetites, including women's appetites for other women, are "bad."

Even before Thelma dies and is transformed into a ghost, her appetite and her role as an outsider reinforce *Hex*'s emphasis on the alienated teenager, a reality that she shares with her friend Cassie but which she also expresses in a different way because of her lesbian identity. She says to Cassie, "You think I'm sort of a loser" ("Pilot") and perhaps this is why Cassie bonds with her early on, since she too is an outsider.

However, unlike Cassie who appears to want to fit into a heteronormative world through her attraction to Troy, Thelma is outrageous; her pink spiky hair and wild fashion sense (her wardrobe includes lacy, sheer blouses and Wellington boots) indicate her extreme state of otherness. She is also the recipient of jokes about lesbians. Her classmates often have jokes at her expense but she usually provides a witty comeback indicating an ability to resist the heteronormative world around her. In one scene, the students in a poetry class joke about Thelma showing another girl the meaning of "suck on country pleasures" ("Pilot"). A male student says, "Thelma will show you later," and another young man adds, "Now that I'd like to see." Thelma quips, "Yeah, you might learn a thing or two" ("Pilot"). Thus Thelma is not only linked to appetite for food (she is sucking on a lollipop in this scene) but to sexual appetite as well. Thelma also loves Cassie (one illustration of her sexual appetite), but Cassie views Thelma as her friend and may "flirt" with her as Thelma says but does not reciprocate this love since she is attracted to men. Thus Thelma's appetite or desire is not satisfied and could be considered "mad" if there is no likelihood that this desire can be satisfied.

The Thelma-Cassie relationship in *Hex* is developed even further through the transformation of Thelma into a ghost.[11] Cassie's visions and her name clearly link her to the mythical Cassandra, but Thelma's identity as a ghost serves as a way of reconceptualizing the Cassandra myth and its associations with madness, appetite and visions. The term "mad" is used synonymously with "insane" and clearly Cassie is worried that her visions combined with her new abilities might constitute some form of mental instability. Yet while still alive, her friend Thelma says that she believes her, and perhaps this is why Cassie in turn believes in Thelma after Thelma dies, which may be why Thelma becomes a ghost that Cassie can actually see. Thus the ancient Cassandra story that is based on no one believing in Cassandra's vision is subverted in a postfeminist fashion through the insertion of Thelma into Cassie's visionary sphere of experience. Thelma may not only be viewed as someone who believes the truth of Cassie's visions ("I believe you") ("Pilot"); she becomes an extension of Cassie's visions and a key presence in the series. In fact, Thelma *is* a postfeminist *vision*, and creates a "third space" or alternate for Cassie to escape the influence of Azazeal.

While Cassie's madness lies in her Cassandra-like belief that no one will believe that she is having visions, not to mention that she becomes the mother of Azazeal's son who is destined to destroy the world, Thelma's "mad" personality is of a different order. She is both a lesbian and a ghost and in this sense occupies a third space or in-between space that falls outside the realm of the conventional, heteronormative world of classmates who mock her sexual orientation. She crosses boundaries and moves between the world of the supernatural and the world of the "ordinary." Thelma is not a witch in the way that Cassie is a witch. Cassie has visions and can perform supernatural acts that involve moving objects or setting objects on fire. Thelma on the other hand is "witch-like" since the link between lesbians and witches has also been established through images of women as witches, hags or crones on the boundaries of patriarchal society (Daly, *Gyn/Ecology*, 180). As a ghost, Thelma is clearly on the border; she may not have visions like a witch, but she is an even more powerful presence than Cassie in many ways since she has *become* a vision of postfeminist difference.

Despite some of the limitations she experiences as a ghost — she cannot touch Cassie and she can only wear dead people's clothes — Thelma is one of the most compelling characters in the series. She actually offers a way of reconceptualizing "madness," through her status as a ghostly vision of a lesbian. As ghost and as a lesbian she appears to be an outsider, but as co-conspirator with her friend Cassie she becomes an insider, thus transforming the Cassandra myth of the completely isolated seer into a postfeminist vision of female friendship which crosses the boundary of sexual orientation. Though dead, Thelma is a life-affirming force in the series. She offers an alternative vision for women and counters the supernatural storyline controlled by Azazeal with her own supernatural involvement as a ghost. Thelma subverts the patriarchal myth of the mad woman as expressed by Cassie's fear that she is going insane, through her images of alterity: her lesbian orientation, her extravagant fashion sense (pink, spiky hair, flashy footwear) and other expressions of excess, particularly her appetite for food and her ongoing screen presence as a ghost. She becomes a paradoxical sign of excess and absence, not only through her ongoing appetite for food, but because of her ghostly identity. While her screen presence is available for the audience to see, she can only be seen by Cassie and a few other characters (Azazeal; Ella, a witch). In this sense Thelma has a complex role as an insider/outsider figure. She is inside Cassie's world of experience but as a ghost also falls outside Cassie's world of the "living" and outside the perception/ experience of others. She thus offers a new postfeminist way of talking about lesbian sexuality, madness and visions in the context of telefantasy.

As a telefantasy, *Hex* creates a hybrid neo-gothic world of ancient and modern images that address the perennial problems of female alienation for a contemporary television market. The U.K. series goes beyond a focus on heterosexual alienation as represented by Cassie, a Cassandra figure and a witch, but also introduces a lesbian character who becomes a ghost that subverts the patriarchal narrative that dominates Cassie's life. While Cassie must fulfill the destiny determined for her (bearing the son of the fallen angel Azazeal), Thelma can exit this kind of narrative by becoming a ghost. After Cassie's death, the series forged on with Ella, a female hero who continued to wage war against the forces of darkness. However, Thelma remains as an important way of redefining the vision of female "presence" and heroism. While Thelma may not be a Cassandra figure who has visions, she *is* the vision (albeit a ghost), and provides a unique representation of female agency. *Hex* thus presents a fantastic, postfeminist transformation of women as vessels or recipients of visions (Cassie) to women *as visions* and unconventional savior figures. Thelma reconfigures the image of possession from one of violence to one of playful excess. Cassie appears to follow the path of the mythical Cassandra since she dies (in the act of saving her son), yet Thelma remains as a fantastic vision in the series as a lesbian heroine who exudes extravagance and excess and who redefines what it means to be a "mad" woman in the twenty-first century.

FIVE

Postfeminist Savior
Seeing the Future and
Reliving the Day in Tru Calling

In *The Power of Myth*, Joseph Campbell describes a hero as "someone who has given his or her life to something bigger than oneself" (151). One of the most common ways a hero demonstrates this commitment is through the desire, duty or ability to save people. *Tru Calling*, the Fox television series that ran from 2003–2004, depicts a twenty-two-year-old woman who works in a morgue and who begins to hear and see dead people. After the dead ask for her help, she experiences the unusual ability to relive the day and has the opportunity to "save" these people from dying. Sometimes she also acts as a mediator and prevents others from making mistakes (whether these mistakes are life-threatening or less serious social *faux pas*). Tru (Eliza Dushku) is also a unique postfeminist reconstruction of the Cassandra figure; she can see into the future not because she is a seer in the traditional sense of a person who has "visions" but because she finds herself in a third space or in-between space of reliving the same day. As a result, she often knows the outcome of events and the fates of individual lives. What she also has in common with the mythic Cassandra is the status of an outsider combined with her frustration that others think she is "mad" or crazy because of her warnings that stem from her knowledge of the future. To people who are unfamiliar with how she knows the future, she appears to be psychic (although she refuses to accept this term to describe her experiences) or at least, incredibly intuitive, and in other cases strange[1] or even crazy. Yet unlike the seer Cassandra who could not prevent fate ("It comes when it comes," Aeschylus, 1250), Tru's ability is more ambiguous. Initially she has a good

70

deal of success in changing the fates of individuals who would have died without her intervention, and her "calling" appears to demand that she save the lives of people who should not be dying. However, over the course of the series, especially with the addition of the character Jack, who serves as male counterpart to her feminine power, her role as a female savior figure and her relationships with family members become more complicated. In a postmodern world of multiple truths, the rules of her universe keep changing.

Tru has the unique ability to know the future because she re-experiences the same day. As a young woman who transcends the usual boundaries of time, she occupies a kind of feminine third space as someone who re-experiences the past in a new present. Over the course of the series, her need to intervene in the lives of others ensures that she must live a rather unstable or unpredictable life. Like many young women of the postfeminist or third wave feminist generation, she has a rather unconventional job (she works at a morgue) and lacks stable relationships with a parent or significant other[2]; these experiences are also depicted in other postfeminist television series like *Charmed* and *Buffy the Vampire Slayer* where the leading female characters do not have a conventional family life or steady jobs. Non-traditional work experiences are also evident among generations of young people that belong to either to Generation X (born roughly 1965–1976) or for Tru's generation, Generation Y,[3] the children of the baby boomers (born between 1978–1989 or 1977–2002). Women from both of these generations have been part of the postfeminist or third wave feminist era. These young people often lack the secure or "desirable" jobs of the baby boomer generation.[4] Tru dreams of getting into medical school, and until she can do so, she passes her time at the morgue, an "in-between space" where she mediates between the living and the dead. Not surprisingly, her work in this rather isolated space reinforces her disconnection from certain social circles and emphasizes her need to work out problems on her own or with assistance from select individuals like Davis (Zac Galifianakis), her socially inept co-worker. Third wave feminists and postfeminists have frequently highlighted the importance of individual expression rather than following the mindset of a collective as part of a third wave feminist focus, and Tru's unusual ability reinforces the fact that she has her own style. At the same time, she is appreciative of the help she receives from an unusual male character like Davis, who lives on the margins of society because of his work in the morgue and his self-consciousness.

Despite Tru's role as an outsider or stranger to most of the people she tries to help, she actually occupies a hybrid space as an outsider / insider. She typically finds herself "in the moment of transit where space and time cross to produce complex figures of difference and identity, past and present, inside and outside, inclusion and exclusion" (Bhabha, 1). As a postfeminist heroine and Cassandra figure, she often knows the fate of others, and consequently negotiates between family members, different social classes, and people of different sexual orientation. She also moves between the world of science and the inexplicable reality of her pseudo-"vision" or knowledge of the future. Tru still manages to establish connections with other people despite their initial resistance to her efforts. As an insider/outsider trying to understand the lives of strangers, she acts as a mediator who wants to resolve difficult situations. Sometimes she has to live with the knowledge that she cannot fix everything. Tru's inside/outside status also makes her a female hero who is adaptable, who can mediate stressful situations, but who cannot save everybody's life or save everybody from harm. (The introduction of the rather sinister character of Jack (Jason Priestley) during Season 1 makes this abundantly clear.) In the case of her own relationships and family situations, she leads a rather fragmented life and as the series progresses, she becomes less certain about her purpose, thus revealing the challenges faced by this postmodern, postfeminist heroine who finds strength of purpose in her memory of her mother.

Changing family structures and relations form an important component of the postfeminist characteristics of the series. Like other female heroes (Buffy, Cassie in *Hex*, Phoebe) in recent television series, Tru's relationship with her dead mother, Elise Davies, plays an important role in establishing Tru as an independent thinker. The series begins with Tru attending her mother's funeral and mentioning that she heard her mother's voice saying everything is okay. Her mother was murdered, and when Tru grows up she believes that perhaps her newfound ability is a kind of legacy or gift she has inherited from her mother. This "genetic" link is confirmed much later in the series in "Drop Dead Gorgeous"

(1.13) when Davis, Tru's co-worker, indicates that her mother had the same ability to experience the rewinding of a day as Tru: "What you could do, she could do it too." The mother-daughter relationship here could easily echo the inter-generational relationship between second and third wave feminists. As many third wave feminists have argued, they recognize the influence of second wavers, but must also express their individuality. Tru attempts to lead this kind of hybrid life; she honors her mother's memory and appears to have inherited her ability. This link to her mother is reinforced when near the end of Season 1, a kind of epic polarization occurs between one side consisting of Tru and her mother (both tried to save people from death), and the opposing faction of Richard, Tru's father, and Jack, who do not prevent deaths. Despite Tru's mythic bond with her mother, it is significant that the mother is absent in this series, and this could reflect a third wave feminist desire to displace the previous generation of feminists or women in order to establish an individual identity.[5] While Tru is loyal to the memory of her mother, she is also a very independent young woman with leadership abilities. She takes on the role of mother to her siblings Meredith and Harrison, and she is not quick to trust others with her secret power. Some of this lack of trust must also be the result of her fractured relationship with her father, who remarried and essentially abandoned the children of his first marriage. Tru indicates that she can prevent death but "can't get [her] father to take interest" in her ("Closure," 1.8). She does negotiate a kind of peace with her father[6] when she leaves a conciliatory message for him on his voice mail-answering machine ("Closure"), thus suggesting a postfeminist acceptance of the unique challenges of being a child in the 21st century. With the absent mother and a living yet absent father who does not appear in the flesh until episode 1.14, "Daddy's Girl," Tru turns to her brother and sister for familial connections. Her rapport with Harrison, her brother, is stronger than her bond with her sister, who ceases to be a regular character in the series near the end of Season 1. Tru's relationship with her siblings is affected by the fact that all of them appear to be dysfunctional in their own way, perhaps a characteristic of certain families in a postfeminist, postmodern age: "like postmodern culture contemporary family arrangements are diverse, fluid, and unresolved" (Stacey 95).

The nuclear family is clearly challenged in *Tru Calling*. For women in the 1990s and the early part of the twenty-first century, the reality of family life is characterized by alternative families, often in the form of absentee parents if the family structure changes. As a result, Tru steps in to play the parent-adult to her sister Meredith and to her brother Harrison, who are not necessarily appreciative of her efforts to "save" them from morally questionable activities. As one of three siblings, she plays the role of mediator-negotiator as she tries to help her brother and sister with their own addictions. Her sister has a drug addiction and her brother Harrison is addicted to gambling; she manages to save her brother from numerous bad decisions that could endanger his life or the lives of others, and she tries to convince her sister to stop using cocaine. However, as the episode "Past Tense" (1.4) reveals, she may be able to warn people of the dangers of their actions, but people will still make their own decisions. For example, Tru warns Meredith about a surprise drug test at her law firm; however, instead of not taking drugs, Meredith finds a creative way of passing the test. Thus Tru's ability to change people is questioned in this episode, allowing the viewer to conclude that free will or choice is still involved in the fate of individuals.

Tru's central role as someone who has knowledge of future events because she can relive the day appears to give her the heroic ability to save others. For example, in the pilot episode she intervenes in the murder and suicide of a pregnant woman, and in "Putting Out Fires" (1.2) she saves one of the characters from being burned in a fire. However, already early on in the series, it becomes clear that she is not able to save everyone and that she can never be sure what "fate" has in store for the dead people who ask for her help. In episode 2, one of the people caught in the fire cannot be saved. Episode 11 ("The Longest Day") complicates the entire matter of Tru's role as a savior even further by indicating the uncertainty surrounding who is meant to live and why. In this captivating episode that echoes the different paths of fate presented in the creative German film *Lola Rennt* (1998), the day rewinds over and over again, and the outcome of each day is different. Tru's inability to know the outcome reinforces the mystery of life and death, and conflicts with Tru's earlier belief that she does know the outcome of events. Unlike more traditional hero figures whose mission or "calling" may become clear (e.g., the instructions Joan of Arc receives to lead an army against the English), Tru represents a new postfeminist, postmodern heroine who must adapt to change; this need to adapt, to be flexible has been identified by postfeminist critics as a quality of the third wave generation. Amanda Lotz indicates that women can "experience their subjectivity differently and dependent on context" (115) and Tru's need to adapt to each different rewind of the same day demonstrates this kind of adaptation. The shifting ground of Tru's "in-between space" as a woman of vision is also a quality of postmodern television which, according to Lez Cooke, destroys "old certainties" (185).

In keeping with the postmodern relativism that pervades *Tru Calling*, Tru's gift may also be perceived negatively as a curse. Far from being completely "normal" herself, Tru is often viewed by others as "damaged" in some way as well. In "Past Tense" (1.4), someone asks, "What kind of freak are you?" Her "gift" or ability to see dead people and relive the day sometimes seems like a "curse" to her ("Valentine," 1.12), especially because her personal relationships often suffer as a result of her need to involve herself in the lives of the dead or potentially dead. For example, her brother Harrison questions her sanity and until episode 9 ("Murder in the Morgue") only half believes her, referring to her as his "crazy" sister who has "crazy days" ("Star Crossed"), thus reinforcing the similarity between Tru and her "mad" mythic precursor, Cassandra. While Tru does not seriously question her own sanity, like most heroes she wonders about her ability to respond appropriately to her "calling" or, as Joseph Campbell has described this phase of the hero's journey, "the call to adventure" (*The Hero with a Thousand Faces*). "The Longest Day" is the episode which tests Tru's resilience as well as her ability to keep using her detective skills and collection of information and her intuition in order to "save" at least one person even though she cannot save everyone. Even when the rules of the game appear to change, as in the multiple rewind realities of "The Longest Day," she must make adjustments and not lose her presence of mind.

Tru's experience of a "do-over day" ("Murder in the Morgue") reveals how this postmodern, postfeminist Cassandra figure has some significant departures from the mythic prototype. To begin with, she does not experience visions of the future in the sense of a "waking" vision, unless one considers Tru's first experience of a day to be synonymous with a vision. However, if one were to extend the concept of the vision to Tru's original experience of a rewind day, then the first experience of the day would be the vision or the experience that most of the other people in Tru's world would reject or dismiss as "unreal"; consequently Tru's second experience of the day would be the "reality" for these people. Because Tru is located in a kind of postmodern, postfeminist "third space," it may not be very useful to discuss her experience in simple binary terms of vision or dream versus reality. One of the features of female characters or heroines with visionary, psychic or alternative cognitive powers is that they inhabit a kind of third space which can either generate the possibility for mediation or the perpetuation of further ambiguities. For example, in "The Longest Day" when Tru has multiple rewind experiences of the day, one could argue that there is no one true ending; perhaps all of the scenarios or endings are equally valid or equally possible as in the case of Borges' famous postmodern story "The Garden of Forking Paths" which presents the concept of an infinite series of times, a "network of diverging, converging and parallel times" (Borges, 98). Perhaps all of the scenarios played out in the episode when a father tries to save the life of his ill daughter are equal visions of fate despite Davis' comment at the end of the episode that one can change events, but one can't change fate ("The Longest Day").

Tru's life is also characterized by the negotiations and a complex reworking of knowledge systems, which reinforce her position in a third space. This contributes to the postmodern, fractured[7] character of the series. The series appears to questions the existence or validity of a single way of knowing or a single truth (Hutcheon, *The Canadian Postmodern*, viii). Instead *Tru Calling* proposes an alternate knowledge system through the female figure of Tru. Tru's newfound ability to hear and see dead people talk to her, and her reliving of the past, or the day more specifically, create an alternate way of knowing. The female visionary has historically been associated with the mystical or the irrational, and even though Tru is not strictly speaking a visionary in the same sense as Cassandra, her "gift" has mysterious, mystical associations. Even when we discover that her mother had this ability and that there could be some kind of "genetic" link or that Tru "was chosen for a reason" ("Valentine,"

1.12) according to Davis, this does not detract from the mystery of how both she and her mother came to possess this ability. Yet this form of mystical-inexplicable knowledge that she is granted because of her ability to re-experience the day merges in an interesting way with the form of knowledge more commonly associated with the world of science. Shifting notions of the "truth" contribute to the postmodern and postfeminist ambience of the series. Like any good detective, Tru must sift through the information in order to arrive at a conclusion. The fact that she uses scientific knowledge and deductive reasoning to arrive at conclusions (sometimes with the help of co-worker Davis) reveals that the female seer has been recast to accommodate the apparently contradictory ideas of intuition and reason. It is particularly interesting that technical terminology is used to describe Tru's ability to relive the day; Davis and Tru refer to her experience of a "rewind day" (1.11).

Another important fact in the postfeminist or third wave feminist recognition of male contributions to feminism may be reflected in the connection between Tru and her "boss" Davis. As Astrid Henry has pointed out, third wave feminists have tried to move away from what they perceive to be an anti-male image of feminism (Henry, 110). In *Tru Calling*, Davis and Tru work more as a team than as a boss and employee, and the similarity between their names Tru "Davies" and "Davis" is probably not coincidental. In fact, one could argue that like Tru, Davis also occupies a kind of "in-between space"[8] since he seems to have no life outside the morgue, the meeting ground of the living and the dead. Tru's knowledge of science because of her interest in applying for medical school dovetails with Davis' clinical knowledge of dead bodies. His awareness of the mysterious element of Tru's ability and his comment "life is better left a mystery" ("Star-Crossed," 1.6) further breaks down a distinct boundary between gender and between two different forms of knowledge.[9] While science has traditionally been a male domain, Tru embodies the merging of previously incompatible spheres of the intuitive and the rational. She uses both her knowledge of science and her supernatural experience of reliving the day to help others, thus breaking down the perception that science and the supernatural are incompatible.

In the postmodern universe of *Tru Calling*, Tru Davies (and some of the other characters) discover that there is no single Truth (or at least not the Truth that people expect to be the Truth); instead, as Linda Hutcheon has argued, there are multiple truths or alternative ways of seeing and knowing (*The Canadian Postmodern*, viii–ix). The episode "Star-Crossed" (1.6) highlights the concepts of truth and knowledge in a particularly interesting and subversive fashion through the theme of lesbian sexual orientation, thus reinforcing the postfeminist focus on diversity in the form of "lesbian visibility in popular culture" (McKenna, 285).[10] The title of the episode incorporates the idea of Shakespeare's Romeo and Juliet who are star-crossed lovers because of their feuding families. One set of young adults at a private school are the children of privilege while another group consists of scholarship holders without the wealthy family connections; apparently the different groups "don't mix." The episode suggests that a boy called Adam and a girl called Jen are star-crossed lovers because of their class differences. Tru's belief that the star-crossed lovers are Adam and Jen is based on her seeing the bodies of these two teens together at the site of a car crash before she experiences her rewind day. Jen's hotheaded brother also mistakenly believes this relationship between Adam and his sister to be true. However, the narrative subverts this "truth" by revealing a secret lesbian relationship between "Juliet and Juliet" (1.6). This representation of a transgressive relationship reflects the postfeminist possibilities and sensibilities of this television series. It is a paradoxical, postfeminist representation of difference through "sameness" and Tru finds herself in the position of playing the role of mediator, not only occupying a third space in order to prevent the deaths of Adam and Jen, but trying to convey an alternative truth to heteronormative thinkers like Jen's brother.

Tru's role as the insider/outsider is represented visually and narratively in "Star-Crossed" and in other episodes. She physically places herself between two cars in the middle of the street to try to prevent an accident that she believes will result in the death of Adam and Jen. In "Haunted" (1.5), she interferes with a young woman's relationship with her friends in an attempt to save her life. She acts as a mediator in bringing a young soldier who has a fatal medical condition and his ex-girlfriend together. Tru is often represented standing outside of a circle of people, looking in as an observer. In fact, in "Haunted," Jake, the dying soldier, even tells her that she is "some sort of angel." Tru is positioned in a third space because of her insider/outsider status not only because she can provide "closure" in a positive way; as the series progresses it becomes increasingly clear that her special "knowledge" is partial and her involvement in the lives of others can create unpleasant situations, not just a beneficial outcome. She can therefore function as a disruptive force in the kinds of relationships she develops with family, friends and strangers. For example, her relationship with boyfriend Luc deteriorates because she has a "higher" calling or an insider's knowledge of a duty to help others and because she feels that she cannot reveal the truth about her gift. She realizes that her supernatural ability cannot necessarily fix or restore relationships that have been broken over time. The episode "Reunion" provides an interesting example of this reality. Tru saves the life of Candace at a high school reunion. Tru and Candace used to be close high school friends but then drifted apart. Despite Tru's help, Candace remains distant and says that "some things change ... some things never will," thus preventing a neat and optimistic ending to the episode. The inability of these ex-friends to become friends again suggests a postfeminist world where nostalgia and a superficial concept of feminine solidarity are both subverted. Tru's role as a savior comes at the expense of individual happiness, and in this sense resembles the lot of the traditional hero figure who has a higher calling and who often has to sacrifice personal pleasure to attend to the lives of others.

At the end of Season 1 and throughout Season 2 of *Tru Calling*, a major shift complicates Tru's role as a postfeminist, postmodern female savior figure even further while also complicating the concept of fate. Tru's identity as a female hero is juxtaposed against the character of Jack, played by Jason Priestley of *Beverly Hills 90210* fame. Tru and Jack appear to be polar opposites since Tru believes that it is her calling to try to save people from death, and in doing so she changes their fate. Tru views Jack as a deadly force, a view that is supported by Harrison who says that Tru saves people and Jack "kills them" ("Two Weddings and a Funeral," 1.20); in the first episode of Season 2, Jack states that he preserves fate ("Perfect Storm," 2.1) by insisting that certain people "are supposed to die"; he is merely "helping fate get what it wants" (1.20). In "Perfect Storm," Tru counters that these people are "supposed to live." Jack's alliance with

Tru's father suggests that Jack must be evil since he is continuing in Richard Davis' footsteps ("You once did what I do," Jack tells Tru's father in "Perfect Storm"). According to this view, the masculine forces would be "evil" and the feminine forces of Tru and her mother (who had the same ability) would be good.

While some viewers might be tempted to align Tru with the force of good and Jack with the force of evil, the series reveals that this kind of dichotomy is not always possible. The series' postmodern and postfeminist qualities indicate that such a dichotomy is not sustained or even possible. Jack says that he is not "the enemy" (1.20) and that he and Tru just see things differently.[11] This is an interesting way of framing the relationship between Tru and Jack. In a postmodern sense, difference and relativism have the potential to subvert the idea of absolutes, whether these absolutes are good/evil, female/male. In a postfeminist context, this statement might argue for a reworking of the relationship between men and women. Instead of polarizing the feminist debate around men vs. women, the relationships have changed, and *Tru Calling* illustrates this by showing how Harrison, Tru's brother, does not follow the male line since he supports his sister instead of his father or Jack (2.4).

It is worth noting that by the end of the season, Tru is still maintained as the ethical force, but like other postmodern, postfeminist telefantasy series, *Tru Calling* recognizes that we may live in a world of uncertainties between spaces. As a woman who has a vision of the future through her ability to re-experience the day, Tru negotiates between saving others and her own obligations. She must think on her feet, because the rules of the "game" may change, and the players may affect the outcome of events. In many ways, *Tru Calling* is less about being able to save the world, than about the ability to make adjustments in life and to accept on a certain level that not everything can be explained.[12] The world of *Tru Calling* reflects a postmodern world of adaptation where everything from the workforce to relationships is in flux, and in order to survive, we must retain some principles while also recognizing the need to change when "the rules have changed" (2.4).

PART 2

Joan of Arc in Contemporary Television

Images of a Reluctant Seer

Six

Teen Visions of God

Postfeminist Heroism
and Genre Crossing in Joan of Arcadia

Cassandra is one of the main mythic ancestors for seer figures or visionaries in television and film. However, the historical figure of Jeanne d'Arc — Joan of Arc — is another key example of a visionary who offers both parallels and points of departure for postfeminist heroines who occupy a third space or hybrid space in fantasy-oriented TV programming.

Joan of Arc, the fifteenth century French heroine who successfully led a French army against the English, was declared a heretic and executed as a witch for her claims that she had divine visions and received instructions from God. She has achieved mythic and iconic significance over time for a number of reasons. Not only was she eventually named a saint by the Catholic Church in 1920 (when her powers were recognized as God-inspired), but she has become an example of a woman warrior figure who crossed gender boundaries through her role as a female soldier. Joan of Arc's popularity in American culture has been discussed by Robin Blaetz in *Visions of the Maid: Joan of Arc in American Film and Culture*. Blaetz demonstrates how Joan of Arc captured the imagination of Americans during the first half of the twentieth century, "specifically in relation to women's roles in wartime" (xii). Her image as a warrior figure is presented through artistic representations such as posters, songs, films and statues.[1]

Joan of Arc continues to serve as an inspiration for Americans as is evident through the creation of the American TV series *Joan of Arcadia* (2003–2005). Its creator-producer-writer, Barbara Hall, called Joan of

Arc "the girl warrior" (Pacatte). Yet the Joan in the TV series is also an example of a young woman who functioned in a kind of "third space" or hybrid space and whose paradoxical status as an "ordinary" heroine (a high school student) is in keeping with a third wave feminist recognition of contradictions.[2] *Joan of Arcadia* creates a narrative that incorporates a modern-day Joan of Arc figure, thus demonstrating how the image of Joan of Arc continues to have mythic significance in a different cultural and historical context.[3] In *Joan of Arcadia*, the new battleground is an American high school and the new postfeminist warrior or "chosen one" is a teenaged girl who hears and sees God in many different guises. As a high school student, Joan wrestles with the difficulty of finding some kind of easily discernable morality, myth or truth because she lives in a postfeminist era full of "compromises and contradictions" (Helford, 7). In *Joan of Arcadia*, Joan of Arc has been reconfigured to adapt to the parameters of contemporary American culture and to the demands for a new kind of heroine as the girl on the margins who negotiates between groups and between worlds (the supernatural and the ordinary). Joan interacts with characters experiencing the trials and tribulations of the teen years and with adults who might need her help. Her hybrid status as an ordinary teenager who has visions of God is a metaphor for the kinds of conflicts experienced by both youth and adults.[4] Her hybridity may also be an extension of the show's mixing of genres. *Joan of Arcadia* has elements of family drama, teen drama, police drama, and telefantasy. By incorporating elements from various genres, it offers a unique form of postfeminist, postmodern, hybrid television to a contemporary teen audience while still sending some "traditional" messages about altruistic behavior, sacrifice and leadership to its teenaged audience (many of the qualities embodied by the heroine Joan of Arc).

The historical Joan of Arc is the very image of an unlikely hero, and this is a feature of the icon that translates into the depiction of the "Joan" character in *Joan of Arcadia*. When Joan was "in her fourteenth year," she received a revelation from God through voices which Joan eventually identified as St. Michael, St. Catherine and St. Margaret (Butler as cited in Leeming, 56). Her voices told her to "throw the English out of France and bring her Dauphin" (Charles VII) to his throne in Rheims (Warner, 3). As Marina Warner indicates in her study of Joan of Arc, many of the details concerning the voices and their manifestations remain hazy. The voice was initially single, then multiple (Warner, 122). Yet these voices have become one of the key elements in maintaining the enduring mythic significance of Joan of Arc.

Joan of Arcadia incorporates the important aspect of Joan of Arc's ability to "hear" divine voices. The historical Joan of Arc apparently heard the voice of God through various saints. At first the voice was single, but then the voices increased in number (Butler in Leeming, 56)[5]; the physical details surrounding the voices were not communicated by Joan to her inquisitors during her trial, and so these visual details seem to have been de-emphasized in these accounts.[6] In *Joan of Arcadia*, Joan Girardi, who is similar in age to the original Joan (the former is 16 and the latter was 14), hears an unknown voice in the very first episode. While this ordinary teenager is sleeping, she hears someone calling her name, and after watching the episode the viewer infers that this was probably God. At the end of the episode, Joan hears a voice again, but this time, the voice is transmuted into the voice of her disabled brother. This effect is an example of how the series fuses the extraordinary with the ordinary. The elements of family drama or teen drama (brother-sister relations) are blended with an element of telefantasy (God's voice) to create a hybrid world where the extraordinary and ordinary exist.

Because of the visual[7] nature of the television medium, the blending of television genres and the dominance of religious pluralism and multi-ethnic realities within American society, it is not surprising that Joan Girardi is not a "Catholic" Joan of Arc figure[8] even though the show's creator-writer-producer Barbara Hall is a Catholic. For Hall, Joan of Arc was not necessarily equated with a particular religion but with the idea of "fulfilling one's own nature" (Pacatte):

> When I was a young girl, I looked around at Cinderella and Snow White and all those girl icons and could not find myself anywhere. The only place I did find myself was with the form of Joan, the girl warrior. She continues to fascinate me.... When my daughter was about to come of age, I began to wonder what it would look like if God tried to grab the attention of a teenager today. What would that process look like, and would a modern teenager be able to have the fortitude to follow that calling? [Pacatte]

In *Joan of Arcadia*, Joan Girardi tells God that she is not "religious" (1.1) and He replies, "It's not about religion, Joan. It's about fulfilling your nature" (1.1). Thus, instead of presenting a uniform fatherly God-figure derived from images in the Judeo-Christian tradition, *Joan of Arcadia* constructs God as a shapeshifter.[9] He is an old man standing outside Joan's window, a cute teenaged boy, or a female, African-American cafeteria worker ("Pilot," 1.1).[10] The variety of representations reinforce cultural pluralism and the crossing of gender boundaries which are consistent with a postfeminist or third wave feminist emphasis on diversity. The theme song for the series, "One of Us" sung by Joan Osborne, reinforces the concept of plurality and ordinariness and the dismantling of hierarchical and perhaps even gender distinctions by asking us to consider the divine in relation to ordinary people. The song emphasizes a God who can become "one of us" whether S/He assumes the manifestation of a slovenly person or a stranger on a public mode of transportation. In *Joan of Arcadia*, God can be a child, an adult, male or female; S/He crosses the boundaries of age and gender.

Genre Blending

Joan of Arcadia crosses other boundaries by incorporating a variety of television genres, but it most resembles the genre of family drama since the Girardis are a nuclear family with two parents and children. The family consists of Will Girardi, the police chief, Helen, the mother who works at the children's high school, and three teenagers, Kevin, Luke and Joan. The communal, ritualistic aspect of the series is emphasized when members of Joan's family often sit down together for a heart-to-heart talk over ice cream.[11] The series resembles some other well-known American family dramas such as *The Waltons* and *Little House on the Prairie* because of its focus on family values and the escapades of the children. These series from the 1970s also incorporated some light comedy and a dose of religious morality, and *Joan of Arcadia* is no different in this respect. However, it departs from this model by depicting the divine in an explicitly fantastic[12] framework, thus suggesting how this established genre has moved beyond the limitation of "realism."

The blending of genres helps create the hybrid environment that places Joan Girardi in a postfeminist "third space" or alternate space since she is a girl who has "visions." Rachel Moseley indicates that a significant number of teen dramas use "supernatural power as a motif through which to explore" concerns such as difference, otherness and personal or community relationships (*The Television Genre Book* 42–43) and this has certainly been the case for telefantasy series that feature heroines with fantastic abilities (e.g., *Buffy the Vampire Slayer, Angel, Charmed, Hex*). In a sense, the term "telefantasy" would appear to be a fitting way of describing Joan's ability to see the supernatural; however, the fact that the supernatural element consists of God rather than witches or vampires places it in an even more unusual genre space. This is because for some viewers, the show is a different kind of telefantasy from *Charmed,* a series about witches or *Buffy the Vampire Slayer* which highlights vampires and demons as supernatural creatures. For many viewers, "God" is part of their "reality" or core belief system and may not fit the definition of telefantasy as a genre that goes against the grain of what most people would accept according to the concept of "socio-cultural similitude" (C. Johnson, 4) or "broader culturally constructed and generally accepted notions of what is believed to be true" (4). *Joan of Arcadia* is in many ways more of a hybrid show than the oft-touted postmodern *Buffy the Vampire Slayer* because (with the exception of an episode like "Normal Again" [6.17] which made viewers question whether Buffy's experience as a vampire slayer was "real" or the imaginings of a "madwoman") most of the *Buffy* episodes do not question the existence of vampires and other supernatural beings, thus firmly placing the series within the domain of telefantasy. *Joan of Arcadia* on the other hand includes a female protagonist who doubts the legitimacy of the "god" figure, and even after she accepts this figure, the series re-introduces the idea that perhaps Joan's visions of God were a symptom of a disease ("Silence," 1.23). This creates a kind of Todorovian fantastic for Joan and for the television viewer who must hesitate between a natural explanation of her visions (Joan experienced hallucinations due to Lyme Disease) and an acceptance of the supernatural in her life.[13] The first episode of Season 2 re-introduces Joan's visions of "God" and suggests that the audience is supposed to believe that Joan really does see and communicate with God. Although Joan initially rejects her earlier visions as a form of madness caused by Lyme disease, the rest of the season incorporates God as part of her "reality" and she once again acknowledges that God is speaking to her. When she tells God (who has assumed the identity of a little girl) that He is "not real," God replies, "So people keep telling me" (1.2). While the episode introduces an element of the supernatural into Joan's life, it is intended to be presented in the context of everyday reality, thus suggesting that the supernatural is to be integrated into the ordinary (and not juxtaposed against the "normal").

Joan's hospitalization as a result of Lyme Disease at the end of Season 1, and her depiction as a crazy high school girl or madwoman, are a postfeminist reconceptualization of Joan of Arc's marginalization as a witch-seer figure. Joan of Arc's visions were explained away by church authorities as the heretical ravings of a witch, and she was burned at the stake. Joan Girardi's visions of God are called "hallucinations" by the medical authorities, a modern way of explaining the unknown. Even after the series resumes in Season 2 and re-establishes that God really is speaking to her, Joan wages an internal battle with herself since she worries that she may have an illness like paranoid schizophrenia. This illness would actually help explain the hybrid life that she leads. If the series repeatedly uses God's appearances and reassurances to show that Joan is not mad, then one could ask why the series even introduced medical explanations for Joan's visions. They may be a way of emphasizing otherness or difference, whether this otherness takes the form of a girl who has visions, a wheelchair-bound brother or a science geek. Another way of looking at the "scientific" explanations is to view them in conjunction with the supernatural. Barbara Hall is an avid reader of physics texts and has discussed the possibility that the divine and the domain of science are not incompatible or diametrically opposed: "Then I went to Mass and was stunned. I had this sense of being completely at home. The experience I had of ritual was actually not unrelated to physics because it had something to do with the manipulation of energy" (Pacatte). Her observations are reflected in *Joan of Arcadia*, which dismantles the boundaries between science and mystical experiences.

Additional factors that contribute to the hybridity of *Joan of Arcadia* and its postfeminist heroine are the many other television genres that form the basis of the show. In addition to the inclusion of telefantasy/fantastic/supernatural components (such as the premise of a girl who sees and hears God in different manifestations), the series introduces elements of other genres that help construct the "third space" that Joan inhabits as a contemporary Joan of Arc. Plotlines involve Joan's communication with God, but also includes traces of police drama. For example, Joan's father is the police chief of the town of Arcadia, and in episode one, he is trying to capture a serial killer. Ironically, his daughter's job at the bookstore actually brings her in contact with the killer, whom she mistakes for God. The case of mistaken identity reinforces the kind of ambiguous "third space" that Joan occupies as a postfeminist heroine who sees God and who must negotiate between the world of the natural and the world of the supernatural.

Like many other episodes, the first episode reveals how Joan is asked to follow God's instructions without being fully aware of God's "plan." She therefore stumbles her way through some embarrassing incidents. However, by the end of each episode, the mysterious purpose is usually revealed. For example, in the premiere episode, God's reason for telling Joan to get a job at a bookstore has nothing to do with helping the bookstore owner (the obvious answer); instead, it appears to be a way of encouraging her recently paralyzed brother to find employment by unwittingly "shaming" him into getting a job since his "little sister" was able to get one (1.1).[14] Her job may have also indirectly led to the eventual arrest of the serial killer. Because a serial killer is brought to justice, *Joan of Arcadia* incorporates an important feature of police drama: "society is protected ... by the forces of law and order" (Lez Cooke in *The Television Genre Book*, 19). The storylines that include aspects of procedural crime drama therefore function as a way of entertaining older viewers who may also enjoy reliving their youth by observing the vicissitudes of teenage life. However, the telefantasy aspect of God's directions to Joan adds another layer to the show and suggest a more complex way of viewing the genre of police drama in relation to a supernatural presence, thus creating a hybrid effect. Joan's ability to hear and see God, and her doubts, help to sustain an element of "mystery" in contrast to a male detective who would focus on *solving* mysteries.

The Heroine in Teen Drama

Despite its association with other television genres like police drama and family drama, *Joan of Arcadia* is very much about the lives of teenagers and more specifically about the life of a teenaged girl who revises the myth of Joan of Arc, the historical visionary. She negotiates between the demands of her supernatural influence (God) and her "ordinary" life in high school and at home. Postfeminist or third wave feminists have discussed the importance of acknowledging "diverse relations to power" (Lotz, 115) and the need for negotiation (Lotz, 117). While *Buffy the Vampire Slayer* and the witches of *Charmed* often have a "kick-ass" or physically oriented approach to their demon enemies, Joan's battles are often more subtle but no less real. Her battlefield is the high school environment and she negotiates between individuals and God. In the episode "St. Joan" (1.9), Joan actually explores similarities between Joan of Arc and her own life; she also wages a battle against the (male) school authorities who suspect that she may have cheated on an exam. Her friend Grace encourages her to engage in a political battle and calls her a "girl warrior" (1.9). Joan, however, is a rather reluctant leader or warrior figure. She does not have the same spirit of resistance as either Joan of Arc or her radical friend Grace, who turns Joan's test situation into a school-wide crusade and ends up acting more like a Joan of Arc figure than Joan does. After God convinces Joan to revisit her original decision to not rewrite the test, Joan ends up losing Grace's respect and the support of her friend Adam who had also rallied behind Joan; however, she does symbolically save the life of her teacher, Mr. Dreisbach, who had almost given up on teaching until Joan's success on her second exam convinced him to rethink his earlier decision. The episode reveals how being a public heroine can be less important than saving "someone's life" (1.9) in a more private manner. This private act can also be a form of resistance. In other words, the life of an individual can displace the symbolic value of a political cause, one of the key messages of many third wave feminists who have been criticized by second wave feminists for showing a lack of feminist activism. Kathleen Hanna, one of the members of the riot grrrl band Bikini Kill, articulates this third wave feminist view when she mentions the different kinds of resistance that can occur:

Resistance is everywhere, it always has been and always will be. Just because someone is not resisting the same way you are (being vegan, an out lesbian, a political organizer) does not mean they are not resisting. Being told you are a worthless piece of shit and not believing it is a form of resistance [Garrison 147].

Hanna takes issue with the view that there should be a collective view of how to define resistance. The deed that Joan carries out by rewriting the exam reveals how a private act can often be just as valuable or more important than a public demonstration of activism. This reconceptualization of "resistance" seems to capture the spirit of Kathleen Hanna's third wave feminist perspective.

Like the historical Joan of Arc, Joan Girardi is a non-conformist. She hangs out with two eccentric characters, Adam, a solitary artist figure, and Grace, a girl with few social skills who is labeled a lesbian. Just as Joan of Arc was considered unusual and demonized and eventually declared a witch, Joan Girardi is constructed as a freak in the opening episode. However, she is not a freak in isolation. Her "difference" or otherness as a girl who has visions of God is presented in the context of other "freaks" in the series and serves as a metaphor for a teenager's fear of not fitting in. Her two brothers Luke and Kevin are freaks of a different variety. Her younger brother, Luke, is a science geek, and her older brother, Kevin, was a "jock," but has lost the use of his legs due to a car accident and is thus transformed into a "freak." Kevin says that Joan is their parents' only hope for "normal" (1.1), and the irony of his remark is not lost on the television viewer or on Joan since she knows that her "visions" of God mean that she is not "normal" according to many people.

Joan's "freak" ability to hear and see God injects humor into the series and highlights the alienation and uncertainty experienced by youth. After Joan returns to school from being hospitalized for Lyme Disease, she describes her visions of the divine to her friend Adam: "Six weeks of crafts and writing down my dreams and crying in front of strangers and being grilled by someone named Dr. Dan? You're asking me to undo that? I can't go back there. I just want to be a normal couple again. You know? You remember normal?" (2.1). Joan's alienation is a symptom of teenaged life, and her moments of difference coincide with the problems experienced by other youth in her school. Postfeminists or third wave feminists have validated alternative identities through their politics of inclusion, and in this sense, *Joan of Arcadia* promotes a politics of inclusion since the series depicts a number of individuals who also seem "different" or disconnected from others. Thus, the show with its illustrations of difference paradoxically reflects the "norm" in a high school situation, where these feelings of alienation are probably experienced by most teenagers.

Joan of Arcadia offers its viewers examples of a hybrid heroine and multiple television genres. There is a blend of the fantastic and the real in the series, yet this departure is presented in the familiar framework of a family drama. *Joan of Arcadia* seems to have been directed at a number of different audiences: teenagers (especially teenaged girls), "ageing 'youth' markets still wishing to live out their teenage fantasies" (Rixon, 57)[15] and the parents or grandparents of teenagers who could be more interested in family drama. Ironically, it was this politics of inclusion that might have been responsible for its demise and "second-season ratings slump" (Mickey O'Connor). The final episode of Season 2, "Something Wicked This Way Comes," which introduced a rather sinister (perhaps evil) character, suggested that this series could have been trying to lure a "younger demographic" (O'Connor) by breaking away even further from more "realistic"-based television with additional telefantasy elements.[16] While this shift or what Rhonda Wilcox calls an "abysmal artistic misstep" (96) may have been somewhat of a departure from the show's previous narrative world, one could argue that this new development simply reinforced the telefantasy elements that were already present in the series. In other words, the blending of the telefantasy, family drama and teen drama genres contributes to the hybrid identity of Joan Girardi as a postfeminist example of "the chosen one" (Bavidge) whose heroism lies in her ability to live the paradox of being both different and ordinary.

SEVEN

Joan of Arc
in Niagara Falls

*Signs of a Seer and
Cross-Cultural Contact in* Wonderfalls

CBS's *Joan of Arcadia* (2003–2005) took the figure of Joan of Arc and refashioned her for an American high school setting through the character of Joan Girardi, a teenaged girl who sees and communicates with God. Shortly after *Joan of Arcadia* aired, *Wonderfalls* (2004), a short-lived series with its own recreation of Joan of Arc, the 15th century teen visionary, appeared.[1] *Wonderfalls* is an American production set in Canada. Like the female protagonist in *Joan of Arcadia* and the women of vision in other postfeminist television series, the heroine in *Wonderfalls* enters a third space or alternate world as she experiences the supernatural, the mystical, or the mythic through visions, voices or altered forms of perception. Jaye Tyler (Caroline Dhavernas) is an apathetic twenty-four-year-old woman who works in a Niagara Falls[2] souvenir shop. The mythic pervades the life of this reluctant seer or cynical heroine whether she likes it to or not, and transforms her from an ordinary, disengaged woman into a postfeminist heroine who is more of a mediator figure than a conventional leader. The postmodern series incorporates, refashions and subverts images of Joan of Arc through new kinds of heroines including a young salesclerk in Niagara Falls and Native American women. The latter resist stereotypical images of the commodified aboriginal woman as martyr. The use of the seer archetype provides an ironic way of exploring the third space or alternate world that Jaye (and other women of vision-seer figures) occupy and also allows the series to comment on the role of feminine passivity and agency in a mythic context and in a postfeminist era.

The universe of *Wonderfalls* is a quirky, postmodern world that lends itself to the branding of cult television in a way that the more conventional, family-oriented drama *Joan of Arcadia* does not. Sara Gwenllian-Jones and Roberta E. Pearson state, "[I]n the media, in common usage, and sometimes even in academia, 'cult' is often applied to any television program that is considered offbeat or edgy, that draws a niche audience, that has a nostalgic appeal, that is considered emblematic of a particular subculture, or that is considered hip" (ix). The Wonderfalls gift shop where Jaye works evokes the emblems and nostalgia associated with Niagara Falls and the legends surrounding the Falls; however, her apathetic, slacker attitude towards her work subverts any "romantic" associations with this setting. The show also incorporates and subverts the "Maid of the Mist" legend about an Indian princess who was sent in a canoe over the falls as a form of sacrifice.

Wonderfalls uses its subversive elements to portray an unlikely post-feminist heroine through the figure of Jaye Tyler. It has been described as a "one hour family dramedy about an underachieving twenty-something souvenir shop worker named Jaye Tyler" (*Wonderfalls, TV Tome*) The innovative aspects of the series reflect the kinds of creative effects generated in other dramedies (e.g., *Northern Exposure, Moonlighting*). As Leah R. Vande Ber states in her discussion of dramedy, "critics ... have quite uniformly praised television's dramedy series' sophistication and innovation. They argue that dramedies have a self reflexivity and a set of intertextual references that require a substantial degree of both popular and classic cultural literacy from viewers for full appreciation of their allusions and nuances." In other words, these critics describe the dramedy as a form of intellectual television. The genre of *Wonderfalls* further facilitates the inclusion of parodic commentary in the depiction of its Joan of Arc character(s). *Wonderfalls* achieves this tension between the serious and the comic through the use of fantastic elements, odd camera angles, and the fast-forwarding of scenes. Thus it creates more of the kind of alienation effects reminiscent of Brechtian theatre or Brechtian performance.[3] These television techniques also highlight the viewer's awareness of the camera through wild or frenetic movements that suggest a "hand-held shot" or Steadicam technique as in *NYPD Blue* (Butler, 129), thus foregrounding the eclectic style of the series. There is also the fast-forward technique, which highlights the fantastic, surreal element of the show. The use of these different camera styles in *Wonderfalls* certainly serves as a means of providing a sense of disorientation which accentuates the "hallucinations" or "visions" experienced by Jaye, who lives in a third space or alternate space.

Todd Holland, co-creator of *Wonderfalls*, openly credits "15th century teen warrior Joan of Arc as an inspiration for his series" (Hart). Holland's protagonist is an example of how "the least likely person" (Hart) can demonstrate human compassion. Bryan Fuller, another co-creator, says that Todd Holland "had a thing for the Joan of Arc legend, and we started talking about what it would mean to have someone called who really didn't want to be called, and who might be the last person you would want to be called, and who was calling them, and all of the elements of that legend and how they might be reinvented today" (Warn). As a rather atypical recreation of Joan of Arc, the self-sacrificing warrior and "maid" of Orleans, Jaye Tyler enters the realm of the fantastic-supernatural when she begins to hear toy animals or animal statues speak. They instruct her to undertake actions intended to help other individuals. Thus, like other postfeminist television series that highlight women with visionary powers that place them in a third space or alternate space, *Wonderfalls* is a telefantasy with a woman who acquires the ability to experience supernatural phenomena presumably as a way of helping or saving others. Jaye puts a modern spin on the term "reluctant hero" who refuses "the call" through her apathy and cynical remarks. In "Totem Mole" (1.12) she says, "I don't want to be chosen. In this instance, I'm anti-choice." Joseph Campbell mentions that the hero in myth may question his or her ability to carry out a particular task or the "call to adventure" (Campbell, *Hero*, 58): "Often in actual life, and not infrequently in the myths and popular tales, we encounter the dull case of the call unanswered" (Campbell, *Hero*, 59). Jaye's cynicism is a reflection of a capitalist, dog-eat-dog world where acts of kindness are not necessarily recognized as such. In "Wax Lion," the first episode of *Wonderfalls*, when Jaye ignores a speaking wax lion's instructions ("A word of advice; don't give her money"), the purse of the customer she was serving is stolen.

However, when she responds to "the call" and tries to return a woman's lost purse, the woman accuses her of stealing the contents, and she is punched in the face. Thus Campbell's theory of a hero responding to a call seems to be subverted by the lack of gratitude the stranger shows to Jaye. As a result, Jaye wonders why she even tried to do a good deed. She is presented as a young woman who tries to play the part of the Good Samaritan but this is a difficult role for her since she is not normally known for going out of her way to assist anyone. As her African American friend Mahandra McGinty asks, "Why were *you* performing an act of kindness?" (1.1).

The answer to Mahandra's question is that Jaye believes that the voices of the toy animals have told her to perform acts of kindness. Yet while Joan of Arc believed that her visions and the voices she heard emanated from a divine source, Jaye is not sure about the source of her visions. Her initial similarity to Joan of Arc appears to be that she hears voices or has visions of supernatural phenomena. However, the voices that she hears are not presented as the voice of God as in *Joan of Arcadia* or as the kinds of voices provided to Cordelia courtesy of the Powers That Be who provide assistance to the forces of "good" in *Angel*; instead the source, if there is any one source, remains indeterminate. Jaye generally hears talking toy animals or animal figurines, with the exception of one key episode, "Totem Mole," where she hears the voice of a dead woman. The episodes bear the name of each animal figure that communicates with Jaye: "Wax Lion," "Karma Chameleon," "Wound-Up Penguin," "Pink Flamingos," "Totem Mole" (actually a totem "bird"), etc. Because most of the messages are conveyed to Jaye through inanimate animals that speak, and because the messages do create some chaos in Jaye's life, there is more of a trickster-like quality about the experience reminiscent of the role of a native American trickster figure who is both creative or chaotic depending on one's perspective.[4]

An excellent illustration of the productive and unexpected consequences resulting from an inanimate object's message to Jaye occurs in "Wax Lion" when the lion statue utters the line, "Make me a match" (1.1) while Thomas, a UPS man, enters the gift shop. Thomas' wife apparently left him and he seems to have fallen for Jaye's sister. After hearing the lion's message, Jaye sets up a date, during which her sister declares that she is a lesbian. Shortly thereafter, the UPS man suffers a violent allergic reaction in the restaurant and must be taken to the hospital. During his stay, his ex-wife comes to visit him, but falls for Jaye's sister. Jaye is initially disappointed, but then Thomas meets a nurse who in turn falls for him. The lion's original message "Make me a match" appears to be fulfilled, but not in the way that Jaye (or even perhaps the viewing audience) initially thought it would be, thus offering a representation of the traditional definition of divine providence: An individual must follow a path he or she cannot understand. Like Joan of Arc, Jaye seems to be following some kind of destiny but it is presented in an unclear fashion.

A major postfeminist subversive element in the "Wax Lion" episode occurs when Jaye acts as a mediator figure who occupies a third space between various individuals. When she follows the wax lion's instructions to make "a match," this unleashes or brings to the surface the concept of repressed lesbian sexuality. Susan E. McKenna has discussed the concept of "lesbian chic" (285) that is visible in popular culture including a series like *Ally McBeal* which "opens up possibilities for other expressions through shifts in long standing lesbian stereotypes" (306). It is in this episode that Jaye's sister Sharon announces to the UPS man that she is a lesbian, and he in turn informs Jaye. The episode also depicts how Thomas' ex-wife falls in love with Jaye's sister, thus undermining the possibility of Thomas ever getting back together with his former girlfriend again. Finally, when Thomas brings his new girlfriend (the nurse) to the gift shop to thank Jaye, Jaye notices the nurse looking at another woman's behind. This scene also reveals the indirect and subversive aspect of the trickster lion's message and how Jaye helps facilitate a postfeminist expression of sexual diversity.

Despite their demand for Jaye's attention, the voices of toy animals or animal figurines remain silent on the topic of whether their messages are derived from a divine or demonic source. For example, in "Wax Lion," after Jaye contemplates the sequence of events involving the return of a purse to a woman, she struggles to comprehend the nature of these speaking animals: "Is that supposed to mean something? Is it a metaphor? Are you Satan? Are you God? If you don't say something in the next four seconds, I'm going to assume you're Satan. One, two three, four ... Oh God, I'm a crazy person (1.1)."

Her conclusion that she is crazy is not an unusual one for the seer figures or psychics in telefantasy (e.g., Cassie in *Hex*, Alison in *Afterlife*) to reach when confronting encounters with the supernatural. Yet Jaye's friend Mahandra willingly listens to her worries, and does not seem terribly disturbed by her claim that she hears voices. Mahandra tells her that perhaps "everything has a soul" (1.1), thus offering an animist perspective or an alternate mythic framework. Furthermore, a bartender continues to express interest in dating her even after she says, "I may be clinically insane; you might want to hold out for someone a little more stable" (1.1).[5]

Jaye may be a modern Joan of Arc because she has visions like her mythical prototype; however, unlike Joan of Arc, she has no particular religious faith of her own, perhaps because she lives in a postfeminist, postmodern world where an emphasis on relativism could create a spiritual vacuum. This open-endedness concerning the reasons for her visions highlights the postmodern element of the series since postmodern narratives typically do not provide final answers (Hutcheon, *The Canadian Postmodern*, x) but usually raise more questions than they solve. For example, Jaye does not know why *she* has been "chosen" to receive visions let alone "who" has chosen her (there is no supernatural authority to tell her). In "Totem Mole" (the second-to-last episode) a seer figure tells her that "she has been sought out for a great purpose" and that she has been chosen for this. She responds "Chosen by what?" thus raising the question if she can even be considered "the chosen one." The reasons for this change in her life remains a mystery except that it is a change that forces her out of her former apathy or indifference so that she will engage with others, and in this sense it is a significant and consciousness-raising transformation.[6] Since Jaye does not know why she is experiencing these visions, she differs from other postfeminist seers in telefantasy whose special powers are part of a legacy or inheritance. Cordelia in *Angel* receives her powers from Doyle, a half-human, half-demon seer. Cassie and Phoebe (from *Hex* and *Charmed* respectively) experience visions or premonitions since they belong to a line of "witches." Even River's psychic ability and fighting skills in *Firefly* and *Serenity* have a possible source: the experiments conducted upon her brain. Jaye, on the other hand, has no line of inheritance from other seer figures although it is possible that, if the series had not been terminated after four episodes, this line of inquiry could have been developed. In one respect, Jaye is more like Tru Davies from *Tru Calling* who suddenly wakes up one day and relives the day in rewind mode, but even Tru learns over time that she shares this ability with her mother. While *Wonderfalls* does not include a God figure like *Joan of Arcadia*, Jaye Tyler's sudden acquisition of the ability to experience the supernatural most closely resembles that of Joan Girardi in *Joan of Arcadia* and this probably has something to do with the fact that both series are based on the figure of the visionary, Joan of Arc.

Joan of Arc and the Legend of the Maid of the Mist

The image of Joan of Arc, the heroine as visionary who is also associated with sacrifice (a young woman going into war and a woman who was burned at the stake for her visions), enters into *Wonderfalls* in a number of different ways and interfaces with the legend of the Maid of the Mist at Niagara Falls. *Wonderfalls* exults in the postmodern play with contradictions and multiple mythologies and offers a postfeminist reconstruction of Joan of Arc and of the Maid of the Mist story. The opening scene describes a questionable legend of Niagara Falls that involves a Native American's sacrifice of an "Indian Princess" to the god of the water, and the god's decision to spare the princess if she lived with him as the "maid of the mist."

As Jaye, the narrator, tells this story to a young boy in the souvenir shop, he replies that Native Americans never engaged in acts of human sacrifice. The narrative insists that the legend is false and simply made up as a tourist trap. This non-native concoction of a so-called Native American myth, was actually presented on Niagara Falls postcards,[7] and reinforces the blending of native and non-native culture in *Wonderfalls*. In *Wonderfalls* the statue which pays homage to this "Indian princess" who went over the falls in a canoe is located near the souvenir shop. The statue is also suggestive of some artistic representations of Joan of Arc. In *Wonderfalls* the statue depicts a woman looking skyward, a combination of strength and vulnerability. She stands tall in the canoe as it topples over the falls with her palms up and the woman appears to be surrendering herself to her destiny or to the spirit of the waters. This statue has some parallels with Anna Vaughn Hyatt's 1915 statue of Joan of Arc on horseback. Even though Vaughn's statue depicts Joan of Arc with a sword in the air, Joan looks as though she is almost standing in the saddle: "sitting so high in the saddle that she seems to continue going up and forward even while the horse remains posed" (Blaetz, 26). In a drawing by G. Engelmann (after Fragonard, 1822) she is tied to the stake but also looks upward and off to the side, "gracefully struggling against her fate" (Blaetz, photo caption, 19). Furthermore, like Joan of Arc, the "Maid of the Mist" is a figure of sacrifice. The latter was sent by her chief to go over a waterfall in a canoe to appease a god of the water. When Jaye tells the story, she says the princess refuses the chief's last-minute attempt to save her: "But Princess wasn't having any of that. She's all, no, no, I surrender to destiny" ("Wax Lion" 1.1). Yet the way the narrative is told by Jaye already suggests a subversion of a simplistic myth of sacrifice and that viewers are not to take the non-native mediated myth too seriously: "Anyway, so then Princess takes the plunge, but it's all good 'cause the god thought the daughter was hot so he spared her life... So she agreed to live with the god in the waterfall and became Maid of the Mist" (1.1). Thus women of sacrifice like the Maid of the Mist and Joan of Arc are incorporated and transformed in *Wonderfalls* into postfeminist hybrid forms. The Maid of the Mist statue depicts an aboriginal woman but also bears some similarities to art depicting Joan of Arc. Jaye's cynical narrative of "The Maid of the Mist" and her comment that the Maid's life was spared because "she was hot" (1.1) captures the ironic tone of *Wonderfalls* and explains how the series subverts a romantic idealization of women as objects of sacrifice.

Jaye's role as a young woman who lives in a third space of experiencing visions of the supernatural is developed even further as she engages in a cross-cultural interaction with contemporary Native American or aboriginal culture. The episode "Totem Mole" introduces several seer figures and the representation of the woman as seer undergoes a humorous postfeminist reconceptualization of the Maid of the Mist legend. In "Totem Mole," she states that she does not consider herself a seer, perhaps because the term suggests a person who has a form of spiritual knowledge that she does not have. Nor does she feel that she has "legitimately" inherited the gift of second sight. She has no ancestors who passed on this gift to her. As a result, she perceives her ability to hear and see strange phenomena (such as talking toy animals or dead people) as a burden that she wants to transfer to another individual. In "Totem Mole" (1.12), Jaye's role as the reluctant visionary or leader is captured to perfection when she ends up seeing the spirit of Gentle Feather, a dead American Indian seer, while visiting the Satsuma Indian Reservation in Niagara Falls. Gentle Feather tells her that another seer must be found to offer leadership to her people. Along with this message from a human spirit, Jaye also hears the words of the speaking bird-like totem pole that says, "Show him who's special." Jaye interprets this message as a reference to Gentle Feather's grandson Bill Hutton, an accountant, and so she tries to convince Bill and the Satsuma tribe that Bill is the true heir to Gentle Feather's legacy. Unfortunately, during a series of hilarious scenes, all signs point to Jaye and not to Bill as the "legitimate" seer figure. In response, Jaye tries desperately to tell tribal members that she is not a leader: "I'm not a leader; I need a leader who can talk to dead grandma and find out how to lift a particular burden of mine." She continues to act as mediator by helping Bill go through various tests to prove that he is the legitimate successor of Gentle Feather. Eventually Jaye thinks that she has accomplished her job of making Bill "feel special" by convincing the tribe that he is Gentle Feather's successor.

The trickster element at play in the episode reveals that the "real seer" and legitimate heir to Gentle Feather's power is neither Bill nor Jaye but a savvy American Indian lawyer called Deanna Little Foot who was at the top of her class in law school. The episode also redefines the image of the Maid of the Mist. In "Totem Mole" the image and story of the Maid of the Mist as represented in the souvenirs sold at Jaye's store is deconstructed. As Jaye's brother, a student of comparative religions, points out, "The Maid of the Mist isn't even a real myth. It was just fabricated by whites to bring in tourists." Instead, the image of the Maid of the Mist is reconfigured into a native Indian context. In a misty sauna scene, perhaps a recreation of a native "sweat" ceremony, Deanna Little Foot sees Gentle Feather, "a vision in the mist." Both Deanna and Gentle Feather are examples of "the maid of the mist." When Deanna emerges from the sauna, she is a reborn woman. Deanna in turn becomes a new postfeminist maid of the mist, and follows her destiny to become a seer and leader for her people. She subverts the myth of the Maid of the Mist since the legend is no longer the idealized construction of "the non-native Indian legend," but a cultural and spiritual alternative that stems from American Indian culture. Yet the episode should not be oversimplified as an essentialist message about authenticity vs. false representation. Deanna is an example of the third space that a post-colonial culture occupies as that culture incorporates both modern and traditional elements which may appear to be contradictory. In the final scene, Deanna emerges from a car dressed in a white outfit with white feathers wafting around her. Deanna's final words in the episode articulate a postfeminist, post-colonial hybrid vision that embraces the traditional and modern: She tells Bill about her "vision" of an accountant who will help the Satsuma people build a casino. As a seer and a savvy lawyer, she expresses the contradictions and the diversity associated with postfeminism.

The image of the visionary who is chosen as the legitimate heir is accomplished through a complex incorporation and subversion of the Joan of Arc myth for Jaye as well as for Deanna. The historical Joan of Arc heard voices and received visions asking her to take action, and was transformed from a girl to a girl warrior. Her role as passive visionary was only one component of her character but was instrumental in her becoming a leader. While Joan of Arc followed her destiny, she did so with some degree of choice. Jaye also feels compelled to heed the voices she hears. Her visions of talking animals and in the case of "Totem Mole," "a talking Native American seer who just passed away" shake her out of her apathetic attitude towards life. Try as she might, she cannot ignore the visions, and so she must become involved in the lives of others (just as the self-absorbed Cordelia character in *Buffy* was transformed into the helpful seer figure of Cordelia in *Angel*). As a result, Jaye ends up reconsidering her desire to part with her visionary ability and thinks that perhaps her gift is not a burden after all, since others seem to value or desire her power.

Wonderfalls presents a postfeminist and postmodern recreation of Joan of Arc through Jaye Tyler, the female protagonist who occupies a third space because she sees and hears the spirit of a dead Native American seer figure along with her ability to hear inanimate objects speak. Unlike Joan of Arc who has become an icon of leadership, Jaye is more of a mediator than a leader, but this reflects the postfeminist experience of women who negotiate between spaces and have "diverse relations to power" (Lotz, 115). An apathetic woman in her twenties, she reluctantly responds to the call for action, but she is not always rewarded for her good deeds, thus demonstrating the trickster-like quality of an unknown power which may have granted her the ability to have visions. In "Totem Mole" Jaye's cross-cultural interaction with Gentle Feather, a dead Native American woman who is a seer, and with the grandson of Gentle Feather suggest that she is chosen but again not in the way she originally thinks. *Wonderfalls* indicates that in a postfeminist fashion there are multiple sites for the expression of the feminine that "can lead women to experience their subjectivity differently and dependent on context" (Lotz, 115). In "Totem Mole" *Wonderfalls* introduces multiple dimensions of the heroine: a respected Native American seer and grandmother, a young white woman who initially sees her visionary powers as a "burden," and a confident Native American woman lawyer who incorporates traditional and modern values. The series subverts cultural and sexual expectations; it undermines heteronormative assumptions about relationships by depicting lesbian identity (through Jaye's sister), and it challenges images of a Native American woman in a non-native mediated legend by recreating the image of "The Maid of the Mist" through depictions of powerful women in aboriginal culture.

PART 3

Investigating the Dead
Mediums and Psychic Detectives

EIGHT

Psychic Women, "Dead" Men and the Search for Truth

Cross-Gender Communication in Ghost, The Gift and Premonition

While television in a postfeminist era has seen a clear rise in the number of series featuring women with psychic abilities or visionary powers, there are also several key American films between 1990 and 2007 which depict women with psychic power. The representation of individuals with psychic abilities is hardly a new phenomenon in film; mediums have been featured in films such as *Ghost Chasers* (1951), *Séance on a Wet Afternoon* (1964) and *The Changeling* (1979)[1] and other psychic-paranormal abilities have been depicted in *Scanners* (1981), *The Dead Zone* (1983) and *The Sixth Sense* (1999).[2] However, three films, *Ghost* (1990), *The Gift* (2000) and *Premonition* (2007), make use of the psychic visionary elements in ways that reflect some of the concerns of third wave feminism about relationships between men and women. While creating new ways to support women, third wave feminists are "committed to building positive connections with men as their friends, romantic partners, co-workers, brothers, and fathers" (Wood, 78). The films examine communication between women and men, different ways of knowing or "seeing," and feminine agency. The psychic woman occupies an alternate or third space either because of her mediation between the living and the dead or because she attempts to navigate between different realities and contradictory kinds of information to arrive at some kind

In *Ghost* (1990), Whoopi Goldberg is Oda Mae Brown, a female con artist who pretends to be a medium. In this scene, she puts on a performance and claims to have made contact with a spirit. Her ability to perform and use a fake identity is useful when she must pretend to be someone else in order to help Sam Wheat (Patrick Swayze), a "real" ghost, withdraw money from a bank account.

of truth. The psychic heroines in these three films offer three very different images of women with special kinds of knowledge and generate new ways of talking about women, agency, their use of "passive" powers and how they negotiate between the "absence" and the overpowering presence of men in their lives. While *The Gift* and *Premonition* in particular still critique certain patriarchal attitudes, along with *Ghost* they engage in an examination of how women with the gift of psychic ability can facilitate the removal of barriers between men and women.

Ghost was released in the early days of postfeminism or third wave feminism. Whoopi Goldberg, who provides a humorous portrayal of the medium Oda Mae Brown, has been identified by Susanne Kord and Elisabeth Krimmer as one of Hollywood's key actresses during the 1990s

(*Hollywood Divas*, 129). Oda Mae crosses gender and racial boundaries by helping Sam, a dead white man (Patrick Swayze), communicate with his living girlfriend Molly (Demi Moore). She also helps him in his plan to track his murderer and protect Molly from harm. Her role is initially that of a "fake" medium; as a con artist she pretends to have genuine powers and deceives individuals who seek to communicate with their dead loved ones. She embraces the clichéd image of the fake psychic until one day she actually hears Sam's voice during one of her phony séances and realizes that she does have the ability to hear the dead. This ability develops since Oda Mae not only hears Sam but also begins to hear the voices of other departed souls.

Oda Mae occupies an alternate or third space in a variety of ways and is able to position herself in a manner that makes her a dynamic postfeminist character. She already presents herself as a mediator between the living and the dead when she pretends to have the powers of a medium. When she becomes an "authentic" medium who can mediate between the living (Molly) and the dead (Sam), she experiences this third space in a more pronounced or "authentic" fashion but she does not entirely leave behind her skills at fakery. *Ghost* appears to be about the importance of finding out "the truth" and revealing lies since Sam needs to communicate to Molly the identity of his murderer. However, the film perpetuates the use of deception especially through the character of Oda Mae. Even after it is revealed that she has "authentic" powers, she uses the element of disguise when she pretends to be someone else by the name of Rita Miller in order to help Sam move around bank funds that the man indirectly responsible for his murder had embezzled. Kord and Krimmer address the "problematic portrayal of a black woman" (13) in a film that depicts Oda Mae as "a small-time crook" (130) and as a woman who "always obliges [Sam] in the end" (130), yet they acknowledge that Oda Mae has certain strengths since she knows "how to adopt disguises" (131) and succeeds "where her white counterparts have failed" (130). As a mediator between Sam and the living world, she demonstrates the strength of purpose that Molly, Sam's lover and the film's other key feminine presence, does not. Molly is quite a passive character who grieves Sam's death and demonstrates little initiative, while Oda Mae redefines the image of the passive medium through her active involvement in Sam's

Oda Mae Brown (Whoopi Goldberg) and Sam Wheat (Patrick Swayze) converse in a scene from *Ghost*. Oda Mae has been transformed from a fake medium into a medium with authentic powers. On the far right is the spirit of the man, Orlando, who later enters Oda Mae's body uninvited in order to communicate with his living wife.

investigation of his murderer and through her ability to re-invent herself.

As a black woman, Oda Mae engages in different kinds of negotiation that reveal how she inhabits a third space. She crosses boundaries racially and in gender terms because of her psychic ability. Kord and Krimmer indicate that Whoopi Goldberg's roles demonstrate how she is "forever taking care of white folks" (photo caption 131) and the part of Oda Mae Brown is no exception in this respect since she helps Sam protect Molly. Oda Mae also learns about the world of "white" collar crime (the embezzlement of funds) and manages to help Sam with his plan to outwit the man behind Sam's murder. Her crossing of gender boundaries is even more complex, however, and while some images in the film suggest the "violation" of the black woman's body, it is also possible to read segments of this fantasy film as examples of how postfeminists deconstruct "binary categories of gender and sexuality, instead viewing these categories as flexible and indistinct" (Lotz, 116). In one scene, Oda Mae's body appears to be "invaded" by a black man who wants to communicate with his wife. He has to cross the boundary of a woman's body to gain access his wife. However, it is probably no accident that the man's name is Orlando. The name is significant because in Virginia Woolf's novel *Orlando* it is the name of a male character who is transformed into a woman. The name suggests the importance of cross-gender communication in *Ghost* and the flexible identity of the woman as medium who can help men transform themselves. Just as she has demonstrated her ability to transcend a fixed category by faking her identity (she pretended to be an authentic medium before she met Sam and she disguised herself as someone else to help Sam), she acquires a hybrid identity when spirits access her mind and body. When she actually allows Sam to use her body to embrace Molly in one scene, one could view the scene as Sam's transformation into a woman just as one could also view Oda Mae being transformed into a man. As Kord and Krimmer point out, the scene of Oda Mae's hands caressing Molly's hands (131) initially suggests a love scene between two women before Oda Mae's body is transformed into Sam's on-screen. The scene of a black woman and a white woman together in a sexual context is a transgressive moment and reveals how Oda Mae functions as a postfeminist medium who introduces the concept of diversity through images of sexual, racial and ontological interactions. The scene operates on multiple levels: It depicts an embrace between two living women (one white and one black), it illustrates the powerful psychic and physical bonds between Sam, Oda Mae and Molly, and it portrays an embrace between people in two different states of being: a dead man and a living woman.

The paradoxical absence and presence of Sam plays a significant role in how Oda Mae positions herself as a medium. She must negotiate between not being able to see Sam (in this sense he is absent) while not being able to shut him out; he is everywhere (almost godlike). Oda Mae only "hears" Sam's voice for most of the film and does not actually see him. Nor does she see any of the other dead spirits. Perhaps this is in order to convey the notion of a psychic's "second sight" as a different kind of perception that is not equivalent to ordinary human vision. What else could be gained by presenting Oda Mae's ability in this fashion? By having Oda Mae only hear voices, the film reinforces her image as a different kind of medium from the "fake" medium represented at the beginning of the story who was supposedly able to "see" all kinds of paranormal phenomena. Yet another possibility for the invisibility of Sam is suggested by Kord and Krimmer who argue that "the entire film is built on the idea of a white man who is condemned to invisibility" (130); thus her inability to "see" Sam throughout the majority of the film is an interesting subversion of the historical invisibility of Afro-American people in white mainstream American society.

It is only by communicating with a member of a marginalized group (Oda Mae is a black woman with self-proclaimed psychic abilities) that Sam is able to communicate with Molly and restore justice. This act of communication and the mediation facilitated by another *woman's* mind and body are all the more significant since one of the major issues for Molly in her relationship with Sam while he was alive was that he only answered her proclamation "I love you" with "Ditto." The conversation between Molly and Sam at the end of the film indicates that through his relationship with Oda Mae, Sam has acquired a greater sensitivity to what Molly needs to hear him say.

The Gift

Like *Ghost*, *The Gift* (2000) depicts a woman who mediates between the world of the living and the dead. The film focuses on the experiences of the recently widowed Annie Wilson (Cate Blanchett), a small town psychic who is also a mother of three boys. Unlike Oda Mae's ability in *Ghost* which is limited to hearing the dead, Annie is a psychic who has visions or waking dreams of the dead, including visions of a wealthy girl, Jessica King (Katie Holmes), who is murdered. Before her premonition of Jessica's murder, Annie's daily psychic activities include giving people readings by looking at Zener cards; these cards consisting of five different designs (a circle, a plus symbol, a double star, a square, and a group of three vertical jagged lines) were designed by Karl Zener in the early 1930s for ESP experiments to test telekinetic skills but were not ordinarily used for psychic readings. However, during the first part of the film, it is unclear whether these cards actually help Annie with psychic predictions or whether some of the advice she gives her clients is simply the kind of common sense that a good listener and sympathetic person might be able to provide. For example, in one case she tells a man to go see a doctor; in another, she tells Buddy, a deeply disturbed young man, that he must discover on his own why he hates his father so much.

Like Oda Mae who responds to the absent (dead and invisible) yet ever-present Sam (she hears him and sees him move objects), Annie is also heavily influenced by men in her life whether they are absent or present. For example, her husband is technically absent since he died in an explosion. However, even though her husband Ben Wilson is dead, he is present in other ways throughout the film. For example, Wayne Collins (Greg Kinnear), the local school principal who is attracted to Annie (just as she is attracted to him), reminds Annie of her husband. She does not explain why this is the case but Wayne had just finished telling her that he does not really believe in psychic abilities; perhaps this lack of respect for what is constructed as a feminine power (Annie is also called a witch in the film) links Wayne to Annie's husband, who died in an explosion at his workplace, ignoring Annie's warning to stay home on that fateful day.

The memory of Ben Wilson is also present in the courtroom when Annie is "blamed" for not preventing her husband's death. Like Wayne, the defense attorney for Donnie Barksdale (Keanu Reeves), the man accused of Jessica's murder, wonders whether Annie knew that her husband Ben was going to die. Annie lives in Brixton, Georgia, a small town defined by male power. A number of men, including Donnie and the town sheriff, make disrespectful comments concerning her "work" as a psychic. Donnie, a known wife abuser, calls Annie a witch and actually punches her for counseling his wife. Even the town sheriff who should be on the right side of the law mocks Annie's gift and makes it difficult for her to concentrate and work when she is asked to help with the investigation of Jessica's disappearance. This demonization of the female psychic and the invalidation of her work only make it all the more remarkable that Annie is unwilling to let Donnie rot in jail because her psychic abilities suggest that he is not Jessica's murderer. Her sense of ethics prevents her from merely seeking revenge on a man who threatened her life and the lives of her children.

Annie clearly occupies a third space or in-between space in the film because her psychic ability generates mixed responses, particularly from the men in the town. On the one hand, some of the men believe that Annie can help them. Jessica King's father wants her to assist in the investigation of his daughter's disappearance and she locates his daughter's body at the bottom of a pond. Her mentally fragile friend Buddy needs to talk to her about why he hates his father so much and in some ways treats her like the nurturing mother he never had. (It is later revealed that Buddy's own mother did not prevent his father from sexually abusing him.) Yet while some of the townsmen depend on Annie's psychic ability (e.g., the men who come for readings) and respond to her positively, this same ability also marginalizes her as a woman because some men view her psychic power with fear and contempt. Donnie calls her a witch and others have difficulty classifying or defining her or her gift. For example, during court proceedings at Donnie's trial, the sheriff says he does not know "what the right word is" and the defense attorney supplies the term "fortune teller." The defense demonstrates his skepticism concerning Annie's psychic ability when he asks Annie how many concealed fingers he is holding up. Annie does not know and later counters that her power "doesn't work that way" but this does not seem to satisfy the male proponents of a rigid "black or white" way of looking at the world where the third space or "gray" space of the psychic's visions cannot be accommodated. Her visions are partial or incomplete since she does not have full knowledge of the identity of Jessica's murderer; when Wayne, Jessica's fiancé, asks her for a reading, she replies, "I can't make it happen." This representation of her ability as passive and partial counters the focus on the aggressive, unambiguous actions portrayed by many men in the film. Even Buddy accuses Annie of failing him and questions her ability: "Why don't you tell me why I hate him?... You're the goddamn psychic." His accusation indicates that Annie inhabits a world that is inhospitable to women, even to women who nurture and attempt to heal others.

Despite the blame and abuse that Annie suffers, she is a survivor and uses her role as a psychic and figure of mediation to speak for other women who are silenced by men. She provides emotional support to Valerie Barksdale, who is repeatedly beaten by her husband, and she speaks in defense of the murdered Jessica King, who transgressed the boundaries of social class and upper middle class respectability by having sexual relations with other men (including a lower class man, Donnie) even though she was planning to marry the school principal. Annie defends Jessica's memory when Valerie says that she is glad the "girl is dead" after finding out that Jessica had sexual relations with her husband. The psychic counters, "No one deserves that," thereby resisting a patriarchally influenced culture which would polarize women into two extremes: the virgin–Madonna figure and the witch-whore.[3] The film's message concerning women from different walks of life (abused wife, widowed psychic, murdered fiancée) seems bleak and the central dead person in the film is a woman (Jessica King) as opposed to the dead man (Sam) in *Ghost*, but this bleakness does not apply to women alone. In this sense it sends a postfeminist message that asks its audience to consider how both men and women are affected by violence. Buddy's abuse at the hands of his father indicates that men can also be victims of violence and that the domestic environment or the home can be a vulnerable place for both.[4] Similarly, women may end up endorsing the violent actions of men: Buddy accuses his mother of not intervening when his father abused him and Valerie, the abused wife of Donnie, sanctions the murder of Jessica by saying that she is glad the girl is dead.[5] The film indicates that men who perpetuate violence must become part of the solution, and third wave feminism has demonstrated "a commitment to building alliances with men and other groups that work against various kinds of oppression" (Wood, 78). "The White Ribbon Campaign" which was created by one such group of men in 1991 has led campaigns that heighten awareness of violence against women; these are campaigns led by "both men and women, even though the focus is on educating men and boys" ("The White Ribbon Campaign"). This movement reinforces many postfeminist sentiments that men must be part of the process in improving lives for women if women are to "meet men in the middle" (Wood, 78). *The Gift* suggests the necessity for this kind of male involvement at the film's climax, when Buddy saves Annie from Jessica's murderer. It is important that Buddy is the one to save Annie and express gratitude for being his friend. He thus redeems himself for blaming her for his earlier act of trying to burn his father. The anger which Buddy had harbored against his father for sexually abusing him, had been misplaced and directed against Annie for not being available when he experienced this earth-shattering revelation.

The last segment of the film, involving Buddy's rescue of Annie, includes elements of the fantastic which help locate the psychic woman's experiences within an alternate space or reality. Like telefantasy series which foreground women with visionary powers, *The Gift* includes the fantastic to legitimize the psychic woman's third space. Annie is convinced that Buddy has escaped from the mental hospital where he had been placed after burning his father. However, when Annie stops at the sheriff's office after her encounter with Jessica's murderer, the sheriff reveals that Buddy had never left the hospital. The fantastic element of Buddy's re-appearance and disappearance near the end of the film is important since it further reinforces the mystery of Annie's psychic ability and the importance of her role in Brixton. Buddy calls her "the soul of this town," thus emphasizing her central role in that community despite the efforts undertaken by other men to marginalize or condemn her. This fantastic or surreal scene also sends a postfeminist, postmodern message that "truth" is a slippery concept. Even the sheriff realizes that "you can know somebody and not know them," thereby emphasizing that there are different ways of knowing something or someone. Thus the sheriff who had earlier mocked Annie's gift, now indirectly validates Annie's psychic knowledge as an alternate way of knowing.

Because of Buddy Cole's "fantastic" intervention, Annie is able to achieve a form of closure in her life; she can make the absent husband visible to her sons by looking at photographs of her husband. Earlier in the film, she had expressed a reluctance to discuss the life of her sons' father with her children because the memory of his death had been too painful. The film seems to be suggesting that the male no longer needs to be a purely oppressive influence, nor does the masculine need to be suppressed (as in Buddy's suppression of his father's abusive acts). Furthermore, there is a postfeminist catharsis in *The Gift* since men and women see past their gendered differences in an attempt to recognize that the member of the opposite sex is not necessarily "the enemy." For example, Buddy acknowledges how Annie helped him, and Annie accepts help from Buddy and also restores the memory of her husband in her life in a positive way through conversations with her sons (a marked contrast to the earlier "guilt" that other men may have made her experience about her inability to predict the exact details of his death).

Premonition

Both *The Gift* and *Ghost* depict psychic women who inhabit a third space between the living and the dead; they become involved in investigations and in both cases dead men influence their lives. *Premonition* (2007), directed by Mennan Yapo, provides yet another version of a woman with psychic abilities and the "dead" man or absent husband in her life. Linda Hanson (Sandra Bullock) is a suburban housewife and mother of two girls who has premonitions of her husband's death. In the early part of the film, she is told by a sheriff, a male authority figure, that her husband Jim (Julian McMahon) had been in a car accident "yesterday" and "died on the scene." The film then moves from this "reality" to Linda's experience of going to sleep and waking up to find that her husband is still alive. Over the course of the narrative, every time Linda wakes up she is not sure what day it is and whether her husband will be dead or alive. The replaying of a day is reminiscent of the depiction of time in the television series *Tru Calling*. *Premonition* thus engages in a postmodern play with time and with various levels of reality to the point that it is not only difficult for the character but also difficult for the viewer to know what reality Linda is experiencing.[6]

Mennan Yapo indicated that his goal in making the film was to focus on "normal, average people" ("Glimpses of the Future: Making *Premonition*," a special feature on the *Premonition* DVD) and their encounter with an unusual experience. Prior to her premonition of her husband's death, Linda seems to have had no psychic ability. Her life had in fact become a routine, and she had lost a sense of what it means to be in love. Her husband is little more than a roommate. The premonition she experiences literally functions as a "wakeup call" since when she wakes up for the first time in the film, she receives the news that her husband is dead. Bill Kelly, the screenwriter, says that "what this phenomenon provides the character is an insight into what is really going on in her life which she otherwise wouldn't have had a glimpse of" ("Glimpses of the Future: Making *Premonition*"). Thus, the premonition serves as a means of getting Linda to re-examine her life and not remain passive.

In the early part of the film, Linda appears to be a classic illustration of a Cassandra figure who receives visions of the future. In this sense, she is a woman with little agency who knows about the imminent death of someone but who cannot prevent fate. If passivity is a common trait of the psychic woman or medium who is often depicted as the passive recipient of knowledge, then Linda seems to be far less active or motivated than Annie in *The Gift* and Oda Mae in *Ghost*. Annie at least has contact with members of her community by providing readings and Oda Mae, though initially a reluctant medium, becomes instrumental in helping Sam the ghost achieve his goals of protecting his wife and bringing his murderer to justice. Linda on the other hand is a far more isolated figure who almost walks through life like a sleepwalker. *Premonition* uses Linda's repeated pattern of falling asleep in order to portray Linda's passivity. When she does wake up, she has little control. She cannot differentiate between reality and a dream or visionary state and lives in an in-between state or third space. Things happen *to* her, and male authority figures play a role in her life which limit her agency. For example, the sheriff's announcement of Jim's death at the beginning of the film is followed by the involvement of a male psychiatrist (Dr. Norman Roth) in her life; he arrives at her home to take her to a psychiatric hospital because of her mother's fear that she might have been responsible for the injuries on her daughter Bridget's face. (Bridget actually sustained the injuries after running through a glass patio door.) The image of Linda restrained by the authorities and with her hands bound suggests the madness of the mythic Cassandra whose visions of death drive her mad. Linda's psychic ability has thus been medicalized and dismissed by a member of the patriarchal establishment (and even by her own mother) as the ravings of a madwoman.

However, despite these overriding images of Linda, the visionary woman as a passive vessel that must receive knowledge or perhaps live with the knowledge that her husband is destined to die, she decides to change the course of her life. Her decision to throw away the lithium that the psychiatrist has prescribed is one indication of her conscious choice to take control, as are her cries to the psychiatrist, "You are not separating me from my kids." When she wakes up again in the next scene, she finds herself back in her own bed and her husband is alive. Initially Linda cannot seem to control the reality that she inhabits or the sense of time; she does not know whether she is dreaming or experiencing "real" time. However, once she fears that she might be separated from her two girls, she starts to take charge of her life by engaging in the act of investigating her premonition instead of remaining passive. She makes a chart consisting of different events and the dates associated with those events that occur before or after her husband Jim's death. After putting together the pieces of the puzzle, Linda discovers that Jim was going to have an affair with Claire, one of his co-workers. In a subsequent scene, Linda stands at a lake and talks to a man who also has two daughters and who moved to the lake area after his divorce. He says, "What a great place to start over." The scene leads her to ponder her relationship with Jim and her own role in that relationship. Later, Linda asks her mother, "If I let Jim die, is it the same thing as killing him?" Her question actually raises important points concerning passivity and activity. Her life has been largely characterized by passive behavior and the premonition serves as a fantastic or extraordinary means of encouraging her to contemplate whether her passive role in their relationship may have been synonymous with the conscious act of destroying their relationship. The question also addresses an important ethical issue concerning passive behavior and its potential contribution to the outcome of an individual's fate. (In *The Gift*, Annie refuses to simply let the man rot in jail for a murder he did not commit.) While people often perceive fate as something over which they have no control, *Premonition* asks viewers to consider that the choices they make, including the choice of indifference or inaction, may have an impact on certain events.

In *Premonition* the visions pertaining to Jim's death and other visual signs (including omens or portents of doom) seem to replace the verbal realm of communication. Unlike *Ghost* where Oda Mae depends on the ability to hear the dead speak, in *Premonition* the visual realm is often more powerful. For example, the sight of Jim's severed head falling out of the casket at the funeral is a graphic image of death, as is the dead crow that Linda finds in the garbage. The bloody, scarred face of Linda's daughter who ran into a glass patio door foreshadows or reinforces the violent event of Jim's car crash. Linda's premonitions or visions function as a means of compensating for the absence of communication between Linda and Jim. One could argue that Jim is already "dead" or absent in her life and that the premonition simply acts as a literalization of what is already figuratively the case. Linda and Jim have all the makings of a typical, comfortable, suburban middle-class existence but their lives are emotionally empty since they cannot even say "I love you" to one another. The film functions as a postfeminist visual narrative on how women and men can reach an impasse and lose the ability to communicate or fight for what is important. While Linda, the suburban housewife, hardly seems like a heroic figure, *Premonition* suggests that the domestic environment can be the space for acts of courage. The premonition serves as a third space that allows Linda to use her powers of investigation to fight for her husband in order to save their troubled relationship.

The film initially presents Linda's cross-gender communication with men in negative terms. This includes her interaction with her husband and her discussions with Dr. Roth, the psychiatrist. However, Linda is able to have a conversation with a priest that is an important step in helping her to reconnect with her husband. What is important about her dialogue with the priest is that it presents information in a secular manner outside the context of any particular religion. He talks to her about "people who have lost their beliefs" instead of identifying a particular religious group. This lack of identification with a Christian, patriarchal system of beliefs facilitates a postfeminist way of re-articulating the role of the male authority figure in the film, thus ensuring that communication between a man and the heroine can occur. The priest tells Linda that the Greeks believed that premonitions may occur in people who are "empty vessels" and therefore are more "susceptible to being taken over."[7] She responds that this "sounds almost like a curse" and the priest replies, "Or a miracle." This statement reinforces the conflicting view of psychic power as represented in television and film. It may be seen as a "gift" or as a "curse" depending on the person's perspective. The curse/miracle dichotomy also captures the postmodern quality and relativism of the film since it acknowledges that a premonition of Jim's death might actually create something positive in Linda's life, even though the image of "possession" or "being taken over" may suggest an initial lack of agency for Linda as it does for seer or visionary figures in general. After her session with the priest, Linda reveals to her husband for the first time that she had a dream that he was going to die. Her utterance or act of finally telling Jim about the premonition (which she calls a dream) demonstrates how she uses the visual realm of psychic visions as a means of re-engaging herself in verbal communication. The successful breaking of the silence eventually results in the renewal of sexual intimacy with her husband, another form of cross-gender communication.

Linda breaks down the communication barrier between Jim and herself, which in turn results in Jim's decision to reinvest in their marriage, both emotionally and financially. He increases his insurance coverage perhaps because he took her concerns about his imminent death seriously. His wife feels comfortable talking to him again and their communication on the cell phone shortly before the finale is probably the most meaningful conversation they have had in years. The film's ending confirms Jim's fate and avoids a Hollywood ending of having Linda save Jim.[8] There is a tragic irony in *Premonition* when Linda tells Jim to turn his car around in order to prevent a car accident and he is still killed. Mennan Yapo intended to portray the idea that one "can't change the course of time" ("Glimpses of the Future: Making *Premonition*") since fate appears to be inexorable. While her intervention may not have prevented his death, it did have the tangible result of a renewal in her relationship with him, however short-lived that miraculous transformation might have been. *Premonition* suggests that there may be a destiny in store for people, but leading life in a passive way is not the way to live. Linda's premonition allowed her to exit her cocooned life and make some conscious choices about actually starting over with her husband. Evidence of this new mindset is further highlighted at the finish when Linda wakes up again and observes that "every day we're alive can be a miracle." The audience sees that she is pregnant[9] and will experience another form of renewal in her life despite any loss that she might have experienced.

The feminine principle thus prevails at the end with the scene of Linda, an expectant mother, embracing her two daughters. As a postfeminist heroine with psychic ability, she may not have been able to prevent the death of her husband, but she has experienced the miracle of life in a different way.

Ghost, *The Gift* and *Premonition* depict three different women characters whose psychic or paranormal experiences with "dead" men ironically contribute to a kind of postfeminist renewal in their lives. *Ghost's* Oda Mae Brown discovers through her ability to hear a ghost or the voice of a dead man that she can in fact inhabit a third space where she functions as a medium and mediator to facilitate communication between the living and the dead. As a black woman, she also serves as a site of sexual and cultural hybridity since she allows Sam, a white man, to use her body for one final embrace with his white lover Molly. Oda Mae proves to be a resourceful woman who ironically employs her skills in the art of deception and disguise (she used to be a fake medium) to help Sam in his investigations.

Annie Wilson, a psychic in *The Gift*, also has connections to different kinds of "dead" men even though the storyline focuses on the murder of a young woman. Her dead husband is used by men in the town to "blame" Annie for her imprecise psychic ability. By engaging in a psychic investigation of Jessica King's murder, Annie saves Donnie Barksdale, a "dead" man, who was wrongfully accused of murdering Jessica. Her life is in turn saved by her friend Buddy Cole, a man abused by his father and emotionally scarred, who reappears as a ghost to save Annie and validate her importance as a psychic within her community.

Linda Hanson's experience in *Premonition* involves foreknowledge of the death of her husband. In this film the dead man is already "dead" or absent in Linda's life because of a dysfunctional or emotionally dead relationship between Linda and a husband who is contemplating having an affair. Her premonition allows her to look at life differently and appreciate the miracle of being alive which in some ways becomes more important than whether or not she can save her husband's life. All three films address ethical questions and show how the three women characters become instrumental in ethical decisions; Linda in *Premonition* realizes that she must become an active participant in life and not a passive observer who would simply accept that she cannot or will not change anything and therefore let her husband die as foreshadowed in her premonition. Annie in *The Gift* reveals to the authorities that a despicable man who threatened her with violence has been falsely convicted of murder and puts aside their personal differences to locate the real killer because this is the ethical thing to do. Unlike *The Gift* and *Premonition*, *Ghost* includes a rather humorous treatment of Oda Mae as a con artist turned heroic medium. Her ability to use disguise and deception actually helps a dead white man uncover the crime perpetuated by another man. All three characters are unique kinds of postfeminist psychic mediators and heroines whose interactions with "dead" men, ironically lead to the transformation and revitalization of their own lives.

NINE

Rescue Mediums
and *Psychic Investigators*
Television for Women
and Paranormal Programming

Women with special visionary or psychic abilities are cast as (heroic) characters in postfeminist American television dramas like *Medium* and *Ghost Whisperer* and in the U.K. series *Afterlife*. These series present women and their powers of investigation through their special gifts or role as mediators between the living and the dead. However, the significant role of women as psychics is also evident in "reality television" or documentary-style series that include psychics and supernatural content. A Canadian specialty channel for women, W Network, showcases the series *Psychic Investigators* (2006–) and *Rescue Mediums* (2006–). W Network offers a variety of programs that are designed to appeal to women between the ages of 18 and 54.[1] As a television network, it offers its female viewers an alternative form of programming. In *Psychic Investigators* and *Rescue Mediums*, female psychics occupy a postfeminist third space or an alternate space in a number of ways. They are presented as being able to communicate with the dead and their ability is presented in the context of an alternate kind of investigation. In *Psychic Investigators*, the storyline is primarily that of a criminal investigation which involves some input from psychics along with commentary by a female narrator; in *Rescue Mediums*, two "internationally renowned" psychics investigate spirits haunting a home. Women's psychic abilities receive acknowledgment in these shows in part because they reinforce the "objective" information that is acquired through other sources like police investigators or in the form of other factual information; however, female psychics in both series also manage to "convert" others to their respective "visions" or ways of seeing. The genre of these shows occupies a unique third space or in-between space as well. The series are ostensibly "reality television" and labeled reality television by the TV industry,[2] yet because the content consists of supernatural phenomena and psychic abilities, these shows could be considered "telefantasy" depending on the perspective of the television viewer or critic.

W Network's *Psychic Investigators* unites the popularity of crime detection series with the paranormal or the supernatural. It is a Canadian-U.K. co-production which includes episodes shot in American, Canadian and British locations. This display of assorted settings and the polyvocality of accents help create an interesting hybrid form. There is also a creative merging of the "natural" (real) and the "supernatural" (fantastic). What is notable from a gender perspective is how women are strategically positioned within the televisual and narrative space in order to validate an alternative form of power: psychic knowledge.

"Jacquie Poole" (1.10) serves as a useful example of how the series incorporates women's views in postfeminist television. In this episode, psychic Christine Holohan becomes involved in an investigation of a young woman's murder that occurred on February 12, 1983. Her voice helps create the narrative of the investigation into Poole's death and simultaneously serves as an alternative narrative to the narrative of the police investigation. Christine lives in the republic of Ireland; she has written about her involvement in this real-life drama in her own book, *A Voice from the Grave: The Unseen Witness in the Jacquie Poole Murder Case* (2006). In *Psychic Investigators* she plays herself, thus reinforcing the "reality" dimension of this reality series. She describes how she heard and saw Poole's spirit who presented herself to the psychic as Jacquie Hunt (Hunt was Jacquie's maiden name). Christine explains how she tried to help achieve closure for the spirit of this murdered woman. Evidence of documentary style techniques can be found in this and other episodes of *Psychic Investigators*. Close-ups of Poole's face (including her eyes or even a single eye) emphasize the personal nature of the story, a common documentary technique. The close-up of the eye may also be a televisual way of reinforcing her psychic ability. Interestingly enough, her version of the story is given further credibility when the police inspector's face is shot with a similar close-up of the "all-seeing" eye. These close-ups reinforce the paradox that these two individuals perceive experiences differently (one is a psychic who is positioned on the left side of the television screen, and the other is a police investigator who in a separate shot is positioned on the right) while sharing the common experience of investigating Poole's death. The close-ups and different televisual positions of two different individuals suggests that truth does not reside in a single source or site; in a visual fashion, both the police superintendent and the psychic are presented as being able to see a "truth" even though they arrive at their conclusions through different means.

The overarching narrative voice in "Jacquie Poole" is that of an anonymous female narrator (the voice is actually that of Canadian actress Jennifer Dale). In the trailer for the episode, the narrator asks, "Would a psychic's paranormal powers or hard forensic science nail Jacquie's killer?" As the episode unfolds, the narrator's commentary negotiates between the psychic's experiences and the voice of male authority represented by London police detective superintendent Tony Lundy. Her voice also serves as a way of empowering the psychic's views. Jonathan Bignell comments that in addition to the "documentary subject which provides an impression of reality in documentary television" (195), the "supporting narration, testimony or expert commentary" also serves this purpose. One also needs to remember that traditionally the voice of documentary has been the male voice of authority or the "voice-of-God commentary" (Giannetti and Leach, 312); thus the voice of the female narrator in *Psychic Investigators* serves simultaneously as a way of co-opting the authority of the male voice of truth while also redirecting the viewer to appreciate Jacquie's unique ability and form of psychic knowledge. The narrator mentions that "murder investigation teams are skeptical over the use of psychics and she [Christine] must risk ridicule." However, the narrator also consistently mentions that Christine knew of certain details that "were not released to the press" and by pointing this out, she validates the psychic's knowledge.

By the end of the episode, the psychic's account has been validated in terms of how closely it corroborates the evidence uncovered by the police investigators. The narrator reveals that according to Tony Batters, a policeman involved in the murder case, 120 of the 130 facts revealed by Christine matched the information on trial. The murderer is not brought to justice until approximately 20 years later, however, because it is only once DNA technology is available that Christine's knowledge of the identity of the murderer can be proven with "hard" scientific evidence. While some might argue that the ability of the female psychic is undermined by the power of DNA technology, the show actually reveals how Christine's knowledge was confirmed by a relatively recent scientific development. Instead of viewing her ability as inferior to scientific knowledge, *Psychic Investigators* presents the science as confirming what a female psychic already knew to be true, thus empowering the psychic's form of knowledge. The narrator also states that Christine's psychic skills "converted Tony Batters into a true believer." This recognition of psychic ability by a police officer thus displaces the idea that police investigation and psychic investigation are two completely separate and incompatible activities. A final illustration of how Jacquie's psychic knowledge displaces a pure science-oriented approach is Christine's claim that she had a vision of Jacquie once the case was solved. The Irish psychic indicates that Jacquie was smiling, happy and at peace. This is the kind of knowledge that the police would not have been able to provide, and it reminds viewers of the often forgotten human element in a murder since typical criminal investigations focus on the gathering of evidence. While DNA evidence may have allowed the police to concentrate on apprehending the male killer, the female psychic was able to privilege the vision and voice of the female victim, thus inscribing the narrative of Jacquie Poole with a woman-centered perspective.

Rescue Mediums

Another supernatural-based series that airs on W Network is *Rescue Mediums* which has been described by its producers as a "reality-based half hour television show" ("Haunted Ontario"). Its central figures are two middle-aged women, Jackie Dennison and Christine Hamlett, who are presented by the narrator and producer Michael Lamport as "internationally renowned psychics" (1.1). At first glance, these two women seem like unlikely hero figures, but they distinguish themselves by working as a team that apparently solves hauntings. They help both the occupants of these ghost-occupied houses and the ghosts who haunt the premises achieve some kind of closure. Thus Jackie and Christine occupy a third space as mediators who try to help both the dead and the undead and whose work involves interactions with unpredictable spirits.

Unlike the voice of the female narrator in *Psychic Investigators*, the narrative voice in *Rescue Mediums* is male and may be more readily identified with the tradition of male narratorial voice in the documentary genre. Producer Lamport's narrative commentary provides a framework for viewing the two mediums much like the "voice-of-God commentary" (Giannetti and Leach, 312) that defined documentary film. In the spirit of documentary television, the "authority" of the narrator "provides coherence and continuity" (Bignell, 196). Yet the series does not subordinate the rescue mediums to the narrator's point of view; instead it relies on a similar interrelationship between psychic knowledge and the tradition of reason and science that informs *Psychic Investigators* and thus provides a kind of hybridization of the known and the unknown. The narrator introduces Jackie and Christine as "psychics who make house calls" (1.1), thus suggesting that their profession is analogous to the medical profession. (Typically, house calls belonged to an era when male doctors performed this service.) He also indicates that these women make use of three primary skills to carry out their roles as "rescue mediums": premonitions, psychometrics and psychic drawings. The premonitions are experienced by both mediums, and they are validated at the end of the program with references to "independent research" (1.1) that confirmed the truth of these premonitions. Psychometrics is defined in episode 1.2 as the use of "inanimate objects to obtain information"; in episode 1.3, for example, the rescue mediums use the technique of dowsing[3] to locate information on a map. They even manage to get a skeptic, the male owner of the haunted house, to hold a ring from a chain in order to assist in the act of dowsing. The episode ends with the mediums convinced that the skeptic may now be a "convert" or a believer in psychic abilities.

The third category of psychic skills mentioned by the narrator are the psychic drawings done by Christine. This "rescue medium" has

Christine Hamlett and Jackie Dennison are the "rescue mediums" who use their psychic tools of investigation (including premonitions and psychic art) to help homeowners who have problems with ghosts. This Canadian example of psychic reality television features two British mediums who visit various Canadian locations and use a variety of skills to help spirits cross over to the afterlife.

described herself as a "psychic artist" who sketches ghosts as they appear to her. These drawings are an important part of *Rescue Mediums*. The visual impact of the sketches (which are apparently completed before the mediums see any photographic documents or other forms of evidence) reinforces Christine's status as a woman with visionary powers. The portraits are sometimes used as dramatic devices near the end of an episode to reveal the uncanny similarities between the sketches produced by Christine and the photographs of the dead people. The psychic artwork also serves as a useful televisual tool that captures the ability of both mediums as women of vision since Jackie's impressions of the dead often coincide with Christine's.

Their psychic abilities are granted legitimacy in other ways that are directly related to the elements of reality television. The reality-based aspect of the series includes different techniques reminiscent of reality TV programs, especially the crime TV variety. *Rescue Mediums* has a narrator figure who serves as a guide for the audience. He explains the abilities of the mediums, summarizes scenes which have just occurred and anticipates or questions the next step to generate a sense of suspense for the viewers. The use of a narrator is a common convention in reality-based investigation programs and helps create an air of authority or credibility. *Rescue Mediums* also makes use of the technique of reconstruction through photographs and fictionalized flashbacks and presents other kinds of physical clues such as the disturbance of a powder that a spirit presumably moved aside in episode 1.2 or the smell of "supernatural" cigars (1.3) that is experienced by multiple people.[4] While viewers might question the veracity of these "physical clues," the fact remains that they are presented as key ingredients in the construction of the program. Episodes also include the dialogue of Jackie and Christine as well as conversations between the rescue mediums and the homeowners or tenants of a haunted house. These apparently unscripted "interviews" or conversations are an important part of documentary television shows and documentary films and create the appearance of authenticity to help "establish their legitimacy as more than fiction" (Jason Mittell, *Genre and Television*, 197). The episodes typically end with Jackie and Christine congratulating one another on a job well done, when they often celebrate their achievement by sampling spirits of another kind (e.g., wine, beer). The conclusions of "rescue and relief" are key aspects of reality TV as John Corner points out when analyzing reality TV that involves "reconstructions of crimes and accidents" (98). The "reality" aspect of *Rescue Mediums* is also emphasized when the series blends the unknown with the familiar through the rescue mediums' down-to-earth sense of humor.

Christine Hamlett and Jackie Dennison celebrate with "spirits" after another successful psychic rescue. Their down-to-earth style and teamwork provide an alternative model of female heroism that contrasts with the traditional image of the solitary male hero.

While investigating a ghostly presence (1.1), for example, they notice an unusual odor in a room and make the humorous observation that they "have a stinky ghost."

While the mediums in *Psychic Investigators* are part of a larger group of investigators which include police officers, Jackie and Christine in *Rescue Mediums* are unmistakably the focus of the show. Their unique teamwork also provides an alternative model of heroism which differs from the traditional model of the single hero who stoically bears his or her burden alone as "the chosen one." Jackie and Christine have their individual personalities, but they work together, thus espousing a postfeminist model of recognizing individual differences while also drawing strength from joint efforts.[5] For example, Christine expresses her abilities through her drawings; Jackie often appears to be the more gregarious of the two while speaking to the owners of the haunted houses. However, both women experience similar responses to psychic phenomena ("We both had sort of headaches before we ... we came into the building" ["Jackson's Landing," 1.3]), and they help one another when a spirit tries to overpower them: "Christine: Don't let him overshadow. Don't. It's not safe to do that" (1.1).

Their powers as a psychic team are also reinforced through the similar clothing that they wear in many of the episodes. This televisual cue captures their shared ability to experience the supernatural world of spirits while also highlighting their connection to one another. It also functions as a sign of sameness and paradoxically connects them as mediums who occupy a third space of difference. At the end of each episode they celebrate their camaraderie and their joint success over a drink or by exchanging concluding remarks. While postfeminist shows about women with psychic or visionary abilities tend to highlight single, central figures (e.g., *Medium, Ghost Whisperer*), some series do draw attention to the importance of the group. Shows such as *Charmed* and *Firefly* indicate that the psychic is very much part of a larger group. The sisters in *Charmed* have their individual abilities but are joined as a "power of three."[6] In *Firefly* and the companion film *Serenity*, River is viewed in the context of the larger group (Mal and his crew). What distinguishes *Rescue Mediums* from these productions — beyond its reality TV features — is that Jackie and Christine are a team of psychics, and share a significant bond as a result of their similar abilities. The fact that there are two psychics involved in the investigation of supernatural phenomena helps legitimize the psychic experiences that each is having.

Another postfeminist reconfiguration of the traditional hero's actions in *Rescue Mediums* is how the show transforms the concept of the mythic hero's "vision quest" into a postfeminist psychic vision quest. Traditionally the mythic hero goes in "quest of a boon, a vision, which has the same form in every mythology" (Campbell, *The Power of Myth*, 157). Campbell says that the hero leaves the world that he is in to "go into a depth or into a distance or up to a height. There you come to what was missing in your consciousness in the world you formerly inhabited" (157). The mediums have left their own homes (in the U.K.) to travel to Canadian locations. They also leave the realm of the everyday and enter the realm of spirits. Yet the knowledge they acquire is not a knowledge that will benefit them either in a spiritual or material sense. It is knowledge used to help others. While the actions of mythic heroes often benefited their societies, much of the allure surrounding hero figures has been their own dynamic presence and the self-knowledge they acquire. Jackie and Christine use the knowledge they acquire to benefit the ghosts and the owners of the haunted houses. They help send ghosts to the light and they often enlighten homeowners including skeptics: "I think we may very well have got a conversion" (1.2).

The exclusive focus on the "haunted" home in *Rescue Mediums* is another feature that distinguishes it from a series like *Psychic Investigators* (which includes a variety of crime scenes) and reveals how the series articulates an aspect of postfeminist domesticity in an atypical fashion. Feminist critics have pointed out the emphasis on the domestic realm and in some cases the new validation of domesticity for women in a postfeminist era (Moseley 421). It is worth noting that W Network, which showcases *Rescue Mediums*, also broadcasts the home improvement shows *Divine Design* and *Colour Confidential* and the self-improvement show *The Smart Woman Survival Guide*. *Rescue Mediums* thus takes the familiar format of women in the home from television home living shows that highlight domestic skills and transforms the format by introducing supernatural elements. Jackie and Christine serve a similar function as Martha Stewart or Debby Travis; they are women who "rescue" homeowners from challenging household situations.

Both *Psychic Investigators* and *Rescue Mediums* represent W Network's woman-centered programming. Women appear to be the chief target audiences for these shows since W Network identifies women between the ages of 18–49 and 25–54 as their chief market. What else is it about these reality-based psychic shows that may appeal to women in a postfeminist era? One could argue that it is the conflation or hybridization of the private and public realms that draws female audiences today. The home used to be a private venue; now it has become public through the preponderance of reality shows which showcase the home environment. These psychic reality shows make what was once a very private belief (e.g., belief in psychic abilities or the paranormal) a more public phenomenon, and try to legitimize what may at one time have been dismissed as "madness."

By broadcasting psychic TV with female psychics, W Network may also be endorsing the feminization of psychic ability as an alternative form of knowledge to what has been traditionally represented as male knowledge (the "science" of police investigation or even patriarchal-based spirituality). The Rescue Mediums speak about converting a skeptic to their way of "seeing" and thus suggest that theirs is not only a form of knowledge but a new kind of spirituality. Their postfeminist approach is represented by the fact that they do not categorically reject a patriarchal form of knowledge (which may have been the practice of second wave feminism); they recognize that there can be multiple and potentially contradictory forms of knowledge in a postmodern, postfeminist era. For example, in one episode they choose to draw on the symbols of Christianity because the ghost of a dead priest would be familiar with these symbols. This strategy suggests a certain kind of flexibility that some have come to associate more with postfeminism or third wave feminism than with second wave feminism.

Some viewers and television critics might argue that these images of female empowerment psychic reality television are questionable since not everyone believes in psychic ability. However, this argument is similar to the idea that women warrior figures like Buffy are not powerful symbols since they belong to the genre of fantasy which has often been viewed as escapist entertainment rather than a genre that draws attention to real-world issues.[7] It is important to recognize that the representational value of these women remains powerful; as John Corner observes, some television genres which highlight spectacle may make "any referential function quite secondary to the attractions of the representation itself" (*Critical Ideas in Television Studies*, 57). How women are represented in television still serves as an important way of presenting alternative models of behavior or heroism even if these alternatives do not at first appear to correspond with lived experience.

Because of the ambivalence surrounding the genre of the psychic investigator show, one could argue that for some viewers, such a show could be classified as a kind of telefantasy (like *Charmed* or *Hex*). Like this genre, reality-based psychic investigator series must therefore also be considered against the concepts of generic and socio-cultural verisimilitude. Catherine Johnson and Steve Neale have argued in their discussion of verisimilitude in telefantasy that it is important to define a genre such as science fiction (a form of telefantasy) against the concept of "socio-cultural verisimilitude" (Johnson, 4) while also considering how generic verisimilitude in a film or television genre is "constructed through the relationship between producer, text and viewer, and between texts that employ conventions of that genre" (Johnson, 4). For example, viewers of science fiction would accept the generic verisimilitude of a genre that allows for an alien to land on Earth; however, such an SF tale would not normally meet the criteria for "socio-cultural verisimilitude" because "while some believe in alien abductions, there is a broader cultural consensus that aliens do not visit Earth" (4).

These concepts of generic and socio-cultural verisimilitude may be applied to psychic reality television shows as well but the issue of "socio-cultural verisimilitude" is more complicated. Such series are presented as reality television and therefore meet the parameters for generic similitude that define the genre of "reality television." In other words, there is a kind of contract between producer, text and viewer (Johnson) that helps define the genre. Jason Mittel emphasizes that "reality TV is a genre because we treat it as one" (197); in other words, it is "the broad cultural circulation of reality TV as a category" that makes it a genre, "not any internal textual unity across programs" (197). He does acknowledge that the production strategies of some of these shows help create what audiences perceive as reality TV; these include the conventions of "serial narrative, verité camera style, and first-person confessional segments" and the downplaying of the "constructed nature of the program via appeals to the 'real'" (197).

These psychic television series also operate within the context of socio-cultural verisimilitude, the "broader culturally accepted belief systems about what is 'real'" (4). But how does one define this broader expectation of what is accepted as "real" in relation to psychic reality shows? Studies have shown that a significant percentage of people believe in some form of psychic ability (premonitions, etc.). If this constitutes Neale's marker of "broader cultural consensus," then such shows do attempt to create a strong sense of socio-cultural verisimilitude. However, if one argues that 57 percent ("Most Believe in Psychic Phenomena") does not constitute a broad consensus, then these psychic reality shows may be viewed as a form of telefantasy since Johnson describes the programs that fall into this genre as "[engaging] with regimes of non-verisimilitude." These reality shows also enter the terrain of telefantasy, because not all viewers will accept the supernatural content even with the addition of non-supernatural "facts" that support the supernatural explanations. In other words, in this day and age, there could probably be a "broader cultural consensus" that psychic phenomena are not "true." But how does one define a "broader cultural consensus"? For the purposes of a television network, the viewers or target audience may well constitute the "broader cultural consensus." Furthermore, the problem with defining these series as telefantasy is that it places too much emphasis on the fantasy dimension and on the concept of "broader cultural consensus" instead of considering the hybridized aspects of these psychic reality shows and how a process of "legitimization" of women and their psychic powers can occur within these shows irrespective of whether one categorizes them as "real" or "fantastic." Whether viewers and critics choose to categorize these shows as telefantasy or psychic reality television, what remains clear is that these psychic reality shows are a hybrid form or genre that creates a third space for women with alternative forms of knowledge and power.

The hybrid aspects of shows such as *Rescue Mediums* and *Psychic Investigators* reinforce some of the values of third wave feminists or post-feminists. The shows' diegetic elements (including their use of spectacle and narration) combine to form a postfeminist cultural product whereby the traditionally male world of rational scientific investigation merges with the feminized, intuitive world of psychic-supernatural phenomena. The inclusion of a female psychic's point of view in these psychic shows and the hybrid aspects of television genre combine to create a third space in which women with visionary powers establish their presence. These series increase recognition of alternative belief systems (belief in the paranormal) and validate women's voices and visions in a post-modern, postfeminist world. In a sense, *Psychic Investigators* and *Rescue Mediums* provide the "conclusions of rescue and relief" (John Corner, *Critical Ideas in Television Studies*, 98) that are common in "reality TV" (98). These psychic investigator series do not merely have a "referential attractiveness" but also appeal to a level of fantasy, which Corner defines as "a stimulation of the viewer towards scenarios which are highly improbable for them in real life" (98). The presence of these series on W Network may suggest that postfeminist viewers do not consider the referential aspects of these series (references to actual crimes, locations, etc.) and the pleasurable experience of the spectacle of the representation incompatible. Crossing boundaries, whether these boundaries are between the worlds of the living and the dead, between genres (reality TV versus telefantasy) or between different forms of knowledge (masculine reason vs. feminine vision) may well be one of the distinguishing features of postfeminist television.

TEN

Resisting the Myth of the Bad Mother

Psychic Visions and Maternal Anxiety in NBC's Medium

In the NBC series *Medium* (2005–), the character Allison Dubois (Patricia Arquette) identifies the importance of the visual in her life by pairing the truth of her visions with the act of watching a television show: "I see the truth; it's a friggin' television show" ("Pilot").[1] Her comment is not only a way of describing how Allison crosses boundaries between fiction and reality in her visions, but also draws attention to the ongoing importance of the women with visionary abilities in contemporary television series, especially those series that focus on the investigative powers of the psychic. The role of the female psychic has entered television and film in various forms, whether through "real" psychics who work with audience participation in a talk show environment or through the clichéd fictional image of the "fake," flaky psychic, "a frizzy-haired, talon-fingered, incense-burning weirdo" (Dubois, 97).[2] Yet Allison Dubois's *Medium* character departs from some of these established images by introducing another dimension to the figure of the psychic: the psychic heroine as mother (who negotiates between her family life, her work in the district attorney's office and the visions she receives as a medium).

Medium is based upon the work of "real-life" psychic and mother Allison Dubois,[3] who assisted the Arizona police in various investigations. While Allison, the main character in *Medium*, shares some of the qualities of earlier "women of vision" like Cassandra and Joan of Arc (not to mention "real-life" psychics who claim to tell the truth), who were marginalized or vilified for their unusual power, she also has a broader range of experiences as a wife and mother that develops the character of a woman with special visions. Her role as a family member suggests the possibility of transforming the image of the female seer who historically and mythically has often been cast as a rather solitary individual into a woman with a family. Yet this transformation is not without its limitations (as was the case with Cordelia's and Phoebe's experiences with maternity in *Angel* and *Charmed* respectively). Allison's nighttime dreams and waking visions repeatedly interrupt her ability to function "normally" as a wife and a mother of three. In many episodes Allison and her husband Joe appear to live on the edge of madness as Allison must listen to the demands of her dreams and visions while negotiating between her "gift" (her second sight) and her roles of spouse and mother. A feminist reading of the series shows how *Medium* makes frequent use of the dream state to associate the character Allison Dubois with the archetypal figure of the Great Mother who is often divided into the binary opposition of the good mother and the bad or terrible mother. (Alison must negotiate between these images and subvert this binary.) Furthermore, in *Medium* the anxiety surrounding good and bad mothering facilitates the representation of Allison's gift as a genetic trait (shared by Allison and her daughter) and as a disease or a form of "contamination." In other words, biological and psychological images reinforce the "demonization" of motherhood, suggesting that even in a postfeminist age, inflexible attitudes towards mothers (not to mention mediums) can still be a reality.[4] Not only must Allison address the powerful images of the bad mother which inform her dreams, but she must see how she can negotiate the third space or hybrid space she occupies as a medium, mother and working woman.

In her book *Don't Kiss Them Goodbye*, the real-life Allison Dubois defines a medium as a person who can "predict future events ... get into a person's mind ... and communicate with the dead" (xx). She adds that she sees "dead people" (xx). Historically, the role of the medium became prominent during the nineteenth century when interest in psychic phenomena developed (partially as an extension of mesmerism), but more so through the emergence of the Spiritualist movement consisting of individuals who claimed to have contact with the spirits of the dead. By the early 1850s, Spiritualism "had begun to spread quite widely through the Eastern United States" (Gauld, 304) and by the mid–1850s, mediums and "home-circles" were to be found throughout Europe. In the late nineteenth century, a medium by the name of Leonora Piper gained wide acclaim in the United States (Gauld 32). During this time, the figure of the medium was incorporated into American fiction as well. For example, Ambrose Bierce included a medium as a narrative device in his short story, "The Moonlit Road" (1893); the medium Bayrolles speaks for Julia Hetman, a character presumably murdered by her own husband. The construction of the medium (like that of other seer figures) has very often been limited to the portrayal of a passive vessel or conduit with limited agency. For example, in Bierce's story, the character of the medium is not developed; she only serves as an interesting narrative device that illuminates the story of a deceased character.

In history, fiction and film, the female visionary has been presented as a rather solitary figure, disconnected from the mainstream society. Joan of Arc has achieved iconic status as "the maid of Orleans," but was burned at the stake for her visions. Cassandra, the mad Trojan seer, has been portrayed by the Greek tragedian Aeschylus as a lonely woman disconnected from her people and suffering from Apollo's psychic violation of her being; he granted her the gift of sight but cursed her since her visions would not be believed, thus enforcing her isolation. Even the more modern character of Oda Mae Brown in the film *Ghost* is initially presented as a "fake" medium-con artist who capitalizes on the sorrow and concern of people wishing to contact their dead loved ones. In her book, Allison Dubois talks about these kinds of callous psychic opportunists who "injure their clients," and she hopes that "by providing some guidelines for young psychics and mediums" she can help "prevent them from becoming the types" who do damage to the field of psychic research (24).

In keeping with Dubois' comments on the stereotypical medium, *Medium* appears to represent a unique movement away from past and even recent constructions of the psychic as a rather eccentric, opportunistic figure who lacks legitimacy, to more wholesome or complex images of the medium as wife and mother. Motherhood, marital rela-

Patricia Arquette plays Allison Dubois in the NBC television series, *Medium* (2005–), based on real-life medium Allison Dubois. Arquette depicts a unique dimension of the psychic heroine in television: the medium as mother.

tionships and psychic activity have not usually been considered in relation to one another. While the biological or genetic connection between a mother and a daughter with unusual abilities was captured in the 1960s series *Bewitched*, this image of inherited supernatural ability was restricted to witchcraft. In her book *Don't Kiss Them Goodbye*, Dubois points out that she did identify with "characters who had special gifts. Whether it was Tabitha on *Bewitched* or Tia in *Escape to Witch Mountain*" (xxi). The recent focus on the link between visionary ability, seers and mother figures in more contemporary series like *Charmed* and *Angel* would appear to suggest the promise of a more sympathetic, holistic, integrated life for these women of vision and a decidedly less clichéd view of the solitary visionary.[5] Yet while the character of the seer-psychic may have acquired another dimension as mother (perhaps recognizing that the psychic ability is an extension of the old stereotype that women are simply more intuitive than men) and tries to negotiate between various roles (mother, wife, medium, woman in the workforce), further examination of individual *Medium* episodes indicates that the representation of the mother is not entirely unproblematic. This is in part because of some of the paternalistic, societal and mythic constructions of the psychic as an expression of the archetypal good Mother and the archetypal bad or terrible mother.

In *Medium*, Allison Dubois, played by Patricia Arquette, is the mother of a busy household of three daughters and the wife of Joe. Combining family life with work outside the home is enough of a challenge for this former law school student who works in the district attorney's office; however, Allison has the additional "gift" or "curse" of being a medium. Allison lives in a third space or in between-space where spirits of the dead invade her dreams and her waking life, and it is actually quite incredible how much of the series takes place in the Dubois bedroom with Allison waking up and her husband constantly asking her, "What's wrong?"

In the pilot, Joe (Jake Weber), an aerospace engineer and the scientist in the family, questions the validity of her dreams or visions by suggesting that they may simply be stress-related. Earlier representations of female seer figures in myth, history and popular culture have also emphasized the believability of the seer's or psychic's message. These include historical figures like Joan of Arc and nineteenth-century psychics Mrs. Leonora Piper (1857–1950) and Mrs. Gladys Leonard (1882–1968). In the case of Joan of Arc, her ability to hear voices and experience visions of the divine was demonized and equated with witchcraft. The American Mrs. Piper and the British Mrs. Leonard underwent tests and monitoring to determine the authenticity or credibility of their psychic experiences as Alan Gauld explains in his studies of these specific mediums. Even in the case of a mythic seer like Cassandra, the issue of believability is important, and the questioning of the seer's message has clear patriarchal implications. After all, it was Apollo, the male god of reason and prophecy, who cursed Cassandra by bestowing upon her the gift of sight without the possibility of being able to find believers. In the series *Medium*, Joe sometimes assumes a patriarchal tone or role that echoes or perpetuates this Apollonian masculinist intervention. While he appears to play the part of the concerned and well-meaning husband in a postfeminist age where an entire generation of women often have the benefit of "enlightened" husbands who contribute in a more hands-on way to the raising of children, his determination to "normalize" Allison's dreams actually invalidates her unusual ability. Throughout the first season of the show, he attempts to separate the vision from the person — his wife — and refuses to recognize the fact that this postfeminist "medium" is the message[6] and cannot be disassociated from her visions.[7]

Allison's marital relations form a significant part of the series and contribute to her construction as a mother, especially an absent mother. She and Joe experience some tension over her nightmares and her frequent need to leave the house and her family abruptly. Her role as mother figures prominently into her dream state and into her non-dream existence. Jungian psychology has established the link between archetypes and dreams, and theorists of myth like Erich Neumann and Joseph Campbell[8] have furthered discussions of the archetypes that are present in myth and dreams. One of these archetypes is that of the Great Mother who can "be terrible as well as good" (45). According to Neumann, "she is the goddess of life and death" (45). The Virgin Mary and the witch in "Hansel and Gretel" are common illustrations of the two sides of the Great Mother, with the Virgin Mary embodying the all-nurturing mother, and the "Hansel and Gretel" witch incorporating the cannibalistic qualities of a terrible or even anti-mother. Other examples of the terrible mother include demonic figures such as the Furies and other "goddesses of the underworld and the dead" (Neumann, 80).[9] Even though feminist mythographers Jane Caputi and Diane Purkiss have critiqued the "patriarchal bias of mythographers" (Caputi, 425) like Neumann and Robert Graves, it is interesting to analyze how this kind of binary has become firmly re-inscribed in a television series like *Medium*. While the inclusion of the figure of a psychic mother appears to be an innovative move for a TV series and suggests a desire to step outside the box (with respect to images of the female medium), further examination of the series indicates that the figure of the medium is still defined according to the binary of good vs. terrible-bad mother in both mythic and sociological terms.

Despite all the praise that the series has received for its "realistic" portrayal of motherhood,[10] actress Patricia Arquette, who is the mother of a teenage son and a toddler daughter, says that the series strikes "at the heart of the guilt and exhaustion she's [Arquette] often dealing with" (McKeon). In a postfeminist age, there still appears to be a link between motherhood and guilt even though mothers try hard to resist the feelings of guilt.

Arquette's remark about motherhood and guilt is particularly relevant since further examination of the dreams and images in *Medium* reveals this noticeable dichotomy of good and bad motherhood in the series. Various episodes show that this dichotomy clearly involves Allison's concern for one of her daughters and the anxiety she experiences over being a good mother (let alone a "great" mother) while trying to negotiate between working and visionary lives. For example, in the pilot, Allison's perceptive, intuitive ability is tied to her experience as a mother; yet she uses the idea of intuition to explain the "logic" of a crime, thereby dismantling the binary opposition between "reason" and "intuition" and challenging the patriarchal structure of the "Law of the Father" (represented by the legal system in general, the police, and the district attorney's office). She explains the actions of a murdered woman on the basis of the woman's probable location which was linked to the mother's response to her baby. Allison explains that the woman must have heard her child crying and was then shot when she went to see why (1.1). Here Allison offers a blend of logic and intuition, thus negotiating between the binaries of "rational" police investigation and the emotional, intuitive response of a mother. She explains the intuition of a "good mother" who instinctively responds to the cries of her child. In many ways, Allison's own visionary ability is constructed as an extreme example of what is presented as a mother's intuition that something is not quite right. This is the image of the "good" mother, a modern configuration of the mythic "Great Mother." This good mother is responsive to her child's cries, and is the very essence of positive, nurturing motherhood. Jane Swigart describes this maternal ideal in psychological terms and presents another established mythos of the "good mother":

> Imagine a woman who wants only what is best for her children, whose needs she intuits effortlessly. This mother adores her offspring and finds them fascinating. She is exquisitely attuned to her children and is so resourceful that she is immune to boredom. Nurturing comes as naturally as breathing, and child rearing is a source of pleasure that does not require discipline or self-sacrifice. She is the Good Mother [6].

While the pilot episode and other episodes do depict Allison as achieving the status of a "good," intuitive mother, many episodes showcase Allison's fear that she cannot live up to such an image; the result is her anxiety around the idea of being a "Bad Mother" (Swigart 7). Allison struggles to balance the demands of home and her psychic imperatives. The boundaries between work obligations and home life blur. "Suspicions and Certainties" (1.2) offers some parallels between the content of Allison's visions, her daily life as a mother, her work environment and her fear of not measuring up. Most episodes begin with Allison dreaming and waking up from her nightmares, daydreams or visions. In "Suspicions and Certainties" Allison dreams of a man having sex with a woman who ends up as a blackened, rotting corpse. The next scene shows Allison screaming and waking up next to Joe and daughter Bridget. These opening images establish the archetypal figure of the crone or hag as repulsive femininity in a patriarchal context. The dead woman is also an indicator of the "Terrible Mother," especially since one of the police officers makes the remark, "Is she underage?" and another answers, "The opposite" (1.2).

While one could argue that the Crone has been "read" in a more positive, feminist light as a sign of "profound transformation and healing" or as a "harbinger of rebirth" (Caputi, 433), subsequent scenes suggest otherwise. In the scene where Allison wakes up screaming, Bridget (who was sleeping next to her) also screams and says, "Mommy, you gotta stop doing the police stuff" (1.2) and Joe concurs, "Yeah, Mommy, could you maybe stop doing that?" (1.2). Furthermore, after this opening dream sequence, Allison's role as an "inadequate mother" is symbolized by the scene of two of her daughters shouting and Allison turning to look at an older man lying next to her, telling her, "Get out of bed. Deal with your children" (1.2). The man happens to be her dead father-in-law (1.2). Now while Allison does tell him off ("That's okay. You already are damned"), his words serve as a patriarchal judgment of Allison as a bad mother. Shortly thereafter, she tells Joe that she is depressed, another sign of a mother who does not meet the ideal of the "all-giving" mother (Swigart, 8). A third example of her "terrible" mother image is her decision to bring her baby to work because she could not arrange for childcare. Although a helpful co-worker takes the crying child off her hands, the disapproving stares of co-workers and the image of an unhappy child suggest that Allison's image as a bad mother (defined in this context as a woman who is not staying home with the children or finding appropriate childcare) has been established.

Allison's visions or dreams, her work life and family life add up to a chaotic existence for her. In her conversation with her mother, Erin Harde talks about "the chaos" of third wave feminism "because it holds so many possibilities" (122). While Allison's husband and her daughter would prefer that she separate her family life from her investigative work as a medium, the series reveals how Allison's experiences — her dreams and her reality — blend into one another in a postfeminist, postmodern fashion. In an age where women and men routinely take their work home with them or work out of the home and have access to cell phones and other kinds of technology, the clear division between work and family is not always possible.

Allison tries to resist the binary opposition between good and bad mothering by highlighting the reality that life cannot always go according to plan. As the series develops, Joe accommodates her unusual ability more easily. However, the first and second seasons of the series reflect how even in a postfeminist era, the pervasiveness of social expectations around motherhood may still contribute to the "guilt" experienced by many working mothers. In *The Politics of Parenthood* (1993), Mary Frances Berry wrote in a prophetic fashion of persistent problems for working women in the twenty-first century, problems that she identified in the 1990s:

> Workplace policies and parental responsibilities are not responding to the reality of employed women fast enough to spread the possibility of real equality of rights beyond an elite. Unless women and men change their attitudes toward children and who cares for them soon, there will be growing discontent in the next decade, and children and their parents will suffer [8].

These are the kinds of attitudes that Allison, a twenty-first-century, postfeminist mother still encounters when she is forced to bring her child to work because of limited childcare options.

Allison's attempts to negotiate the challenges of being a medium and a working mother are explored even more fully in "Night of the Wolf" (1.4). This episode develops the image of the "Terrible Mother" further by linking it to psychic motherhood in psychological, mythic and genetic ways. One of the storylines deals with Allison's middle child, six-year-old Bridget, who appears to be somewhat of a social misfit because she does not have any friends at school. Allison blames herself for not recognizing the signs of a problem and for not intervening sooner: "This is my fault. I should have been out there, making playdates, arranging sleepovers" (1.4). Here Allison's guilt takes on a patriarchally induced quality, since she feels that it is her role as mother to take the blame for this and concludes, "Maybe this wasn't the greatest moment to go back to work" (1.4). Interestingly enough, Joe does not experience the same kind of self-blame, but ends up blaming Allison as well. Historically women have often been conditioned to take sole responsibility for any kind of child-related problem that might suggest a deviation from the norm, and this is evident in Allison's conviction that Bridget's lack of friends is her fault. Jane Swigart points out how this notion that mothers are responsible for the shaping of their children has contributed to the myth of the "Bad Mother":

> The truth is that child-rearing is a collective endeavor in which fathers, extended families and the whole society plays a role, either by taking an active part in the well-being of children or by refusing to do so. The myth of the Bad Mother hides this crucial fact: The early years of a human life are the most important and formative. They should be the concern and responsibility of more than one isolated, devalued, unsupported person [8].

Allison's anxiety reflects society's typical image of the "Bad Mother" and the attribution of blame to the mother. Her daughter's "problem" reaffirms her image of herself as a "terrible mother." Allison's fears seem premature and subside temporarily when she observes her daughter playing with a little boy called Bobby in the schoolyard. In the course of the narrative, however, Allison realizes that her daughter also has an ability to see the dead. This blurring of the lines between "reality" and the surreal world of Allison's visionary experience reflects the unusual world of fantasy, or in the case of a fantastic television series, telefantasy, where there is "an engagement with and dislocation from culturally constructed notions of what is perceived as reality" (Johnson 7).[11] More importantly, this telefantasy episode of *Medium* establishes the genetic connection to psychic or visionary ability. Allison fights with Joe about how to approach Bridget's new powers. While she explains how the ability to communicate with the dead is special, Joe stigmatizes Bridget and by extension Allison by expressing his dismay that Bridget can see dead people. Bridget's earlier status as a social misfit with no friends combined with Joe's concern about her ability to see a dead boy suggest that she is not "normal" and has inherited the abnormal "condition" of psychic ability. Allison ironically responds, "Sorry to have polluted the gene pool" (1.4).

Another representation of the "terrible" mother in "Night of the Wolf" (1.4) involves a wolf in Allison's nightmare. This nightmare serves as an introduction to the secondary storyline. *Medium* adopts the classical paradigm that is so common in film and features "double plot lines" (Giannetti and Leach, 43).[12] The dream depicts Allison dressed as Little Red Riding Hood running away from a wolf, and even though this is simply a short scene in the entire episode, it incorporates one of the common features of a classical plot structure: "a chase" (Giannetti and Leach, 43). The mother figure is present through Allison's appearance in the dream. She may play the role of Little Red Riding Hood in the dream, but the television audience knows that in the non-dream state, Allison is a mother. Consequently she becomes a composite of both Red Riding Hood and a mother. The fear of the terrible mother and by extension, Allison's own earlier fears of being a terrible mother, are made visible through the predatory figure of the wolf. In the fairy tale versions of "Little Red Riding Hood," the wolf is disguised as a good mother figure; he assumes the role of a grandmother or a "good" mother, thus transforming the conventional good mother into an image of "terrible" or monstrous maternity. He is a perversion of motherhood and appetite as symbolized by the rocks in his stomach. The rocks signify an unequivocal departure from the "normal" context of food. Allison's fear of the wolf in her dream may be viewed as her symbolic fear of becoming this kind of monster.

Like many episodes, "Night of the Wolf" indicates that there is the possibility of escaping and even defeating the monsters of our nightmares. Just as Allison helps a woman escape from a man called Wolfe, she is also able to help her daughter Bridget. In the course of the episode, Allison attempts to subvert society's image of the bad mother by explaining the nature of their common powers to her daughter; she even shows Bridget how she (Bridget) can help the dead find peace. Allison's positive approach to her ability demonstrates that women who have special ways of "seeing" can challenge the stigma of being a social misfit. Instead, difference is something that should be embraced, one of the key messages of third wave feminism. Allison's support of her daughter's "difference" in "Night of the Wolf" shows how the series challenges some of the earlier images of inadequate motherhood.

The outcome of "Night of the Wolf" reveals that Allison is triumphant in her heroic defeat of the "wolf" and, by extension, is able to stop worrying about the effectiveness of her mothering skills, at least for a while. However, negative images of motherhood reappear later in the series (and not just in conjunction with Allison), indicating that she and other postfeminist mothers must continually address ongoing social anxieties surrounding the trope of the bad mother. The unsettling depictions of motherhood presented in "Night of the Wolf" are developed further in the second season of *Medium*, thus suggesting that there is still a level of instability associated with mothers and by extension with Allison, the series' central mother figure. In "Raising Cain" (2.13), a mother shoots and wounds her seven-year-old son, Tyler, because she believes that he will grow up to be a killer. The mother has based her conviction that her son is evil on a dream, similar to one that Allison experiences. Yet in another dream, Allison witnesses a different outcome for the boy when she sees him in the role of class valedictorian for his high school. John Muir argues that this episode reveals the complexity of the series and Allison's dilemma: "If she fingers the mother as the shooter, the boy (who has miraculously survived the attempt on his life) could grow up and indeed become a killer. If she doesn't, the mother has a second chance, an opportunity to embrace the boy (instead of condemning him and evil)." The episode does indeed indicate a complex relationship between nature and nurture. Is the boy "naturally" evil, or does his mother "make" him this way? "Raising Cain" is all about choices that people make, and for "heroines of the nineties and the new millennium" there are often "too many choices" (L.S. Kim, 319). Furthermore, in a postmodern, postfeminist world of relativism, it is not always clear whether there is a "correct" choice. As Shugart and her co-authors argue, third wave feminism is about "the power to make choices, regardless of what those choices are" (195).

Medium has taken the figure of the female medium into an interesting direction by presenting a new kind of female hero, the medium as mother. As a woman living in a postfeminist era, Allison lives in a third space or in-between space where her visions intersect with her family and with her work outside the home. In her dreams and in her daily interactions with other women and with her own daughter, she confronts images of the "bad" mother and the guilt that results from this construction. *Medium* still presents some disturbing messages for working mothers in particular and for mothers in general; it would appear that the special gift of the character Allison Dubois has become a metaphor or a postfeminist cautionary tale—a tale for other working women who are also mothers and wives, and whose "visions" of a life "outside" the family home might be perceived as threatening to a patriarchal system of guilt surrounding maternal responsibility. The construction of "bad mothers" is also achieved through horrifying mythic images, and through psychological and genetic images of contamination. Despite her concerns that she might be a bad mother, Allison is able to struggle against this negativity and act as a positive role model for daughter Bridget. In Season 3, the mother-daughter bond as expressed through the ability of "second sight" extends to Allison's other daughter Ariel, thus suggesting even more possibilities for the exploration of psychic abilities as a unique representation of postfeminist difference.

ELEVEN

Looking for Closure

Investigating Mothers, Daughters and Disease in Ghost Whisperer

Launched in the same year as the NBC series *Medium*, CBS's *Ghost Whisperer* (2005–) features a young newlywed by the name of Melinda Gordon, who also has the gift of being able to communicate with the dead. While she is not called a medium in the series, she functions as a mediator between the living and the dead much like Allison Dubois in *Medium* and Alison Mundy in the U.K. series *Afterlife* and therefore occupies a third space or in-between space as she negotiates between different worlds of experience.

The preamble for all of the episodes after the series pilot demonstrates Melinda's role as a mediator when she addresses the television audience and says "to tell you my story, I have to tell you theirs" (1.2). She tries to obtain closure for the dead by solving their cases to help them "cross over" into the light. Melinda Gordon (played by Jennifer Love Hewitt) is a younger postfeminist heroine than the women in *Medium* and *Afterlife*, sporting low-cut outfits that have often been identified with the body-conscious television characters of the third wave or postfeminist generation (e.g., Buffy, the witch sisters in *Charmed*, Tru Davies in *Tru Calling*). However, the series is not just about showcasing a young woman's body; it deals with serious topics such as communication or lack thereof between mothers and daughters and the role of technology as a means of communication or as an investigative tool in a postfeminist, post–9/11 world. The desire for closure in *Ghost Whisperer* through the depiction of an empathetic medium figure may be a response to the kind of cultural anxiety that characterized the American public's need for answers in the wake of 9/11. The series reinforces the need for Melinda to achieve closure for dead spirits and for the survivors of the loved ones left behind, and she is generally successful in accomplishing this; however, in her own relationship with her biological mother, such closure or stability cannot be achieved. Various first-season episodes suggest that the mother-daughter bond can only be experienced in an altered or mediated fashion, and in this sense, Melinda's relationship with a mother figure is articulated through the language or imagery of disease or dis(ease). As such, the mother-daughter relationship may serve as a representation of the uneasy relationship between second wave and third wave feminists while also reflecting the cultural anxiety surrounding the unknown in a post–9/11 world.

Perhaps more than some of the other postfeminist television series which foreground a woman with visionary powers, *Ghost Whisperer* seeks to achieve closure as part of its telefantasy format. The supernatural world of ghosts and the idea that the dead need to cross over to achieve closure for themselves are the driving force of the show, and Melinda is the woman who must facilitate this

Jennifer Love Hewitt stars as Melinda Gordon, the owner of an antique store who communicates with the dead in CBS's *Ghost Whisperer* (2005–). Melinda helps the living and the dead achieve closure. Her own relationship with her living mother proves a bit more challenging, however, so she turns to her dead grandmother for emotional support.

with her unique ability to see the dead. The concept of "closure" is mentioned repeatedly. As a postfeminist heroine and medium-detective figure, Melinda frequently uses the tools of technology to find the answers. She accesses her laptop and the Internet to search for pertinent information on the identity of the dead and to assist in the location of their loved ones. Technology is presented as an integral component of her life. The world of technology is not necessarily diametrically opposed to her fantastic ability. In fact, even spirits are shown as being able to manipulate technology, thus demonstrating the interface between the world of the supernatural and a world where technology is usually synonymous with the rational and the natural rather than the supernatural. For example, Melinda often mentions how spirits can communicate through electrical forces or gadgets. Some examples include strange voices on answering machines, the mysterious operation of household appliances and lights, and the sending of messages on a computer. Melinda is a kind of postfeminist cyborg[1] who uses technology and human psychology and empathy to find answers and to provide closure for spirits or ghosts who haunt the living.

As a postfeminist heroine, Melinda is comfortable with computer technology, but also enjoys what appears to be a diametrically opposed interest: a fondness for antique objects. She runs an antique store, an occupation that seems to reinforce her role as an individual who has a connection to the dead, since she often acquires antiques at auction houses after someone has passed away. Melinda's hybrid nature (one foot in the world of technology, and one foot in the world of antique culture) demonstrates how she can be part of two worlds or in between worlds and how she can successfully bridge the gap between the world of the living and the world of the dead. Like third wave feminists, Melinda does not subscribe to an "either/or" mentality but crosses boundaries and recognizes multiple alliances or "constellations of identity" (Purvis, 118).[2] For example, in "Voices" (21.9) she communicates with a technologically gifted dead mother who is trying to reach her son. In this episode, the sounds of voices on an answering machine and noises emanating from a computer and television screen actually make Melinda ill, yet she helps transmit a mother's message to her gay son to help rebuild a relationship with the boy's father.

Melinda can offer comfort to dead mothers and their children. Yet while she derives satisfaction from helping the dead and their living friends and relatives, she does not have the same kind of success in her relationship with her own mother. Like other female heroes with visionary powers, Melinda has the unique ability to see things that others do not see and, like Tru Davies in *Tru Calling*, her ability is inherited.

Melinda believes that the gift can be traced back to her grandmother, and not her mother. Initially, she thinks that she has inherited the power from her grandmother and that the "gift" has skipped a generation because her mother does not admit that she too can hear ghosts. In many ways, Melinda's grandmother serves as more of a mother figure than Melinda since the series casts her as a nurturing figure who explains the gift to Melinda, and it is her grandmother who appears to her at various times to provide support when Melinda needs support or once Melinda has helped a spirit cross over. In this sense, Melinda's bond with her grandmother could symbolize the kind of bond between women that has characterized some aspects of the feminist movement or the general continuum of feminism. The strong bond with the grandmother actually reinforces the awkward relationship between Melinda and her mother. Like the mothers in other postfeminist series such as *Buffy the Vampire Slayer*, *Tru Calling* and *Charmed*, Melinda's mother is absent or at least removed from her daughter for much of the series. The series begins with Melinda attending a funeral, and her grandmother is the supportive "mother" figure in this scene. Melinda's mother only enters into the series in a significant way during "Melinda's First Ghost" (1.14).

The postponement of the introduction of Melinda's biological mother in the series and the refocusing on other kinds of mother-daughter relationships reinforces Melinda's distant relationship with her own mother. One can view Melinda's experiences with other mother figures throughout Season 1 as a female hero's sublimated search for "the mother," a feminine version of the mythic male hero's search for the father (Joseph Campbell).[3] Campbell describes the father in various myths as "the invisible unknown" (*Hero*, 345) and indicates how the hero's journey involves the realization or knowledge that he "and the father are one" (349), part of Campbell's notion of atonement or *at-one-*

ment: "the savior figure who eliminates the tyrant father and then him-self assumes the crown is (like Oedipus) stepping into his sire's stead" (353).[4] In Season 1, this search for the male parent is reworked in a post-feminist, postmodern fashion into a search for the mother figure. Like the male hero's search for the father, Melinda's search or role as investi-gator involves dealing with the maternal unknown in various manifes-tations. She also makes an attempt to displace the mother in some cases, but the relationship between mother and daughter in this postfeminist television series is complicated and ambiguous.

As previously mentioned, Melinda's mother does not have any screen presence until the episode "Melinda's First Ghost" (1.14). Prior to this episode, Melinda does have other encounters with mother figures, whether these figures are the dead or ghost mothers of the living, the liv-ing mothers of dead children, her grandmother and her mother-in-law. This focus on a variety of mothers reveals a postfeminist reconceptual-ization of mother-daughter relationships, since for women of the third wave generation, the structure of family is a more fluid idea: "Whether children are born to a single mother, a single father, two mothers, two fathers, or a mother and a father, a family is defined by love, commit-ment, and support" (Baumgardner and Richards, 316). In other words, the essentialized, biological mother may not be the primary influence. The displacement of the biological mother in *Ghost Whisperer* may also symbolize a third wave feminist way of challenging the views of the sec-ond wave feminist "mother," whether this mother took the form of a bio-logical mother or a symbolic mother. As Baumgardner and Richards indicate when discussing Christina Baker Kline's book *The Conversation Begins*, "[M]any of the daughters said they sometimes felt abandoned by their feminist mothers, and frequently overshadowed" (*Manifesta*, 212).

Even though Melinda may have difficulty accessing her own mother, she serves as an important mediator figure for other mothers. An inter-esting treatment of living mothers occurs in "Homecoming" (1.6) when a boy who dies from an allergic reaction to bee stings searches for his biological mother even though his adoptive mother contends that she is his "real mother." The episode reveals how Melinda serves as a media-tor between the two mothers, between the dead son and his adoptive mother, and between the dead son and his biological mother. While adoption is not a phenomenon limited to the twenty-first century, alternative family arrangements have become a more visible reality in the lives of North Americans, and the image of alternative families has been reproduced in postfeminist television. For example, even though Buffy Summers in *Buffy the Vampire Slayer* has a mother, her primary parental connection is to the librarian Giles who becomes a father figure. The *L Word* depicts lesbian parents and in *Charmed* three sisters form the chief family unit. In *Ghost Whisperer*, Melinda's ability to negotiate between the family members of the people she helps indicates the increasing need to recognize the diversity of families, a reality for third wave feminists who may belong to such families themselves. In "Homecoming" she is able to ensure that the mother and son communicate with each other through her despite the fact that the biological mother was an absent figure in the son's life while he was alive.

An example of an episode that presents a physically "dead" mother is "Voices" (1.9). The mother uses technology such as television screens, answering machines and other electronic gadgets to communicate with her son, Kirk; she represents the emergence of women in the field of technology. What is interesting about her method of communication is that even though Melinda is able to eventually communicate with her, the electronic media cause her to have headaches. As Melinda's husband Jim says to her, he has never seen her "gift" make her sick before. Her sickness ends when the dead mother finally convinces her son Kirk to communicate an important message about his sexuality to his father. Melinda's suffering or headaches also serve as a way of reinforcing the uneasiness or dis(ease) she experiences with her own mother. The son's difference or homosexuality can be equated with Melinda's difference as a woman of vision, and his conflict with his father echoes the lack of communication she has with her mother. Kirk indicates that his own mother was his "map even when [he] felt like a freak." Melinda wishes that she and her own mother had a relationship like this.

Another conflict between mother and child occurs in "Demon Child" (1.16): Melinda helps an angry dead boy communicate with his living mother who is a busy working mother and who runs the risk of not paying enough attention to her daughter. The episode may serve as a critique of the career-obsessed woman, an image often associated with second wave feminists who chose work over domestic life. Work life vs. home life was a clear dichotomy for second wave feminists and in order to establish themselves in the work environment, some chose not to have children. Third wave feminist Rebecca Walker indicates that since second wave feminists understood "that motherhood had been used to keep women within a limited paradigm of femininity ... it was natural for them to break away from the idea of woman as primarily a child-rearing machine" (Bussel). However, work outside the home was not only a priority for second wave feminists. The reality of nanny culture for working mothers is a post–1990s phenomenon.[5] Women of the third wave generation also struggle with the work/family dynamic. Some have tried to validate domestic life (which was often rejected by their second wave feminist foremothers), and others have looked for ways to make their work lives accommodate family.

Melinda finds herself in an in-between space in this episode, not just because of her role as mediator between the living and the dead, but also because she tries to communicate a dead son's concerns about his work-obsessed mother, while she (Melinda) also prefers the idea of work to having a child in her life. She resists the idea of having a child even though her husband Jim is interested because she loves her work in the antique store, not to mention her vocation as someone who sees and communicates with ghosts.

Other mother figures who are more closely related to Melinda and who have an impact on her life include her mother-in-law Faith, who is introduced in "The Crossing" (1.2). In this episode, Jim tells Melinda to be "normal" for his mother, a request that is very difficult for Melinda since she cannot ignore the ghosts who require her assistance. While Melinda and Faith get off to a rough start in this episode, Faith eventually reveals that she sometimes feels that her husband and dead son are watching over her. In later episodes, Melinda develops a fairly close relationship with Faith and is in some respects closer to her than to her own mother, thus suggesting that mother-daughter relationships can take various forms that may even be stronger than the bond between a daughter and her biological mother.

Melinda's grandmother Nana is the mother figure who is most instrumental in ensuring that Melinda recognizes that her ability to communicate with the dead is a gift. Melinda speaks out loud to her dead grandmother and says, "You're the only person that doesn't make me feel like I'm crazy" (1.3). Nana is the "closest thing to a twin" (1.3) she ever had, an image that reinforces the psychic connection between Melinda and her grandmother. As a child, Melinda was nurtured by her grandmother; for example, the pilot episode shows a young Melinda and her grandmother observing a dead man's ghost at a funeral; Melinda does not "understand," but her grandmother assures her that she will. Once Melinda is an adult, her grandmother appears as a ghost a number of times to offer support. In "Ghost Interrupted," for example, Melinda's dead grandmother visits her and says, "Take everything I've given you and make it your own" (1.3). These words of wisdom reflect an interesting relationship between two generations of women. On the one hand, the younger generation is expected to receive the knowledge transmitted by an older generation of women, yet there is also recognition that the grandchild must have her own input and not merely imitate the former. This is the kind of rapport that second wave feminists and third wave feminists might strive for since it recognizes that the third wave generation of women has inherited something from the earlier generation or wave while still following their own path. It is interesting that the statement "Take everything I've given you and make it your own" pertains to a grandmother-granddaughter relationship, however, rather than to a mother-daughter relationship. The absence of the mother in this relationship also suggests that Melinda's power to see and hear the dead is a more ancient power, a power that can be traced back to Tessa, one of her female ancestors who was considered a "witch" in her day ("The Weight of What Was," 3.5). *Ghost Whisperer* therefore validates a primeval image of the mythic mother or the woman with special powers, but in validating this relationship with other foremothers or alternate mother figures, the series maintains the gap between Melinda and her biological mother, thus suggesting that this mother-daughter relationship remains dysfunctional and lacks closure.

Ghost Whisperer's focus on the grandmother rather than the mother as Melinda's benevolent maternal influence may be a way of recognizing alternative mother relationships in the lives of young women who can have many female mentors in their lives now that feminism has helped provide access to the working world. At the same time, the distance between Melinda and her mother may echo the need of some third wave feminists to distance themselves from their second wave "mothers" in order to define themselves. As Amber E. Kinser indicates, for some third wave feminists "that space is located somewhere between the rock that has been second-wave feminism, and the hard place that feminism and its dissidents have led us to" (127). In *Ghost Whisperer*, this third space takes the form of Melinda's relationships with substitute mothers and her special ability to communicate with supernatural elements.

While the presentation of a biological mother-daughter relationship is postponed in *Ghost Whisperer*, it is addressed for the first time in a more developed fashion in "Melinda's First Ghost" (1.15). A key component in the Melinda-Beth relationship is the introduction of the discourse of disease. Like other women of vision in postfeminist television, Melinda sometimes has a difficult time viewing her ability as a gift. Like Tru Davies in *Tru Calling*, she is not sure whether her ability to relive the day and see the future through the past is a gift or a curse. Other women of vision even raise the question of madness in conjunction with their abilities. Joan Girardi in *Joan of Arcadia* and Jaye Tyler in *Wonderfalls* worry about going insane, and Allison Dubois in *Medium* feels that her husband views her gift and her daughter's ability to see the dead as a disease.

"Melinda's First Ghost" shows the distance between Melinda and Beth because of their different views of Melinda's "gift." Beth discourages her daughter from talking about her visions, and the episode shows flashbacks in which Beth criticized her own mother for talking about this ability at a birthday party. While Melinda goes to her mother for information about Sarah Applewhite, a childhood friend, who died of leukemia, she actually makes a personal discovery of her own. She had always believed that her gift had skipped a generation and that her mother never had this ability. However, as she conducts an investigation for information about Sarah and her family, Melinda discovers that Beth can actually hear the dead and that she has blocked this out over the years. Beth's decision to ignore the ghosts and their voices may be the reason she experiences headaches. She chooses not to hear them because she fears them and says that acknowledging them makes her feel that she is "crazy" (1.14). Beth's denial of her "gift" explains why she cannot value what Melinda does by helping ghosts; Beth's uneasiness with her power or her dis(ease) has in fact resulted in her tendency to pathologize the ability to talk to spirits. Her headaches are a manifestation of this dis(ease).

The episode's focus on a diseased child (Sarah Applewhite) and her mother who acquires the same disease after Sarah's death ("I'm the reason Sarah got it") is interwoven into Melinda's relationship with her own mother. Melinda helps Sarah and her mother achieve a sense of closure despite the possibility that Sarah's mother might die of the same disease. Sarah wants to make sure that her mother will reunite with her father and not feel guilty about being happy. Here the child with Melinda's help is the agent and the series seems to suggest that the children can provide guidance for the older generation. If this mother-daughter relationship is examined in the context of second wave feminism and third wave feminism connections, it suggests that mothers have something to learn from their symbolic and biological daughters. By extension, Melinda believes that her mother might want to re-evaluate her own ability to hear the dead, a talent the mother has perceived as a medical condition like "allergies" ("The Vanishing," 1.19).

"The Vanishing" is an interesting episode in which the image of disease and Melinda's unique ability reappears. The story begins with Melinda in the hospital. She is in a coma and has a near-death experience. After she leaves the hospital, Melinda's ability to see ghosts disappears; as a result she is unhappy and feels incomplete ("like a big fake"). Beth on the other hand experiences "blessed silence" as well as a period free of headaches because she does not see or hear ghosts any more. Everything even tastes better to her, which is often the case for people who are no longer ill. The absence of spirits in Beth's life makes her happier and more inclined to share her life with Melinda. She confesses how she kept her "visions" a secret from her husband (Melinda's father). This "secrecy" surrounding Beth's visions suggests the kind of secrecy involving disease that is presented in "Melinda's First Ghost." In this story, a mother keeps her leukemia a secret from her husband. However, their dead child, Sarah, is instrumental in helping reveal the truth.

Ghost Whisperer shows how the concept of what is "normal" is relative according to the person involved. Grace, the sick mother, blames herself for her daughter's death because she feels that their conditions were genetically linked. Yet for her daughter, her mother's disease becomes a way of re-connecting with her parents in an effort to normalize relations with her mother and father. Like Grace, Beth focuses on the negative aspects of her situation. She views her ability to see ghosts in negative terms, while for Melinda, the return to a "normal" state is defined by her ability to see ghosts. Both she and her mother briefly see spirits in this episode, thus sharing a moment as women who occupy a third space or an alternative way of seeing. It would appear that *Ghost Whisperer* upholds Melinda's concept of the apparently "abnormal" or odd as the norm, and Beth must reluctantly accept this perspective. This validation of the younger woman's perspective suggests the need for mothers to value the views of their symbolic or biological children; the scene can also be interpreted as a postfeminist generation's comment on how second wave feminists need to validate the opinions of their third wave feminist "daughters."

While *Ghost Whisperer* shows no signs of the Melinda-Beth relationship achieving the kind of sentimental closure that the series espouses for other kinds of families or situations, it does suggest that Melinda herself is working on achieving a kind of mythic mother status that transcends biology. She may not be ready to be a mother herself in "Demon Child" (1.16), but she is a nurturing mother figure to many children (both dead and alive) in the series. Melinda assumes the role of a mother figure in a number of different situations perhaps as a way of demonstrating a different kind of mother-daughter relationship than the one she experienced. She does not have her own children and makes a point of telling her husband Jim in "Demon Child" that it is not the right time. She is probably reluctant to have a child because of her strained relationship with her own mother. However, she reaches out to ghost children and to living children in a number of ways throughout the series.

One of the most obvious instances occurs in "Lost Boys" (1.5), an episode that positions Melinda as a Wendy figure in relation to several "lost boys" who are ghosts in an abandoned house that used to be an orphanage. "Lost Boys" incorporates the timeless fantasy of Peter Pan and describes changing attitudes towards family in a postfeminist age and what it means to be a mother. As she reads a story to the young boys, thereby fulfilling their search for a mother, Melinda tells them that Wendy was more than a mother to the "Lost Boys" in "Peter Pan," she was their friend. Melinda's own relationship with the boys (including her willingness to sleep in a house occupied by ghosts) indicates that Melinda does not need to be a biological mother to express maternal feelings. *Ghost Whisperer* may also reflect the increasing interest in adoption in a postfeminist world among celebrities (e.g., Angelina Jolie and Madonna) and non-celebrities alike (North Americans who adopt children from China and Third World countries). While their second wave foremothers often rejected family in favor of work, women of the third wave have embraced the diversity of family structures, whether this means adopting a child from another country or embracing blended and extended families that can result from divorce ("What Happens Next: Information for Kids about Separation and Divorce").

Melinda's desire to act as mediator, which often includes interacting with mothers and children or even acting as a mother figure herself ("Lost Boys"), helps define her as a postfeminist heroine. Even though the direction of Melinda's relationship with her own mother who shares her gift remains less clear, Melinda's success as a postfeminist heroine lies in her ability to help achieve closure for others including parents and their children. The narrative desire for closure, which runs counter to Melinda's rather unstable relationship with her own mother, may reflect the contradictory emotions experienced by Americans as well as other nations in a post–9/11 world. There was and still is a need to heal and recognize the heroic efforts of individuals after the cataclysmic event of the September 11, 2001, plane disasters and the ongoing threat of terrorism against Americans. However, there is also the reality that Americans live with the fact that many questions will remain unanswered. This human desire to have answers to questions that cannot be answered may be fulfilled by a television series like *Ghost Whisperer* which introduces Melinda's ability to help ghosts cross over to another world as a means of providing some sense of closure.

It is significant that Melinda's powers develop even further near the end of Season 1 when she begins to have waking visions as well as dreams that go beyond her previous ability to see spirits or ghosts. Her powers exceed those of her mother and her grandmother, and in the last two episodes of Season 1 she acquires an almost mythic status as she tries to solve the case of a plane disaster and solve the case of spirits who are disappearing. The previous theme of disease or illness in *Ghost Whisperer* has developed into a focus on cultural dis-ease or disaster. "Free Fall"[6] (1.20) and "The One" (1.21) resonate with the mood of disaster that captures the unsettling atmosphere of 9/11. In addition to her importance as a mediator between the living and the dead, Melinda is imbued with a mythic status as a female hero-mother figure since she is identified as "the one" who needs to save ghosts that could be led away by a sinister male spirit sporting a wide-brimmed hat. In the course of "The One," Melinda manages to solve the mystery of why a plane crashed by talking to the ghost of the pilot. The episode appears to offer some form of closure for a senseless disaster. But human relationships cannot be resolved as easily, and this explains why Melinda still has unresolved issues with her mother that continue into Season 3.

Ghost Whisperer offers its audience a postfeminist heroine who is able to achieve closure for many of the dead with whom she has communicated. She bridges the gap between technology and the world of ghosts to help both the dead and the living, thus serving as an illustration of a postfeminist heroine and mediator. Melinda's search for closure may reflect the desires of Americans looking the answers in a post–9/11 world where such a dream or vision cannot be realized. However, even in Melinda's universe, she cannot achieve complete closure; relationships with certain living human beings such as her mother, for example, prove more complex. The series' emphasis on other kinds of mother-daughter relationships reveals the inadequacy of a biological mother-daughter relationship and Melinda's need to experience mother-daughter relationships in alternative ways, either through her grandmother or mother-in-law or through her dealings with mothers and daughters who may be dead. This establishment of relationships with pseudo-mothers or other people may reflect a new postfeminist approach to family where the ideal of motherhood has been displaced, perhaps as a way of emphasizing that women who are part of a third wave feminist generation need to find a third space or alternate space and distance themselves from their biological or symbolic mothers in order to find their own paths. Instead of asking their mothers "Why can't you value what I do?" (1.14), postfeminist women may need to re-define what it means to be "normal" in a postfeminist and post–9/11 age.[7]

TWELVE

A Medium's Visions
of a Third Space
Finding Family in the U.K. Series Afterlife

"Psychic TV" has not only become a phenomenon in the United States through series such as *Medium, Ghost Whisperer* and psychic talk shows (e.g., *Crossing Over with John Edward*); it has also become a popular form of entertainment in the United Kingdom. Documentary-style shows such as *Most Haunted* (2002–), Stephen Volk's *Ghostwatch* (1992), the British-Canadian co-production *Psychic Investigators* (2005–) and the U.K. broadcast of the Canadian show *Rescue Mediums* (2007–) are proof of the widespread depiction of paranormal phenomena in U.K. television. A recent British television drama series which presents a female medium as its central character is creator-writer Stephen Volk's award-winning series *Afterlife* (2005–2006).[1] Like most U.K. series, it had a short run (only two seasons with a total of 14 episodes). Comparisons between this show and the American series *Medium* are inevitable since *Afterlife* debuted shortly after *Medium* in 2005 and both medium figures have the name Alison (albeit with different spellings: Allison Dubois and Alison Mundy). However, *Afterlife* is a much darker show than *Medium*, perhaps because Volk creates a Gothic aura of isolation through the character of Alison Mundy (Lesley Sharpe), who lives alone and has no obvious family members living with her. The concept of family in this series undergoes a postmodern, supernatural and postfeminist transformation as the notion of a traditionally stable family consisting of a husband, a wife and "living" children is replaced by alternate family structures. *Afterlife* also reflects some of the experiences of third wave feminists (in the U.K. and North America) with alternative families (e.g., divorced parents or parents who have adopted a child).

The series furthermore explores a changing male-female dynamic through the development of a male-female friendship that is not based on an obvious sexual attraction. Alison follows the stereotype of the rather solitary psychic, yet over the course of the show, despite some setbacks along the way, she creates a new sense of family. Her feminine powers are validated and suggest the importance of re-evaluating the concept of the heroine. Unlike the youthful confidence of the victorious American postfeminist woman warrior heroine Buffy, Alison's unassuming nature and British identity demands a different kind of reading. As Belinda Acosta points out, "Alison is Buffy at midlife" and suggests that "[e]ven superheroes age." Her unusual powers are questioned by the scientific community, and she struggles in her own third space as a medium to keep her sanity and to subvert traditional notions of family and class. As a medium, she negotiates or mediates between different classes of people and between the different worlds of the living and the dead.

Afterlife is set in Bristol, England, and focuses on Alison, a medium who appears to be in her 40s, and her scientifically minded psychologist "friend" Robert Bridge (Andrew Lincoln), who studies Alison and her unusual ability.[2] While the series includes some wonderful visual effects that make this such a well-crafted series, its most intriguing aspect is clearly the storyline that emphasizes the relationship between Alison and her psychologist friend Robert. It begins out of scientific curiosity but becomes a friendship and even a special kind of love that distinguishes it from other, more conventional relationships (husband and wife). The series makes a statement about an alternative relationship between women and men in a postfeminist age. Despite the personal suffering and conflicts that the two characters experience as a result of different points of view, the series still captures how Alison and Robert offer one another a form of support that is made available through the unique third space that Alison inhabits as a medium.

While Homi Bhabha uses the term "third space"[3] in relation to hybrid difference and contradictions in post-colonial societies, the term is also useful in understanding Alison's role as a medium, and as a way of viewing her in the context of a feminine third space where she resists and engages with the largely patriarchal knowledge system of science. Negotiation, or the embracing of contradictions, is also a practice that is highlighted as an important component of third wave feminism, and as a way of conceptualizing the role of the medium who has one foot in the world of the living and one in the world of the dead. It is probably also significant that the last name of the psychologist Robert Bridge suggests an interest in venturing beyond the safety of science (a traditionally male domain) as he writes a book about an unconventional woman, a medium, whose very abilities challenge and reshape much of his rational thinking.

For most of the series, Robert views Alison's abilities through the lens of science as he attempts to explain her visions through psychological analysis. He thinks that Alison's belief in her ability to communicate with the dead may be signs of a psychological breakdown, or represent unresolved issues that Alison may have with her dead mother and with her father who is still alive. However, at various times, particularly near the end of each season, Robert's views become less certain and reflect the validation of Alison's "in-between space" as a medium. Each of the two series or seasons begins with Robert's doubting of Alison's ability; in the first season he doubts Alison's ability to see his son, and in the second season, Alison's own mental well being is questioned as the narrative suggests the possibility that her belief that her dead mother is tidying up her house is merely a sign of an obsessive compulsive disorder. In both seasons, Alison is presented as a woman who lives in isolation. The door of her flat has multiple locks and she is a fragile woman who fears that she is losing her mind.[4] Feminist critics might argue that this is hardly the representation of an empowered woman. Yet her ability as a medium is eventually legitimized through her influence on Robert's life.

The gender relations between Alison and Robert produce some interesting ways of reading the series as a narrative about alternative families, and alternative forms of knowledge which challenge traditional scientific belief systems as well as the boundaries between the classes in British society. Their reciprocal relationship is suggestive of a new approach to male-female relationships that may be the result of third wave feminist ideas that suggest women and men must often work together in a climate of mutual respect. This is a departure from the commonly held perception that second wave feminism chose to promote an anti-male image of feminism (Henry, 110). Alison's knowledge or experience threatens the certainty that is associated with scientific knowledge conveyed by Robert and by his colleague Barbara Sinyard (Kate Duchêne). Barbara's less than hospitable attitude towards Alison suggests an inability to tolerate this new kind of power which is not grounded in the scientific tradition and which is feminized through Alison. Of course, Dr. Sinyard's hostility is only partly related to her scientific training; it is also the result of her loyalty to Robert's ex-wife Jude and is based on Barbara's belief that Alison is the "other woman" trying to threaten the renewed bonds between Robert and Jude. Thus it soon becomes clear that as a medium, Alison occupies a third space between Robert and his colleague, between Robert and his wife, and between the world of science and faith or belief in the afterlife because she threatens to break down some of the easily established binaries between these worlds. Hers is a world of ambiguity, a third space where creator-writer Volk is able to suggest that the crossing of boundaries can occur.

The class differences between Robert and his circle of friends and Alison are a key illustration of how the female medium occupies a third space, and breaks or challenges traditional boundaries in this postmodern series. According to Lez Cooke, British postmodern television has destroyed "old certainties" and eroded "cultural hierarchies" (195). One such hierarchy consists of class differences, and another involves differences in occupation. In *Afterlife*, Robert is a well-educated psychologist and his ex-wife's circle of friends belong to an educated, well-heeled class as well, while Alison's less polished accent and her awkwardness in social situations may suggest a "working class" background. For example, in "The 7:59 Club" (1.6) Alison does not have the same social graces[5] as Robert and his friends, and finds herself in an in-between space as a result of her relationship with him. She is Robert's object of study for his book and they appear to have a close working relationship, yet Robert makes it clear that she is overstepping her boundaries when she interrupts his tutorial session with a student: "This is totally unacceptable. You have no business invading a tutorial like this" (1.6). Alison, however, disregards all social niceties and refuses to leave. In an act of postfeminist resistance in which she challenges both the hierarchy of class and a paternalistic attitude, she replies: "No, no, no, I'm not going, I'm not going anywhere actually" (1.6). This scene demonstrates the importance of class divisions and social etiquette in British society, a distinction that is not as evident in American series such as *Medium* and *Ghost Whisperer*. Yet despite the depiction of class distinctions, *Afterlife* makes an attempt to show how these distinctions are eroded through the introduction of a third space, the validation of Alison's alternative form of knowledge as a medium. Over the course of the series, Alison disrupts the clear division between the elite who think that theirs is the only valid system of knowledge, and individuals who are less privileged. Alison's way of "seeing things"[6] becomes a way of life that Robert accepts as well at certain stages of his life: when he speaks to his dead son through Alison, and near the end of his life, when his brain tumor causes him to see and experience life differently. The two-season structure of *Afterlife* reveals how Volk organized the series with his two characters, Alison and Robert, as key focal points. While Alison appears to be *Afterlife's* primary focus, the term "afterlife" does not simply have to be restricted to "life" after a physical death. Robert must start a "new life" after the death of his son, and Season 1 of the series seems to concentrate on the difficulty he experiences living after his son died in a car accident. In an interview, Stephen Volk admits that he is "extremely skeptical about the objective existence of any 'afterlife' or 'next world' in the religious sense" ("Interviews"); he appears to be more interested in using concepts of the supernatural as metaphors that allow him to comment on the human condition. In Season 1, Alison establishes herself as a presence in Robert's life and the episodes in this season often show how Robert's beliefs are "being slowly shot away from under him" (Volk "Interviews"), while Season 2 focuses more on Robert's increasing involvement in her life. This is an observation made by actor Andrew Lincoln who plays Robert: "He's far more concerned with her well being ... particularly because she went into a coma" (*Afterlife: Behind the Scenes*). As Lincoln indicates, at the beginning of Season 2, viewers discover that Alison went into a coma as a result of her séance session with Robert's son, Josh; and as Lincoln suggests, this establishes an even stronger bond between the two characters.

In Season 1, Alison makes use of her power as a mediator to help Robert achieve some form of catharsis and closure in his mourning for Josh, who died in a car accident. She regularly sees Josh, either while his father is present or when he is not, and tries to encourage Robert to communicate on the subject of his son. Robert resists throughout the season even though Alison has knowledge of incidents that she could not have through any other source. In the final episode of the series, "The 7:59 Club" (1.6), Alison finally convinces Robert to communicate with his son through her; he accompanies her to a séance not to try to contact his son, but to help her deal with the traumatic memory of her experience and the injury she suffered in the train crash six years earlier. This episode conveys that Alison's psychic ability or her power to communicate with the dead occurred after a traumatic accident in her life. The crash, which took place between Manchester and Preston, resulted in the deaths of 35 people. (This episode may have been based on the London train crash of October 5, 1999, which killed 31 people.) A specific national context for *Afterlife* which distinguishes it from the American series *Medium* and *Ghost Whisperer* is its incorporation of a train disaster.[7] "The 7:59 Club" depicts the strange third space Alison occupies when she is asked to hold a séance with the loved ones of people who were killed in the train crash that she had survived. Just as planes have a new resonance in the American imagination since the tragic events of 9/11 (two episodes at the end of Season 1 in *Ghost Whisperer* highlight a plane crash), trains remain powerful symbols in British culture because of the commuter culture and the geographical proximity of cities in Europe versus the longer distances in North America.

The culmination of Alison's ability to help Robert and her crowning achievement as a medium is presented through the use of a good old-fashioned séance in the final episode of Season 1, "The 7:59 Club." The participants are a group of people who lost loved ones in the crash, and Alison is able to speak in the voice of the dead spirits in order to address the living relative who is part of the séance circle. After speaking in the voices of various people who died in the train crash, she adopts the voice of a child but turns to Robert and says, "You're my daddy." Speaking in the voice of Robert's dead son Josh, she manages to get Robert to let his son go so that he can cross over into the afterlife. Alison has helped facilitate what Robert could not accomplish on his own: letting go of the pain associated with the loss of his son.

In this scene, the female medium takes on an interesting transgendered experience. By crossing gender boundaries to allow Robert's son to speak through her, Alison reflects what Amanda D. Lotz has identified as one of the key attributes of postfeminism: "Texts with postfeminist attributes deconstruct binary categories of gender and sexuality, instead viewing these categories as flexible and indistinct" (116). While one could argue that this attribute may simply be the attribute of a medium, it is this particular example of breaking down gender boundaries combined with the series' depiction of the interdependence of Alison and Robert that allow one to read *Afterlife* as postfeminist television.

The final episode of Season 1 is understandably quite dramatic since there is a possibility that Alison has died. Stephen Volk says that he deliberately created an ending that would permit him to end the series if ITV chose not to renew *Afterlife* (Volk, "Interviews").[8] However, with the renewal of the series, Volk was able to develop the relationship between his two leading characters even further. Season 1 ended with Alison's ability to serve as a kind of spiritual mediator; she heals Robert by creating some form of "closure" for Robert and his grief over the loss of Josh. The second season, however, focuses on Robert's increasing involvement in Alison's life as she experiences a mental breakdown, later attributed to the suppression of the childhood trauma of witnessing a death. Robert's life is also transformed as he discovers that he has a brain tumor, which means that he could die any time.

There is a direct contradiction or discrepancy between the backstory of Alison in Season 1 and the backstory created for her in Season 2, which may disrupt a viewer's sense of consistency in the narrative, but perhaps that is the point. In Season 1, Alison apparently gained her special power through a near-fatal injury received in the train crash; Season 2 creates another backstory that indicates how Alison had her ability since childhood and that it was an ability that her grandmother and aunt also possessed. Alison's illness or "madness" in Season 2 is an exaggeration of the medicalization of Alison's ability as abnormal in the first season. Like *Ghost Whisperer*'s Melinda, whose mother treats the power to communicate with the dead as a medical condition, Alison is also perceived by members of the scientific community as falling outside the realm of the "normal." However, Volk uses this alternate space to explore different notions of what is considered normal[9] and to suggest that the world we live in is gray, not black and white. The extreme sense of solitude and personal dislocation experienced by Alison are a departure from the more typical or familiar nuclear family drama format of *Medium* (husband, wife and children) and suggests the influence of the Gothic in British television and film[10] as well as Volk's deliberate move away from the "larger-than-life" or "glossy world" of American series (*Afterlife: Behind the Scenes*).

Alison's image as a "broken" individual throughout the series might give some feminist critics pause; however, the interplay between Alison and Robert (who is "damaged" in his own way) suggests a reconstruction of female-male relationships that are part of a postmodern and post-feminist experience, thus reflecting Volk's own interest in showing how the supernatural can be used as a metaphor to explore and undercut notions of certainty that dominated a pre-postmodern existence. The dynamic and mutually dependent relationship between Alison and Robert reveals how Alison's life in an alternate space, the third space of a solitary female medium with no husband or children of her own, may serve as a way of re-evaluating Robert's life.

Family

Despite the lack of traditional family structure in her life, Alison's relationship with her psychologist and her ability to see Josh suggest the creation of an alternative (albeit somewhat dysfunctional) family and an alternative way of knowing. Third wave feminists have been raised in an era where the "standard" two-married parents, two-child family is not the only reality. This series captures this shift in the composition of the family through the mediating influence of the female psychic who creates a third space to accommodate a different sense of family. Alison has no children of her own; the sixth episode of Season 1 reveals that she is not able to have children of her own because of the injuries she suffered in the train accident: "In the train crash there was this big thing, this metal spike... It tore through my womb" (1.6). Since she has no children, it seems rather appropriate that she should "adopt" Josh as her own. Alison and Robert are not married, yet as a medium-psychic who occupies a third space (between Robert and his pregnant ex-wife, and between Robert and his son), Alison becomes a surrogate "mother figure" for the dead child who needs to reconnect to his father through Alison. She tells Robert about Josh when she sees him, and Robert often discounts the information that she presents to him. However, she is able to communicate with him about the child in a way that is not possible for Robert and his ex-wife, Josh's mother. For Robert and his ex-wife, talking about Josh is far too painful, especially since she is also expecting the child of her new husband. As a result of Alison's ability to speak in a childlike voice, Robert can finally let his son go in the final episode of Season 1 ("The 7:59 Club," 1.6). The visual effect of this séance scene is quite remarkable since it shows the image of Josh in a mirror; the viewer then sees Josh step out of the mirror once Robert confirms that he loves his son "more than anything." However, Robert does not "access" his son directly; he does so through the mediating presence of Alison who does not speak in Josh's actual voice, but only approximates his voice, thus reinforcing the concept of how the medium occupies a third (often contradictory) space. The camera moves between Alison, Robert and Josh, thus intensifying the connections between these "family" members.

Alison almost loses her own life in this unusual act of familial communication (Season 2 reveals that she was in a coma); while she is hardly an action heroine, her role as a communicator and facilitator is no less heroic than the actions of the "kick-ass" heroines from other television programs that highlight the power of women (Buffy, Xena). The séance scene also shows her heroic ability to perform an act of self-sacrifice (Campbell, *The Power of Myth*, 151), a longstanding quality of all kinds of heroes including "mothers" throughout the ages.

Season 2 continues the first season's concern with the medium and family; many of the dead people that Alison sees have some kind of family trauma, whether they are the victims of a family suicide (1.1) or the victims of a train accident (1.6). It is therefore perhaps not so surprising that Alison has her own family trauma to address. In Season 2 in particular, Alison must negotiate between her own trauma and childhood ghosts and the energy required to help others. She continues to respond to living and dead people who need to achieve peace or closure in their lives; she attends meetings organized by Robert to discuss her abilities or to do "cold" readings. Yet she must grapple with her own inner or external demon as the case may be; throughout Season 2 she claims that her dead mother is appearing to her and rearranging the house. Robert is convinced that Alison is simply experiencing a breakdown due to some childhood trauma, and the depiction of Alison's rearranged things is done in such a way that the Todorovian[11] sense of the fantastic is maintained. In other words, it is not easy to determine whether Alison is actually seeing her mother, which would be an example of Todorov's definition of the marvelous, or whether she has simply had too much to drink or has become mad, an example of the uncanny. When Alison's father visits, this becomes less of an uncertainty since he claims that he too saw Alison's mother. Mr. Mundy says that his wife killed herself and he found the body; however, through Robert's counseling sessions, Alison finally admits that she witnessed her mother's death (2.6). After this revelation and cathartic experience, Alison is at peace once again. This is an interesting parallel to the moment that Robert experienced during the séance when Alison facilitated the healing process for Robert over the loss of his son.

Heroes

Viewers may find that by focusing on Alison and on what Robert perceives as her descent into the madness of an obsessive compulsive disorder, the writers (Volk and others) have undermined the credibility of the medium, or the female protagonist's power, and that she is merely a mad Cassandra figure. However, even in the mythic narratives of the male hero, such a descent into the underworld, whether this is a physical journey as in the case of Herakles and Orpheus or primarily a psychological one as it for the male hero in the film *What Dreams May Come*, the experience of "darkness" is a necessary part of the hero's development. The hero must journey into the darkness before going into the light. *Afterlife* does challenge Joseph Campbell's theory of the journey in some respects since even at the end of the series, when Robert joins his son, and Alison witnesses this reunion, she is not venerated the way that traditional heroes are. This may be part of the postmodern uncertainty that pervades *Afterlife*. While Alison has facilitated the completion of Robert's journey, she is not easily accepted by the other women in Robert's life, Jude and Barb. Barb espouses the "rational" view, calls Alison mad (2.8) and feels that she has come between Robert and his work and between Robert and his relationship with Jude. Robert's ex-wife is overwrought when Alison tells her that Robert appeared to her after his heart stopped the first time (2.7) and told her that he was not ready to die. Jude replies: "He came to you. He came to *you*. You bitch" (2.8). Near the end of the series, Robert has the opportunity to start afresh with his ex-wife, but it is Alison who sees Robert right before his death. Despite opposition from these other women, Alison stays true to Robert just as he stayed by her side in the first season. The series thus questions a feminist ideal of a community of women which may not have welcomed all women. Alison serves as an illustration of "difference"; she may not be a woman of color, but her unusual ability as a medium place her in a different category that is not understood by either Jude or Barbara. One postfeminist message in *Afterlife* seems to suggest that instead of bonding with other women, women in a third wave feminist era may cross gender lines for friendships, and that women should not feel that they are betraying a feminist cause by having friendships with men.

While one could read *Afterlife* as the journey of the hero Robert Bridge, it would be more appropriate to see the series as a narrative about the psychologically intertwined journeys of two heroes, Alison and Robert, whose divergent views near the beginning of the series converge near the end because of Alison's influence as a woman of vision on Robert's life. As a medium, Alison is a postfeminist heroine who offers Robert a new way of seeing; the series suggests that for some, this new way of seeing may be related to a scientific, biological explanation, such as a brain tumor; for others, it is a gift of vision attributed to psychic ability. During the last months of his life, Robert feels elated (he claims that this feeling is caused by his tumor) and he experiences life outside his own body, the very experiences that have characterized Alison's life (1.7). While Stephen Volk has indicated that he is not a believer in an afterlife *per se*, he and other writers for the series have imaginatively presented the supernatural or the fantastic as another way of challenging the boundaries of life, whether those boundaries are created by family, social class, medical science or gender.[12] In *Afterlife: Behind the Scenes*, Volk states that Season 2 does not end with a resolution; it actually raises more questions. During his final moments of life, Robert expresses this open-endedness, which Alison's own experiences of the afterlife have suggested all along: "I thought it would be so clear, but it isn't. I thought that all the questions would be answered but they're not."

Conclusion

Representations of women with visionary powers, psychic ability or other special ways of "seeing" and "knowing" in television and film since the 1990s reveal diverse ways of defining the female hero in a postfeminist era. Yet the element of racial or ethnic diversity has not kept pace with other elements of postfeminism or third wave feminism outside of the visual media. Postfeminism or third wave feminism has been receptive to "the multiple ways ethnicity, class, education, sexuality, age or generation, marital status, motherhood, and ability position women in society" and offers ways of "illustrating disparate perspectives on female experience and social opportunities" (Lotz, 115). Despite the presentation of women of color in television and film (including an African-American medium in *Ghost* and Native American seer figures in *Wonderfalls*), most representations of difference occur in other ways. The primary expression of difference in these telefantasies and fantasy films is the visionary ability itself, which presents the central female character as unique. She occupies a third space or in-between space that allows her to negotiate between worlds or experiences. If she is a medium figure like Oda Mae in *Ghost,* Allison Dubois in *Medium*, Alison Mundy in *Afterlife* or Melinda in *Ghost Whisperer*, she has access to the living and the world of the dead. She may have knowledge or premonitions of future events like Tru in *Tru Calling*, River in *Firefly* and *Serenity*, Annie in *The Gift* and Linda in *Premonition*. Phoebe in *Charmed* has knowledge of both future and past events. Joan Girardi in *Joan of Arcadia* sees God as many different people, and Jaye Tyler in *Wonderfalls* receives cryptic messages from trickster-like animal figures, one of which encourages cross-cultural contact with Native American society.

The U.K. series *Afterlife* addresses difference through class distinctions and shows how a postfeminist medium negotiates this issue in post-modern British society. In another British series, *Hex,* Cassie, the seer-witch figure, offers a way of validating relations between women through her friendship with a lesbian ghost. Thelma, the ghost, *is* the vision that resists the traditional narrative of possession or the story of the seer who receives visions from a patriarchal source. In *Ghost* the African-American medium Oda Mae "deconstructs binary categories of gender and sexuality" (Lotz, 116) while she merges with a man's spirit to embrace a woman.

Occasionally in television (*Wonderfalls, Afterlife*) and film (*Premonition*), the female visionary signifies difference because she and others think that she may be mad or mentally disturbed. While television series and films may introduce the familiar Cassandra-like image of the mad seer as a way of defining the woman who has visions as "other," most of these narratives show that the woman of vision has more agency than the mythic prototype of Cassandra and that she is able to change the way other people look at her psychic or supernatural experiences. These women eventually challenge a narrow definition of what constitutes "normal," thereby encouraging others to accept different ways of seeing. As hero figures, they help or save other people in the process.

As women with visionary abilities, the characters in postfeminist television and film also break down the boundaries between the world of science and mystical or spiritual experiences. Melinda Gordon's use of technology combined with her ability to converse with the dead in *Ghost Whisperer* allows her to solve mysteries that benefit both the living and the ghosts that she encounters. Characters like Alison in *Afterlife* challenge an established system of knowledge (the science of psychology) and offer new ways of bridging the perceived gap between science and the world of psychic experience. The two mediums in the reality television show *Rescue Mediums,* the psychic Christine Holohan in *Psychic Investigators* and Annie in *The Gift* also question the divisions between the work of police investigators and their own investigative skills as psychics. Occasionally they even convert skeptics over to their way of seeing. This results in a bridging of the communication gap that has existed between men and women, and serves as one of the goals of third wave feminism.

The genre of telefantasy and the hybrid form of psychic reality television shows that incorporate supernatural elements can offer transformative experiences for women since their central female "characters" can cross boundaries more easily in these artistic forms than women outside the context of television or film. Fantasy television and film allow for a process of identity re-invention. Fan responses to the women depicted in several television series suggest that they often find these women of vision are more compelling than other characters in the same series, even when these female characters experience certain setbacks. The genre of psychic reality television offers a new way of validating alternate forms of knowledge by presenting these women as legitimate investigators. These shows often blur the lines between the world of psychic investigation and the "science" of police investigation.

This is not to say that all depictions of the seer, witch or psychic in television and film are unproblematic. In addition to constructions of the mad seer, postfeminist constructions of motherhood in television series like *Medium* still suggest that women struggle to resist images of the "bad" mother as they negotiate between the demands of family, work and (in Allison Dubois' case in *Medium*) the demands of the dead. One of the creative ways in which the woman of vision is used in film and television is to suggest the changing concept of family in a postfeminist era. Just as postfeminists recognize a diversity of views among feminists, they also know that there are many kinds of families in addition to the nuclear family. In visual media, family is redefined through a medium's connection with the father of a dead child, or through an individual's association with a crew of unrelated people (River's experience in *Firefly* or *Serenity*).

The visionary woman also plays an important role as a new kind of heroine in a postfeminist age. She may incorporate some of the standard qualities of the traditional hero in myth. She is often a savior figure or a healer and in the case of Melinda from *Ghost Whisperer* may serve as a symbol of the kind of healing and closure Americans were looking for in the wake of 9/11. The woman of vision may take the form of a mother like Allison Dubois in *Medium* who negotiates between competing demands. Often, she may be more of a mediator or a facilitator than a Joan of Arc–style "leader," as she helps others develop their potential in the process. At times a character with special sight is a reluctant heroine not unlike the reluctant male hero in myth. She can even be more of an anti-heroine than a heroine. A figure like River in *Firefly* and *Serenity* is able to help others with her psychic ability but her instability can also be perceived as "dangerous." As one can see, there are different models of heroism for seers, witches and psychic women in visual media, because the women in these series and films represent a spectrum of women: teenagers, single women, mothers, married women, women in their twenties, thirties and forties, and middle-aged women. In other words, women represented with visionary powers in postfeminist television and film are not limited to a single generation, unlike the "woman warrior" figure who tends to be limited to younger characters.

Depictions of women who have visions in film and television offer a way of connecting women across age groups and across nations (the U.S., Canada and the U.K.) while still acknowledging differences that may be dependent on specific cultural or national contexts. One of the goals of third wave feminism as articulated by Jennifer Purvis is to "imagine a new signifying space [and] create a point of convergence and contestation" (119). The postfeminist seer, witch, psychic, or medium in television and film most certainly occupies this kind of space and uses her difference to make connections with others, especially with individuals who are also constructed as different.

Chapter Notes

Introduction

1. I address the figure of Lorne, a male demon-seer figure in *Angel*, in my analysis of Cordelia, the female seer figure in *Angel*. A television series such as *Psych* (2006–) does not legitimize psychic ability but is based on the subversion of such a possibility since the protagonist uses reason or logic to fool others into thinking that he has psychic abilities.

2. Mesmerism is defined as "a system of healing" (Spence, 597) founded by Friedrich Anton Mesmer (1733–1815), a German physician trained in Vienna who expounded the principles of animal magnetism. He applied magnetic plates to the bodies of people to heal them (Lewis Spence, ed., *Encyclopedia of Occultism and Parapsychology*).

3. In "Old Myths, New Powers: Images of Second-Wave and Third-Wave Feminism in *Charmed*" (in *Investigating Charmed*), I examine how the response of the postfeminist witches or Charmed Ones to the figure of the hag is problematic.

Chapter 1

1. Yvonne Tasker and Diane Negra refer to the "irony and self-reflexivity that characterize so much of postfeminist and postmodern culture" ("Postfeminism and the Archive for the Future," 171).

2. Phoebe, the witch who has premonitions in *Charmed*, is a bit of a departure from the conventional seer since she is able to actively call up a vision by touching an object.

3. Cordelia crosses over as a character from *Buffy the Vampire Slayer* to *Angel*; however, Charisma Carpenter's transportability as a seer figure is evident in the series *Charmed* where she plays a seer by the name of Kira. The actress also appeared in the film *Voodoo Moon* (2005) as a woman with psychic abilities. Other characters who cross over from *Buffy* to *Angel* include Faith, Spike, Darla, Drusilla and Harmony.

4. Cordelia also seems to have inherited the suffering of her namesake, Cordelia, the daughter in *King Lear* who suffers the false accusations leveled against her by her father.

5. In "Becoming the Other: Multiculturalism in Joss Whedon's *Angel*," Jane Stadler argues that *Angel* can be "interpreted as a critique of xenophobia, the fear of foreigners" and uses Lorne as an example of a person of color in a positive central role.

6. The Powers That Be are generally considered beneficent forces that send visions; however, they are also cynically referred to as "The Powers That Screw You" by the female character Fred in "Deep Down" (4.1) since there appears to be an arbitrariness about them not unlike the will of the gods of classical Greek mythology.

7. In *Angel* it is not always clear whether

Cordelia's visions are generated by good or evil forces. Cordelia experiences another hybrid moment when she discovers that the visions that have caused her so much pain were not sent by "The Powers That Be" but by a man with a split skull (another image of hybridity), who happens to be the pawn of Lilah, one of the sinister characters from the law firm Wolfram and Hart. The unpredictability of Cordelia's postmodern world suggests that there can be no easy identification of good or evil forces. Cordelia finds herself in multiple in-between spaces in *Angel* and lives in a world with shades of gray since it is often difficult to determine who is behind certain fantastic or supernatural phenomena.

8. It is worth noting that prior to Cordelia's role as the suffering seer in *Angel*, she already identified herself as a person who suffered in *Buffy the Vampire Slayer* when she complains about suffering through a "beachless" vacation: "No one has suffered like I have suffered" ("When She Was Bad," 2.1). Of course in *Buffy* the statement can be dismissed as Cordelia's self-absorbed attitude, while in *Angel*, the gradual deterioration of her brain, her burned skin and the boils on her face in "That Vision Thing" demonstrate extreme suffering as a result of her visions. The irony of Cordelia's words about her perception of extreme suffering in *Buffy* is clear when one views the words of this cheerleader in relation to her extremely visible, heroic suffering as a seer in *Angel*.

9. Studies have shown a direct link between humor and healing. (See Athena Du Pré's book, *Humor and the Healing Arts: A Multimethod Analysis of Humor Use in Health Care*.) Comedians who have suffered from a disease like cancer or comedians who belong to minority groups have also used humor or irony to empower themselves in the face of adversity.

Chapter 2

1. There are hints of River's increasingly important role in "Objects in Space," the last episode of *Firefly*.

2. In her conference paper "Never Been Kissed: Sex and the Smart Girl on Teen TV," Cindy Conaway offers some interesting analysis of "smart girls" in postfeminist television (Popular Culture Association, 2006). Sherrie A. Innes' collection *Geek Chic: Smart Women in Popular Culture* (Palgrave-Macmillan 2007) includes essays on this cultural phenomenon and extends the discussion to an analysis of older "smart" women.

3. Elyce Rae Helford reads Tank Girl as a young woman who "displays the aggressive individualism and 'projected' sexuality of rock-me / postfeminism" (8). The film *Tank Girl* (1995) is based on the British comic by Alan Martin (with drawings by Jamie Hewlett) which debuted in 1988.

4. Aristotle believed that characters, including tragic heroes, should be consistent. River's character is so unstable that she cannot meet this criterion unless one argues that she is consistently inconsistent, much like Aritha van Herk's postmodern picaresque heroine Arachne Manteia in her novel *No Fixed Address*.

5. When River was a child, she played a game with Simon and claimed that the Alliance crew had to "resort to cannibalism" ("Safe").

6. In the novel version, "Dorothy ... was truly frightened to see the Witch actually melting away like brown sugar before her very eyes" (Baum, 134).

7. Fan discussion thread, "Crazy Is as Crazy Does: River Tam." Television Without Pity: *Firefly*. http://forums.tele visionwithoutpity.com

8. In her conference paper, "'It's just an object. It doesn't mean what you think': The Male Gaze and Female Language in *Firefly* and *Serenity*," Alyson R. Buckman

offers further analysis of the important role of River and the use of "place" in "Objects in Space."

9. River suggests Early's patriarchal dominance when she uses a sexual image to describe his presence on the ship (or in her since she *is* the ship): "You crawl inside me uninvited." Early also threatened Kaylee with rape.

10. River is not the only one of Whedon's characters in the *Serenity/Firefly* universe who lives in an ambivalent space; even the operative in *Serenity* is fluid, since he seems to be transformed from enemy to anti-hero. One could also argue that the crew members of *Serenity* occupy an indeterminate space between hero and anti-hero. When Zoe says a hero "gets other people killed," this could apply to Mal. On the other hand, some critics might argue that this is really more of a definition of an anti-hero. The subtitle of the *Firefly* collection *Finding Serenity: Anti-Heroes, Lost Shepherds and Space Hookers in Joss Whedon's Firefly* suggests the pervasive presence of the anti-hero in the series.

Chapter 3

1. *Charmed* has been televised or released in DVD format in countries such as Canada, the U.K., Germany, Sweden, the Netherlands and Japan.

2. Phoebe's name is the clearest indication of her power of sight and reveals the mythological connections to her identity. The name is derived from the Greek word for light (*phoibe*), and translates as "brilliant, shining." The masculine version of the name is Phoebus, part of the name of the Greek god, Apollo. Apollo was known as the seer-god who spoke through a priestess, the Delphic Oracle (Cotterell and Storm, 43). Phoebe is also an alternative name for Apollo's twin sister, Artemis, the goddess of the moon, thus establishing an important connection to the feminine realm. According to Bar-

bara Smith, Phoebe "was the daughter of heaven and earth (Gaia) and the mother of Leto, thus grandmother of Artemis and Apollo, from whom the god takes his epithet *phoibos*. She was a moon deity, like Selene" (Smith in Carolyne Larrington, *The Feminist Companion to Mythology* 86, 65–101).

3. Series like *Angel, Firefly, Tru Calling, Joan of Arcadia, Wonderfalls, Medium,* and *Ghost Whisperer* suggest that the seer or visionary is a compelling character type for television, perhaps because of her mythic or iconic stature. Clearly, there is some variation from series to series but the seer's visions and premonitions suggest feminine empowerment in the context of a rather passive form of knowledge. This heightened ability or knowledge can simultaneously make the character central and marginal, resulting in a figure identified with instability (such is the case of the mentally unstable River, a character from *Firefly*).

4. In this chapter on *Charmed*, I focus on Phoebe because she is the central female seer over eight seasons of *Charmed*; however, two other seer figures appear in the series: the Seer (Debbi Morgan) and Kira, the seer (Charisma Carpenter).

5. With the arrival of Paige at the beginning of Season 4, Phoebe's visions often appear less central to the storylines, perhaps because of the need to integrate the new sister Paige and her abilities into the series.

6. One of the most famous examples of a mythic seer's involvement in the life of an ordinary individual is Tiresias' knowledge that Oedipus was responsible for the plague in his city. (He was later revealed as the murderer of his father Laius.)

7. In *Angel*, the sexual ambiguity of the seer figure is an interesting dimension; Lorne, the demon lounge singer with an affinity for gay culture (Stan Beeler, 88–100) has the ability to see into the future when he hears a person sing. He may

be an interesting reconstruction of the Tiresias figure who was able to live part of his life as a man and part of his life as a woman.

8. Josh Whedon, the creator of *Angel* and *Firefly*, extends this image of passivity in his depiction of Cordelia, who is the recipient of painful visions, and through the "mad seer" character of River, an unstable, mentally and physically unpredictable character in his apocalyptic series *Firefly*. River's passive power is actually transformed into a violent outburst, thus demonstrating that the binary opposition between active and passive is an oversimplified way of viewing the seer's ability vs. other kinds of powers.

9. Andy tells Prue, "Phoebe's premonition was one you couldn't stop, after all. Weren't supposed to stop."

10. Phoebe's dissatisfaction with her premonitions reappears in the latter portion of the series as well, including Season 8. However, in "Vaya Con Leos" (8.10), it is related to the perceived inaccuracy of her visions when her marriage to Dex Lawson (the result of a spell) does not translate into the fulfillment of the romantic fantasy that she had envisioned for herself.

11. Phoebe's expression of wish fulfillment and some of the ensuing problems may reflect what Rachel Moseley has called the "postfeminist difficulties of 'having it all'" (421).

12. In her analysis of postfeminist popular culture, Diane Negra identifies the shift from the image of the career-driven woman (a common goal for second wave feminists) to the valorization of women in the home: "With discourses of ideal femininity clearly tilting away from the professional path, retreatism has become a recognizable narrative trope. Accordingly, both film and television have incorporated fantasies of hometown return in which a heroine gives up her life in the city to take up again the role of daughter, sister, wife

or sweetheart in a hometown setting" ("Quality Postfeminism" #5).

13. Yet another figure called the Seer appears in Season 7 of *Charmed*, and this is a character played by Charisma Carpenter who also played the role of Cordelia, a seer figure in *Angel*. The Charisma Carpenter character in *Charmed* passes on a vision to Phoebe about a group called the Avatars who try to eradicate evil in the world but who end up creating a world with its own disturbing characteristics.

14. The series is not very specific about how the supernatural cross-fertilization took place.

15. Kate Donovan indicates the tension between good and evil and the concept of moral ambiguity in her description of Cole Turner: "But even when he became the Source of all Evil, it wasn't because he wanted power for himself. It was to save Phoebe" (Donovan in Crusie, ed., *Totally Charmed*, 107).

16. Cassandra, the famous Trojan seer, is usually presented as childless and unmarried; however, in one variant of the myth, she was the mother of Apollo's children.

17. See the thread "Phoebe's Powers" on *http://Charmed-net.com/en.*

18. According to Shugart and her coauthors, the "politics of difference that drive third-wave feminism thus are manifest in an embracing of contradiction so that apparently inconsistent political viewpoints coexist in the name of third-wave feminism" (195).

Chapter 4

1. John Kenneth Muir notes the parallels between Cassie's relationship with Azazeal, the fallen Angel, and Buffy's relationship with "the sometimes good/sometimes soul-less vampire, Angel." He also mentions the link between Thelma, the lesbian character and friend of Cassie, the central female character in *Hex*, and

Willow, Buffy's friend who becomes a lesbian later in the series. Director Grant indicates that despite the setting of an old English house, he sought to create the "feel of an American college" ("Making of *Hex*") and audience members may think that some of the lighter moments are even reminiscent of the humor in *Buffy the Vampire Slayer*.

2. In the tragic Greek play *Agamemnon*, for example, Cassandra functions as the Trojan War "prize" slave of Agamemnon, the Greek king; she sees the death of the king and her own death (Aeschylus, 1274).

3. The DVD version of *Hex* repackaged episodes 1 and 2 as the pilot, whereas when the show first aired in the U.K. only episode 1 was the pilot.

4. Cassandra feels the presence of the god when she sees visions, "his *fire*!— sears me, sweeps me again — the torture! Apollo Lord of the Light, you burn" (*Agamemnon* lines, 1269–1271). In *Angel*, Cordelia's also experiences terrible pain when she receives a vision (Chapter 1).

5. The cutting of the finger may also be an allusion to Sleeping Beauty's pricking of her finger on the spindle. This act may be interpreted as a symbolic sexual initiation.

6. Aeschylus' Leader character in *Agamemnon* assumes that Cassandra bore Apollo a child and in fact in some versions of the myth she is a mother. *Hex* may be incorporating this allusion in its depiction of Cassie and the child she bears out of a union with Azazeal.

7. The ancient Greek physician Hippocrates argued that women were prone to hysteria or a form of madness because he believed that a woman's uterus could wander around in her body, thus causing a physical and emotional imbalance. The word hysteria is derived from the Greek word for uterus (hystera).

8. Meredith A. Powers describes Circe as "a gorgeous willful witch with both

charming and diabolical ways" (*The Heroine in Western Literature*, 72)

9. The name Troy for Cassie's man of choice is interesting since the mythical Cassandra was a Trojan.

10. *Hex* has been compared to *Buffy the Vampire Slayer*. In the film *Buffy the Vampire Slayer*, Buffy is also portrayed eating junk food and one of the scenes shows her sucking on a lollipop as well. This film (like *Hex*) draws explicit parallels between sexual appetite and appetite for food.

11. One cannot deny that there is a certain tragic element in Thelma's situation when she says, "Dead people still have desires, you know," and remarks that she "can only wear dead people's clothes" (2.1). Other fantasy shows like *Buffy* have been criticized for the negative portrayal of lesbians (through the death of Willow's lover in *Buffy*).

Chapter 5

1. A male character in "Putting Out Fires" (1.2) describes Tru as "weird but hot."

2. The women who are part of the postfeminist era which crosses over with Generation X and Y have often been children of families that do not resemble the nuclear family: "No longer is there a single culturally dominant family pattern to which the majority of Americans conform and most of the rest aspire" (Judith Stacey, 96).

3. Generation Y is known for a different attitude towards employment: "Change, change, change. Generation Yers don't expect to stay in a job, or even a career, for too long.... They don't like to stay too long on any one assignment. This is a generation of multitaskers, and they can juggle e-mail on their BlackBerrys while talking on cell phones while trolling online" (Stephanie Armour).

4. Tru's brother Harrison is an illustration of a young person who seems

to have a difficult time holding down a job.

5. See another example of how the "third wave feminist" witches displace the second wave generation in the television series *Charmed*. Karin Beeler, "Old Myths, New Powers: Images of Second-Wave and Third-Wave Feminism in *Charmed*."

6. Tru's improved relationship with her father is based on a lack of knowledge on her part; she does not know that he arranged for a hitman to kill her mother. Her father is also the opposite of Tru and Tru's mother; he used to have Jack's job of ensuring that individuals die as fate would have it. One could argue that Richard and Jack reinscribe the traditional image of fate as inevitable that was part of the ancient Greek belief system. Tru tries to subvert this kind of inevitability by arguing that there are individuals who are taken before their time.

7. While Tru is clearly a heroine of a postmodern, postfeminist time, the postmodern relativism that characterizes the show has some similarity to one of the traditional elements of a hero, the fact that a hero's strength may also be viewed as a weakness. For example, the mythic hero Oedipus is a proud man who is a decisive leader. However, pride may also be an individual's downfall and hasty decisions can be fatal as is the case when Oedipus kills his father/King Laius after the latter forced him off the road.

8. In "Two Pair" (1.16), we discover that Davis is his *middle* name.

9. This idea is discussed further in the chapter on the U.K. series *Afterlife*.

10. Both *Buffy* and the U.K. series *Hex* have re-presented lesbian sexuality as a key aspect of their woman-centered series. In *Buffy*, Willow and her friend Tara are witches who have a lesbian relationship, and in *Hex*, lesbian desire is articulated through Thelma, the dead friend of Cassie, a Cassandra figure.

11. The series even goes so far as to suggest that even Jack may not be a completely reprehensible character when he experiences uncertainty over the fate of a woman dying of leukemia ("Last Good Day," 2.4).

12. The genre of fantasy in literature, film or television emphasizes the existence of the inexplicable in our lives.

Chapter 6

1. For example, Anna Vaughn Hyatt Huntington's statue of Joan on horseback (1915) reinforces an important political tie between the United States and France based on their affiliation during World War I and their common values of liberty and democracy ("Joan of Arc, 1915," New York Public Art Curriculum).

2. Helene Shugart, Catherine Egley Waggoner and D. Lynn O'Brien Hallstein refer to "the third-wave proclivity for contradictions" ("Mediating Third-Wave Feminism," 198).

3. Other recent depictions of Joan of Arc can be found in the animated television series *The Simpsons* and in *Wishbone*, a children's television show. In *The Simpsons* ("Tales from the Public Domain," 13.14), the character Lisa Simpson takes on the role of the famous French heroine. Like Joan, Lisa demonstrates the independence of spirit and courage that are part of the iconic or mythic proportions of this historical figure; as Joan, Lisa leads the French army and defeats the English. However, this American comedy series puts a contemporary spin on the rest of the Joan of Arc narrative that reflects the ironic values of a postmodern American comedy series (that has an audience of both young and adult viewers). Marge Simpson, Lisa's mother, retells the story so that Joan of Arc is not burned at the stake. Lisa asks her father, "What happened, Dad? They didn't really burn her, did they?" Marge replies, "Of course they didn't, honey. Just then, Sir Lancelot

drove up on a white horse and saved Joan of Arc, they got married and lived in a spaceship, the end." The story as retold by Marge may not sustain an image of an independent Joan, but in a typical postmodern fashion, it does not uphold a fairytale ending either, since it introduces the unusual, non-medieval element of a spaceship.

The American children's series *Wishbone* features a small dog called Wishbone who (along with his human friends) adopt the roles of various characters in history or in famous works of literature. The series functions primarily as a way of introducing North American children to "great authors" or to the classics of literature. The *Wishbone* episode retelling the story of Joan of Arc was released under the title "Bone of Arc" (1996) in video format and under the book title *Joan of Arc: Wishbone Classics* (1996). This series is based on Samuel Clemens' (Mark Twain's) fictional biography of Joan of Arc called *Personal Recollections of Joan of Arc* (1896), which Clemens wrote under the pen name of Sieur Louis de Conte. According to Robin Blaetz, Clemens' primary interest in Joan is linked to a Romantic desire to "return to a time when the most troubling of questions could be answered through faith in the supernatural" (205). Yet the fact that Clemens' narrative has in turn helped generate another Joan of Arc story is also important because it emphasizes how Joan of Arc has become a part of American culture as well as French culture. In the *Wishbone* Joan of Arc episode, the dog plays the devoted friend of Joan of Arc, who is played by a young girl.

Joan of Arc is also recreated in the American-Canadian co-production *Wonderfalls* (2004), which is aimed at a twentysomething audience. This series is the focus of the next chapter.

4. Rhonda Wilcox mentions that at the very end of the series (Season 2), "Joan is told that she has superpowers rather than being an average teen" ("God's Clothes, God's Bones," 96), thus robbing her of her ordinariness. However, one could argue that Joan's "superpower" already exists in her ability to see God.

5. As Warner's analysis reveals, accounts of Joan's voices and their physical manifestation as described at her trial are sometimes inconsistent; in one version, the voice appears to emanate from a cloud (120); in other accounts Joan provides more physical details of the individuals associated with these voices (Warner, Chapter 6).

6. In Butler's account of one version, a blaze of light accompanied the voice which was initially singular (Leeming, 56).

7. Robin Blaetz indicates that two recent films about Joan of Arc, Besson's *The Messenger* and Duguay's *Joan of Arc*, "are occupied less with the relation between women and war than with Joan of Arc's psychological state and the visualization of the supernatural" (182). This emphasis on the visualization of the supernatural certainly takes place in both *Joan of Arcadia* and in the series *Wonderfalls* which also depicts a woman (Jaye Tyler) who is a unique recreation of Joan of Arc. Joan Girardi and Jaye Tyler's visions of the supernatural reflect the psychological uncertainty of living in an increasingly fragmented or fractured world.

8. Joan of Arc's voices included the voices of St. Michael, St. Catherine and St. Margaret.

9. Films such as *Oh God!* and *Bruce Almighty* paved the way for presenting God in the context of the ordinary. In *Oh God!* George Burns plays God as a short, cigar-smoking Jewish man and in *Bruce Almighty* Morgan Freeman as God appears as a black janitor, thus subverting the image of God as a white male patriarch.

10. Some might argue that the emphasis on Joan's direct interaction with God could represent a more Protestant orienta-

tion and a rejection of the Catholic faith where individuals have mediators like priests and saints to communicate with God. However, series creator Hall indicated that one of the "commandments" for the series was to present a God who cannot be identified or limited to a particular religious faith (*Joan of Arcadia, TV Tome*, 1.1). Thus a pluralist or multi-faith culture might be a more appropriate way of contextualizing the God figure(s) in *Joan of Arcadia*.

11. The act of sharing ice cream seems to be a common ritual in American television, as is evident in *Judging Amy* (1999–2005), another family-oriented series that Barbara Hall wrote and produced.

12. The word "fantastic" applies to the series in two different ways. Eric Rabkin's definition of the fantastic as an alternative world (to the parameters of the real world established within a text) is valid in the sense that Joan's experience of God is uniquely different and outside the parameters of "normal" even though the notion of God is an accepted part of the "real" world. Yet Tzvetan Todorov's notion of the fantastic as a hesitation between the rational and the supernatural is also relevant for part of the series. This is because it is not always clear to viewers whether Joan's visions are "real" (thus resulting in a reading of the series as the supernatural explained) or whether these visions should be dismissed as the experience of abnormality. For example, during Season 1, Joan's visions of the supernatural may be questioned by the viewer when she is diagnosed with Lyme Disease, and her visions are ascribed to hallucinations which may be brought on by the disease, thus generating even more hesitation in the viewer's realm of experience. When Joan continues to hear and see God after she has been "cured," the series seems to return to the realm of the marvelous (the supernatural accepted), where the supernatural is "accepted" as part of the convention of the series.

13. Todorov's definition of the fantastic (unlike Catherine Johnson's definition of telefantasy) is dependent upon a hesitation between a natural explanation (the uncanny) of an apparently supernatural phenomenon and an acceptance of the supernatural (marvelous). Madness and hallucinations caused by drugs or alcohol would be examples of rational explanations. Fairy tales or science fiction would be examples of "marvelous" works in which there is an acceptance of supernatural creatures such as witches or aliens.

14. A scene between Joan and her brother makes for an interesting use of the theme of "voices." In episode one, Joan hears "God's voice" but when she opens her eyes, she sees her brother. In other words, God's voice and her brother's have blended together, thus erasing the clear distinction between the fantastic and the real.

15. Rixon's examples include *Buffy the Vampire Slayer, Angel, Dawson's Creek* and *Roswell High*.

16. Like *Joan of Arcadia*, the postfeminist series *Tru Calling* (which is examined in Chapter 5) introduced a mysterious male character who functioned as an antithesis to the heroine.

Chapter 7

1. The show first aired in March 2004 and ended in April 2004, since it was cancelled by the Fox network. However, a DVD of 13 episodes, including nine that never aired, has since been produced (20th Century–Fox, 2005). The series also aired completely on Sky1 in the U.K., on the religious channel Vision TV in Canada, and in the U.S. on Logo (2005) which showcases gay and lesbian programs. Stan Beeler argues that the curious variety of "subcultures" (religious network, gay and lesbian) that have responded to the series help reinforce its cult status. Stan Beeler, "Wonderfalls," *The Essential Cult Television Reader*.

2. The American money and images of the American flag on postcards are indicators that the series is supposed to be set in the United States; however, the series was filmed in Toronto and in the Canadian Niagara region ("Canada's Vision TV Will Show All of *Wonderfalls*").

3. The term "Brechtian distanciation" is used in television studies to describe series such as *It's Garry Shandling's Show* (1988–90) and *Malcolm in the Middle* (2000–2006) where a "watered-down form of Brechtian distanciation" (Butler, 49) or the *Verfremdungseffekt* is presented by comic remarks made directly to the television viewer by the characters (Butler, 49).

4. The trickster "behaves in a most anti-social manner, systematically violating all accepted human values, and relies on cunning deceptions and mean tricks to reach his goals" (Penny Petrone, *Native Literature in Canada*, 16).

5. When the family discovers that Jaye fainted at work, they appear less sympathetic. Her brother's response is "It's not physical, it's emotional — she lives in a trailer park" and her father, a doctor, asks her, "When was the last time you had an orgasm?" (1.1). The brother's explanation suggests an emotional breakdown while the father's is linked exclusively to a physical reason. The father's explanation is more disturbing than the brother's focus on Jaye's environment since it suggests that not having sex must affect a woman's stability, but the comment serves more as a way of ridiculing the father's outdated, sexist ideas than Jaye's sexuality.

6. The death and subsequent "rebirth" of the female protagonist George in *Dead Like Me* (2003–2004) as a Grim Reaper makes her value experiences she once took for granted or dismissed as irrelevant. Bryan Fuller, one of the producers of *Wonderfalls*, was executive producer and one of the writers for *Dead Like Me*.

7. As Marian Bredin indicates in her conference paper "Popular Memory and Aboriginal Heritage: A Case Study of the Niagara Falls Indian Village," the story behind the Maid of the Mist, as depicted on a postcard, circa 1924, was an example of romantic idealization of native people: "A highly sexualized image as part of the popular narrative of an Iroquois maiden sacrificed by her father to appease the angry spirits. The story conveys a message of barbarism of Aboriginal people along with the romantic notion of 'ancient' traditions. The misty maiden is clearly an extension of the natural landscape. The representation of the Maid of the Mist as an 'Indian legend' was finally dropped by the Niagara Falls tour boat company in 1995." http://butler.ac.brocku.ca/pcn/MemoryAndHeritage/IndianVillage.html

Chapter 8

1. See Tom Ruffles' book *Ghost Images: Cinema of the Afterlife* for further discussions of films about ghosts and mediumship.

2. *The Sixth Sense* (1999) starring Bruce Willis was a seminal film about a young boy's ability to see "dead people." While it did not feature a psychic woman as its focus, it has undoubtedly had an impact on other directors and television series creators who depict psychic characters. One of the directors of the series *Afterlife* acknowledges that they took their cue from *The Sixth Sense* so that the audience would not know if an event was "real" or "supernatural" (*Afterlife: Behind the Scenes*).

3. The madonna whore complex describes a man's idealization of woman on the one hand (something akin to Pygmalion's desire for ideal beauty that could not be found in any real woman) versus woman as a sexual creature with evil intentions. It is important to note that Annie's ethics apply equally to women like Valerie Barksdale and to men since she had earlier spoken out against Donnie Barksdale

rotting in jail for a murder that she believes he had not committed, despite his vile treatment of Annie.

4. Donnie breaks into Annie's house, vandalizes it and threatens to skin her children.

5. Interestingly, if there is any feminist solidarity in this film, it also occurs in a third space since Annie's visions of Jessica King's murder allow her to connect with Jessica and sympathize with her ("No one deserves that") in a way that was not really possible when she met Jessica before her murder. Social class differences between Jessica, the daughter of a wealthy man, and Annie, the town psychic struggling to make ends meet, are quite obvious and these women would probably have had difficulty relating to one another.

6. Mennan Yapo the director has indicated that in order to provide some sense of continuity in the filming of *Premonition*, he chose to shoot the footage in the order of the chronological timeline since the film's scrambled narrative presented enough challenges. "Glimpses of the Future: Making *Premonition*." Special Features. *Premonition* DVD.

7. Although the priest's reference to the Greeks' view of some people as empty vessels is not gender-specific, the concept of the empty vessel was applied by the Greek physician Hippocrates to women to explain the disease known as hysteria. In *Diseases of Women*, he argued that if the womb was not filled (as in the case of unmarried women) it could wander and cause this condition (Lefkowitz and Fant, 233–240). While it is possible to read the depiction of Linda's experience of premonitions as the manifestation of hysteria, this limited kind of reading ignores the film's subversion of the hysterical woman by representing Linda as a woman who resists her psychiatrist and whose visions or premonitions prove true. Furthermore, the concept of the empty vessel has been used to describe the spiritual experiences

of both men and women in Western and Eastern belief systems.

8. Mennan Yapo says that "in terms of Hollywood you would expect her to save him and the film goes totally the opposite and says no you can't change the course of time" ("Glimpses of the Future: Making *Premonition*").

9. Apparently Sandra Bullock had input in this creative decision ("Glimpses of the Future: Making *Premonition*").

Chapter 9

1. The W Network website indicates that their target audience consists of women "aged 25–54" and "18–49" (*http://www.network.com/corporate/producer_info/index.asp*).

2. *Psychic Investigators* has been classified as reality TV (Kenneth Nguyen).

The producers of *Rescue Mediums* apparently called the show "a reality-based half-hour television show" ("Haunted Ontario") and Brian Medel, writing for *The Halifax Chronicle Herald* newspaper, calls *Rescue Mediums* a "reality TV show" as well. The "reality-based" label is not included in the description of the show on a *Rescue Mediums* website, however (*http://www.rescuemediums.com/index2.html*).

3. Dowsing is usually defined as searching for hidden water with a forked twig, but in this case it suggests the use of an object to pinpoint a location on a map.

4. Jonathan Bignell lists some of the "codes and conventions" of a reality TV show like *Crimewatch UK*. These include "photographs of stolen property, security camera footage and physical clues [that] also appear in television police fiction" (197). He also mentions the fictional aspect of reconstructions of the crime in these reality shows.

5. While some scholars have highlighted the focus on individualism in postfeminist culture or among third wave feminists (Shugart, Waggoner and O'Brien

Hallstein), Jennifer Purvis argues that feminists of the third wave have remained committed to "coherent" feminist political agendas (100).

6. See Susan J. Wolfe's essay on the balance of the individual and the collective in *Charmed*: "*Charm*ing the Elders: Girl Power for Second-Wave Feminists."

7. In *Fantasy: The Literature of Subversion*, Rosemary Jackson mentions the familiar argument that fantasy is often regarded as escapist and purely entertaining and that it has been dismissed for not highlighting real-world issues. She argues, however, that fantasy does correspond to so-called real-life concerns: "Like any other texts, a literary fantasy is produced within and determined by social context" (3).

Chapter 10

1. This is the kind of meta-textuality or meta-reference with which postmodern audiences are all too familiar. Many contemporary television shows make self-reflexive references to television within their narratives. In *The Sopranos*, for example, organized crime head Tony Soprano regularly watches TV shows with content that can be juxtaposed in an ironic manner to the narrative or storyline of his character.

2. Psychics have often graced the stage of established talk shows, and someone like Michelle Whitedove "has hosted her own spiritual talk shows: 'Between Worlds' on UPN-TV, and 'Angel Talk' on PAX-TV since 2001." *http://www.safesearching.com/michellewhitedove/about/*

3. One of the more obvious comparisons one could make in an analysis of *Medium* is between the character of Allison Dubois and Allison Dubois, the actual psychic on which she is based. The fact that the character has the same name as the "real psychic" follows in the spirit of a show like *Da Vinci's Inquest*, based on a famous LA coroner. (This interest in the

"real" as evidenced by the surge of reality shows, as well as the existence of real-life psychics and their programs, may be the basis for this popular interest in a show such as *Medium* that combines the psychic figure with the suspenseful plots of a detective series.) The real Allison Dubois has also written books about her experiences as a medium: *Don't Kiss Them Goodbye* (New York: Simon & Schuster, 2004) and *We Are Their Heaven: Why the Dead Never Leave Us* (New York: Simon & Schuster, 2006). While it may be of interest to compare and contrast the real Allison with her fictional representation (especially since both are mothers), such comparisons between real people and fictional creations assume that television or film will necessarily capture the "truth" about a real individual just because the character is based on a real person. This chapter-length analysis of *Medium* is much more interested in exploring the female psychic in a larger context of how such a visionary has been constructed in history and myth, and how *Medium* incorporates and criticizes some of these key features while also promising to go beyond these limitations. An analysis of the series will point out how Allison resists the stereotype of "bad" motherhood but this discussion of *Medium* also reveals how images of the "bad" mother pervade the series.

4. Jennifer Baumgardner and Amy Richards suggest that third wave feminism (or postfeminism) has a more inclusive approach than second wave feminism: "As Third Wave women, we no longer have to measure our success by how far away we got from our mothers' lives" (*Manifesta*, 214); yet *Medium* suggests that some of the criticism of "mothers" still prevails in this era, even among other women.

5. In *Charmed*, Phoebe is a witch who has premonitions, and Cordelia in *Angel* is the character who (through demonic intervention) acquires the ability to see visions.

6. Marshall McLuhan's famous statement "the medium is the message" ("Understanding Media") can be applied to the way a medium's body and identity can become one with the message she conveys.

7. A dismissive attitude on the part of one of the female lawyers who works with Allison on police investigations further reinforces a patriarchal view of the medium as she makes reference to one psychic as another "Tom, Dick and Harry Housewife" (1.1).

8. Campbell's work on myth has had a significant impact on myth studies and on the popular study of myth. It draws on Jungian views of myth (discussions of the unconscious). Bill Moyers' interviews with Campbell in *The Power of Myth* (in book and home video format) have included discussions on ancient myths and contemporary cultural phenomena such as *Star Wars* and the mythic significance of American architecture.

9. Shari L. Thurer draws on Neumann's ideas in her book *The Myths of Motherhood: How Culture Reinvents the Good Mother*. She says that "in the image of the Great Mother ... Neumann saw an archetypal figure, an eternal symbol, a signifier of psychic issues we all associate with mothers" (24).

10. The series creator Glenn Gordon Caron says that for him, the home "was the meat of the thing. Family is a big part of who she [Allison] is" (McKeon). A number of *Medium* fans and reviewers have commented on how Allison's depiction as a mother is "realistic" because when at home, she often wears rumpled clothing, and she resists the image of perfection associated with motherhood.

11. In her discussion of the genre of telefantasy programs, Catherine Johnson indicates that they "contain significant representations of 'fantastic' events and objects that confound culturally accepted notions of what is believed to be real" (4). For example, while "some believe in alien abductions, there is a broader cultural consensus that aliens do not visit Earth" (4). This statement could be rephrased to accommodate *Medium* and to argue on behalf of its fantastic quality. While some people believe in the power of mediums or psychics to see dead people, the "broader cultural consensus" would probably be that this is not possible.

12. According to Giannetti and Leach, the classical double plot line often included a romantic love story that was developed to parallel the main line of action (43). In *Medium*, there is usually a plot line that incorporates a police case, and a plot line of a more personal, family-oriented nature.

Chapter 11

1. Donna Haraway conceives of a cyborg as half-human, half-machine ("A Cyborg Manifesto," 1991). Melinda also demonstrates an important human quality: the ability to reach out to people and to spirits. Her use of computer technology as a tool to help with her research into the supernatural and her humanity make her a new kind of hybrid heroine in a postfeminist age. Melinda's use of technology empowers her just as it has influenced a whole generation of women who have been raised with technology at their fingertips. Third wave feminists have made use of online technology to create innovative forms of publication such as feminist ezines, periodical-style publications on the web, and blogs and websites that function as online diaries.

2. Jennifer Purvis mentions the importance of difference for third wave feminism: "[W]e may rethink feminism as a process of becoming, multiplying, negotiating change, and mediating difference that is open to debate and to new methods and strategies, where expressions of difference do not stagnate in disagreement and disunity" (119).

3. While Season 1 focuses on mother figures in Melinda's life, Season 3 incorporates the mythic search for the father as Melinda and her half-brother Gabriel embark on this quest.

4. The myth of Oedipus involves a son's discovery that he has unwittingly slain his father and bedded his mother. By marrying his mother, he has become one with the father and at the end of Sophocles' play *Oedipus Rex* he experiences atonement for his crime by blinding himself and honoring the sentence he had imposed on the murderer of King Laius (his father); he is driven out of Thebes.

5. A nanny's experiences are described in the novel *Nanny Diaries* (2003), co-written by former nannies Emma McLaughlin and Nicola Kraus. *Searching for Mary Poppins: Women Write About the Relationship Between Mothers and Nannies* (2007), edited by Susan Davis and Gina Hyams, is a collection of essays by women writers (including third wave feminist Rebecca Walker) who discuss their relationships with nannies.

6. "Free Fall" is an eerie evocation of the people who fell from the heights of the burning Twin Towers in New York. In one of her visions, Melinda actually sees a man falling from a theatre building. The image of this falling man brings to mind the controversial photographs of people falling from the World Trade Center, including the one known as "The Falling Man" that appeared in the September 2003 issue of *Esquire* magazine.

7. E. Ann Kaplan calls for the development of a "fourth wave" feminism that would bring "second and third wave feminists together" (55) to recognize global interconnectedness "in the era of terror" (56).

Chapter 12

1. Lesley Sharpe, the lead actress in the series, won a Royal Television Society award and a Monte-Carlo TV Festival Golden Nymph award for best actress in a television series. Producer Murray Ferguson won a Monte-Carlo TV Festival award for best European producer of a drama series.

2. The study of psychic phenomena has burgeoned in the U.K. The College of Psychic Studies in London has witnessed an increase in courses over the last ten years, from 11 courses a term to 61 courses. *Living with the Dead (Psychic Night)*. Producer-Director: Damon Thomas. Channel 4, U.K. August 23, 2003.

3. See the discussion of Bhabha's term in the introduction of this book.

4. Alison Mundy could be a postmodern extension of the madwoman in the attic from Charlotte Brontë's novel *Jane Eyre*. Like *Hex*, *Afterlife* is a British series and may be influenced by the nineteenth century depiction of madness in Brontë's novel.

5. Alison comes bursting into Robert's tutorial with a student when she re-experiences the trauma of the train accident she survived six years earlier (1.6).

6. There was a 1981–1987 Canadian series about a psychic detective called *Seeing Things*.

7. Children's fantasy series set in the U.K. such as *The Lion, the Witch and the Wardrobe* and *Harry Potter and the Philosopher's Stone* emphasize the mythic presence of the train in British society, probably because train travel is so common in the U.K. as opposed to North American society where the car is "king."

8. Volk indicated that he had "designed the 'arc' of the series very much that episode six would be a big climax." He also said, "Early on I had the last scene of the last episode really clearly in my mind, of Alison being carried out of the séance house into the middle of the road by this big guy in a plastic mask... Of course we all wanted there to be the possibility of doing more, but I also wanted there to be

an 'ending' if we didn't get the chance to continue."

9. The topics of normalcy and madness were explored in "Normal Again" (6.17), one of the most controversial *Buffy the Vampire Slayer* episodes. The storyline places Buffy and the audience in the position of wondering whether her life fighting vampires is her reality, or whether it is merely an imagined story, since the episode also depicts Buffy in another reality, a mental hospital where the doctors are treating her for schizophrenia.

10. Volk's other projects included work in the fantasy genre such as the film *Gothic*

and a television story called "Massage" for the BBC1 *Ghosts* series.

11. Todorov's theory of the fantastic is dependent on the reader's hesitation between an uncanny/natural explanation of a seemingly supernatural event and an acceptance of the supernatural.

12. Amber Kinser says that many of the women of the third wave generation have "grown up with a vocabulary for talking about sexism, reproductive rights, sexual autonomy, fair treatment, lesbian-gay-bisexual-transgender issues, workplace equity, global awareness and intersections of race, class and gender" (134).

Bibliography

Abbott, Stacey. *Reading Angel: The TV Spin-off with a Soul.* London: I.B. Tauris, 2005.
_____. "Walking the Fine Line Between Angel and Angelus," *Slayage* 9 (August 2003) 3.1 *http://slayageonline.com/essays/slayage9/Abbott.htm*
Acosta, Belinda. "TV Eye: Midlife Geists." *The Austin Chronicle. http://www.austin chronicle.com/gyrobase/Issue/column?oid=oid%3A426622*
Aeschylus. *Agamemnon.* Trans. Robert Fagles. New York: Viking Press, 1975.
_____. *The Oresteia.* Trans. Robert Fagles. New York: Viking Press, 1966.
Afterlife: Behind the Scenes. Dir. Louise Ireland. Prod. Vernon Antcliff. ITV Productions for ITV3. 2006
"Afterlife." Episode Synopsis and Directors Notes. *http://afterlife.itv.com*
"Angelus Arcanum." *Fireflyfans.net* Forum. http://www.fireflyfans.net/thread.asp?b= 10&t=3687)
Armour, Stephanie. "Generation Y: They've arrived at work with a new attitude." *USA Today. http://www.usatoday.com/money/workplace/2005-11-06-gen-y_x.htm*
Arts Education Partnership. *http://www.aep-arts.org/resources/toolkits/thirdspace/*
Bartel, Pauline. *Spellcasters: Witches and Witchcraft in History, Folklore, and Popular Culture.* Dallas: Taylor Trade Publishing, 2000.
Baum, L. Frank. *The Wizard of Oz.* New York: Ballantine Books, 1956.
Baumgardner, Jennifer, and Amy Richards. *Manifesta: Young Women, Feminism, and the Future.* New York: Farrar, Straus and Giroux, 2000.
Bavidge, Jenny. "Chosen Ones: Reading the Contemporary Teen Heroine." *Teen TV: Genre, Consumption and Identity.*
Beeler, Karin. "Old Myths, New Powers: Images of Second-Wave and Third-Wave Feminism in *Charmed" Investigating Charmed: The Magic Power of TV.* Eds. Karin Beeler and Stan Beeler. London: I.B. Tauris, 2007.
_____, and Stan Beeler, eds. *Investigating Charmed: The Magic Power of TV.* London: I.B. Tauris, 2007.
Beeler, Stan. "Outing Lorne: Performance for the Performers," *Reading Angel: The TV Spin-Off with a Soul.* Ed. Stacey Abbott. London: I.B. Tauris, 2005.
_____. *Wonderfalls.* In *The Essential Cult Television Reader.* Ed. David Lavery. University of Kentucky Press (forthcoming).
Berry, Mary Frances. *The Politics of Parenthood: Child Care, Women's Rights, and the Myth of the Good Mother.* New York: Viking Penguin, 1993.
Bhabha, Homi K. *The Location of Culture.* London: Routledge, 1994.
Bignell, Jonathan. *An Introduction to Television Studies.* London, New York: Routledge, 2004.

Bibliography

Blaetz, Robin. *Visions of the Maid: Joan of Arc in American Film and Culture*. Charlottesville: University Press of Virginia, 2001.

Borges, Jorge Luis. "The Garden of Forking Paths." Ed. Anthony Kerrigan. Story Translated by Helen Temple and Ruthven Todd. *Ficciones*. New York. Grove Press, 1962.

Bredin, Marian. "Popular Memory and Aboriginal Heritage: A Case Study of the Niagara Falls Indian Village. Paper presented to the 2004 Southwest/Texas Popular Culture/American Popular Culture Association Annual Conference, San Antonio, Texas. April 8, 2004. http://butler.ac.brocku.ca/pcn/MemoryAndHeritage/IndianVillage.html

Brooks, Ann. *Postfeminism: Feminism, Cultural Theory and Cultural Forms*. London, New York: Routledge, 1997.

Buckman, Alyson R. "'Big Damn Heroes' and Little Witches: The Male Gaze and Female Language in Joss Whedon's *Firefly*." *Investigating Firefly and Serenity*. Eds. Rhonda Wilcox and Tanya Cochran. London: I.B. Tauris, 2008.

_____. "'It's just an object. It doesn't mean what you think': The Male Gaze and Female Language in *Firefly* and *Serenity*." Conference paper. Southwest/Texas Popular Culture Association. February 2006.

Bussel, Rachel Kramer. "Rebecca Walker: Baby Love and Other Observations from Writing While Pregnant." 04/30/2007 Independent Media Institute. http://www.rebeccawalker.com/article_2007_Baby-Love.htm

Butler, Alban. *Butler's Lives of the Saints*, cited in David A. Leeming, *Mythology: The Voyage of the Hero*. Philadelphia: Lippincott, 1973.

Butler, Jeremy G. *Television: Critical Methods and Applications*. Second Edition. London, New Jersey: Lawrence Erlbaum Associates, 2002.

Campbell, Joseph. *The Hero with a Thousand Faces*. Princeton: Princeton University Press, 1972.

_____. *The Power of Myth*. Ed. Betty Sue Flowers. New York: Anchor Books, 1991.

Caputi, Jane. "On Psychic Activism: Feminist Mythmaking." In *The Feminist Companion to Mythology* Ed. Carolyne Larrington. London: Pandora Press, 1992.

Carroll, Valerie A. *Re-Presenting and Representing on Girl Power TV: Examining Portrayals of Resistance and Domination from "Dark Angel," "Charmed" and "Buffy the Vampire Slayer."* Dissertation. Saint Louis University, 2005.

Chevalier, Jean, and Alain Gheerbrant. *The Penguin Dictionary of Symbols*. 1982. Trans. John Buchanan-Brown. London: Penguin, 1994.

"Christine Hamlett." *http://www.starnow.co.uk/profile/ProfileDetailPrint.aspx?m_id= 582911* (No longer available).

Clark, Stuart, ed. *Languages of Witchcraft, Narrative, Ideology and Meaning in Early Modern Culture*. London: Macmillan Press, 2001.

Cooke, Lez. *British Television Drama: A History*. London: BFI, 2003.

Corner, John. *Critical Ideas in Television Studies*. Oxford: Clarendon Press, 1999.

Cotterell, Arthur, and Rachel Storm. *The Ultimate Encyclopedia of Mythology*. N.p. Anness Publishing Limited, 1999.

"Crazy Is as Crazy Does: River Tam." *Television Without Pity: Firefly*. http://forums.televisionwithoutpity.com

Cruisie, Jennifer. "The Assassination of Cordelia Chase." In *Five Seasons of Angel: Science Fiction and Fantasy Writers Discuss Their Favorite Vampire*. Ed. Glenn Yeffeth. Dallas: BenBella Books, 2004.

Bibliography

Daly, Mary. *Beyond God the Father: Toward a Philosophy of Women's Liberation.* Boston: Beacon Press, 1973.

_____. *Gyn/Ecology: The Metaethics of Radical Feminism.* New York: Anchor Press, 1979.

Davis, Glyn, and Kay Dickinson. *Teen TV: Genre, Consumption and Identity.* London: BFI Publications, 2004.

Donovan, Kate. "Evil: Can't Live with It, Can't Quite Vanquish It." *Totally Charmed.* Ed. Jennifer Crusie. Dallas: BenBella Books, 2005.

DuBois, Allison. *Don't Kiss Them Good-bye.* New York: Simon and Schuster, 2004.

Du Pré, Athena. *Humor and the Healing Arts: A Multimethod Analysis of Humor Use in Health Care.* New Jersey, London: Lawrence Erlbaum Associates, 1998.

Early, Frances H., and Kathleen Kennedy. *Athena's Daughters: Television's New Women Warriors.* Syracuse: Syracuse University Press, 2003.

Elliot, Lisa M. "Transcendental Television? A Discussion of *Joan of Arcadia.*" *Journal of Media & Religion* 4.1 (2005): 1–12.

Espenson, Jane, ed. *Finding Serenity: Anti-heroes, Lost Shepherds and Space Hookers in Joss Whedon's Firefly.* Dallas: BenBella Books, 2004.

Fagles, Robert, and W.B. Stanford. "A Reading of the *Oresteia*: The Serpent and the Eagle." In *The Oresteia* by Aeschylus. Trans. Robert Fagles. New York: Viking Press, 1966.

Faux, Marian. *Childless by Choice: Choosing Childlessness in the Eighties.* New York: Anchor Press/Doubleday, 1984.

Feasey, R. "Watching *Charmed*: Why Teen Television Appeals to Women." *Journal of Popular Film and Television* 34.1 (2006): 2–9.

Flower, Michael. *The Seer in Ancient Greece.* University of California Press, 2008.

_____, and John Marincola, eds. *Herodotus: Histories Book IX.* Cambridge University Press, 2003.

Frye, Northrop. *Anatomy of Criticism: Four Essays.* Princeton: Princeton University Press, 1957.

Garrison, E.K. "U.S. Feminism-Grrrl Style! Youth (Sub)Cultures and the Technologies of the Third Wave." *Feminist Studies* (2000): 26.1: 141–170.

Gauld, Alan. *Mediumship and Survival : A Century of Investigations.* Paladin, 1982.

Giannetti, Louis, and Jim Leach. *Understanding Movies.* Second Canadian Edition. Toronto: Prentice Hall, 2001.

Gibbs, John, and Douglas Pye, eds. *Style and Meaning: Studies in the Detailed Analysis of Film.* Manchester: Manchester University Press, 2005.

"Glimpses of the Future: Making Premonition." Special Features. *Premonition.* Dir. Mennan Yapo. DVD. 2007.

Gonick, Marnina. "Between 'Girl Power' and 'Reviving Ophelia': Constituting the Neoliberal Girl Subject." *NWSA Journal* 18.2 (Summer 2006): 1–23.

Haraway, Donna. "A Cyborg Manifesto: Science, Technology, and Socialist-Feminism in the Late Twentieth Century." *Simians, Cyborgs, and Women.* New York: Routledge, 1991.

Harde, Roxanne, and Erin Harde. "Voices and Visions: A Mother and Daughter Discuss Coming to Feminism and Being Feminist." In *Catching a Wave: Reclaiming Feminism for the 21st Century.* Eds. Rory Cooke Dicker and Alison Piepmeier. Boston: Northeastern University Press, 2003.

Hart, Hugh. "Sassy Samaritan, talking toys." http://fan-sites.org/wonderfalls/sassy.html

Bibliography

"Haunted Ontario." *http://hauntedontario.netfirms.com/rescuemediums.htm*

Helford, Elyce Rae. "Postfeminism and the Female Action-Adventure Hero: Positioning *Tank Girl*" in *Future Females, The Next Generation: New Voices and Velocities in feminist Science Fiction Criticism*. Ed. Marleen Barr. Lanham: Rowman and Littlefield, 1999.

Henry, Astrid. *Not My Mother's Sister: Generational Conflict and Third-Wave Feminism*. Bloomington: Indiana University Press, 2004.

Hesford, Wendy. *Framing Identities: Autobiography and the Politics of Pedagogy*. Minneapolis: University of Minnesota Press, 1999.

Heywood, Leslie, and Jennifer Drake, eds. *Third Wave Agenda: Being Feminist, Doing Feminism*. Minneapolis: University of Minneapolis Press, 1997.

Hills, Matt. *Fan Cultures*. London and New York: Routledge, 1999.

_____, and Rebecca Williams. "*Angel*'s Monstrous Mothers and Vampires with Souls: Investigating the Abject in 'Television Horror.'" *Reading Angel: The TV Spin-off with a Soul*. Ed. Stacey Abbott. Palgrave Macmillan, 2005.

Hodgkin, Katharine. "Reasoning with Unreason: Visions, Witchcraft, and Madness in Early Modern England." In *Languages of Witchcraft*.

Hollows, Joanne, and Rachel Moseley, eds. *Feminism in Popular Culture*. Oxford: Berg, 2006.

Holman, C. Hugh, and William Harmon. *A Handbook to Literature*. Sixth Edition. New York, London: Macmillan, 1992.

Holohan, Christine. *A Voice from the Grave: The Unseen Witness in the Jacquie Poole Murder Case*. Dunshaughlin, Co. Meath, IE: Maverick House, 2006.

Hutcheon, Linda. *The Canadian Postmodern*. Don Mills: Oxford University Press, 1988.

_____. "Postmodernism." In *Encyclopedia of Contemporary Literary Theory: Approaches, Scholars, Terms*. Ed. Irena R. Makaryk. Toronto: University of Toronto Press, 1993.

Innes, Sherrie A. *Geek Chic: Smart Women in Popular Culture*. New York: Palgrave Macmillan, 2007.

Jackson, Rosemary. *Fantasy: The Literature of Subversion*. London, New York: Routledge, 1981.

Jancovich, Mark, and James Lyons. *Quality Popular Television: Cult TV, the Industry and Fans*. London: British Film Institute, 2003.

"Joan of Arc, 1915." *New York City Public Art Curriculum*. http://www.blueofthesky.com/publicart/works/joanofarc.htm 14/05/2005

Joan of Arcadia. *TV Tome*. http://www.tvtome.com. 15/05/2005

Johnson, Catherine. *Telefantasy*. London: British Film Institute, 2005.

Johnson, Merri Lisa. *Third Wave Feminism and Television: Jane Puts It in a Box*. London: I.B. Tauris, 2007.

Jones, Sara Gwenllian, and Roberta E. Pearson, eds. "Introduction." *Cult Television*. Minneapolis, London: University of Minnesota Press, 2004.

Kaplan, E. Ann. "Feminist Futures: Trauma, the Post-9/11 World and a Fourth Feminism." *Journal of International Women's Studies* 4.2 (April 2003): 46–59.

Kaye, Debra. "Childlessness Transformed: Stories of Alternative Parenting: A Cross-Cultural and Historical Overview of the Roles of Childless People." http://www.eheart.com/BOOKS/childless/history.html

Kinser, Amber. "Negotiating Spaces For/Through Third Wave Feminism" *NWSA Journal* 16.3 (Fall 2004): 124–153.

Bibliography

Kord, Susanne, and Elisabeth Krimmer. *Hollywood Divas, Indie Queens and TV Heroines: Contemporary Screen Images of Women.* Lanham: Rowman and Littlefield, 2004.

Larrington, Carolyne, ed. *The Feminist Companion to Mythology.* London: Pandora Press, 1992.

Lavery, David. *Reading the Sopranos.* London: I.B. Tauris, 2006.

Leeming, David. *Mythology: The Voyage of the Hero.* Third edition. New York: Oxford University Press, 1998.

Lefkowitz, Mary R., and Maureen B. Fant. *Women's Life in Greece & Rome: A Source Book in Translation.* Second edition. Baltimore: Johns Hopkins University Press, 1982, 1992.

Lotz, Amanda D. "Postfeminist Television Criticism: Rehabilitating Critical Terms and Identifying Postfeminist Attributes." *Feminist Media Studies* 1.1 (2001): 105–21.

Makaryk, Irena R. ed. *Encyclopedia of Contemporary Literary Theory: Approaches, Scholars, Terms.* Toronto: University of Toronto Press, 1993.

"Making of *Hex*." *Hex.* The Complete First Season. London: Shine/Sony Pictures Television International. 2005.

McKenna, Susan E. "The Queer Insistence of Ally McBeal: Lesbian Chic, Postfeminism, and Lesbian Reception." *Communication Review* 5.4 (2002): 285–314.

McKeon Charkalis, Diana. "The Mother in the 'Medium.'" 20 June 2006. *USA Today.* http://www.usatoday.com

McLuhan, Marshall. "Understanding Media." *Essential McLuhan.* Eds. Eric McLuhan and Frank Zingrone, New York: Basic Books, 1995.

Mead, Margaret. *Male & Female: A Study of the Sexes in a Changing World.* Greenwood, 1971. Reproduction of 1949 edition.

Medel, Brian. "Hey Ghost, Smile for TV." *The Chronicle Herald.* May 30, 2007. http://209.85.173.104/search?q=cache:DBRQ9mYl2s0J:www.loyalistinnshel burne.com/docs/herald_rescue.pdf+brian+medel+hey+ghost&hl=en&ct=clnk&cd =1&gl=ca&client=firefox-a

Meyer, Michaela. "'Something Wicca This Way Comes': Audience Interpretation of a Marginalized Religious Philosophy on *Charmed* in *Investigating Charmed.* Eds. Karin Beeler and Stan Beeler. London: I.B. Tauris, 2007.

Mittell, Jason. *Genre and Television: From Cop Shows to Cartoons in American Culture.* New York, London: Routledge, 2004.

Moseley, Rachel. "Glamorous Witchcraft: Gender and Magic in Teen Film and Television." *Screen* 43.4 (Winter 2002): 403–422.

"Most Believe in Psychic Phenomena" *CBS News.* April 28, 2002. http://www.cbs news.com/stories/2002/04/29/opinion/polls/main507515.shtml

Muir, John Kenneth. "Raising Cain." January 24, 2006. http://reflectionsonfilmand television.blogspot.com/search?q=medium+raising+cain

_____. "TV Review: *Hex* (BBC America)." August 18, 2006. *http://reflectionsonfilmand television.blogspot.com/2006/08/tv-review-hex-bbc*-america.html

Mulvey, Laura. "Repetition and Return: Textual Analysis and Dougals Sirk in the Twenty-First Century." In *Style and Meaning: Studies in the Detailed Analysis of Film.* Manchester: Manchester University Press, 2005. Gibbs and Pye, eds. 228–43.

Neale, Steve. *Hollywood and Genre.* London: Routledge, 2000.

Negra, Diane. "'Quality Postfeminism?' Sex and the Single Girl on HBO." *Genders* 39 (2004). *http://www.genders.org/g39/g39_negra.html*

Bibliography

Neumann, Erich. *The Great Mother: an Analysis of the Archetype.* Princeton University Press, 1963.

Nguyen, Kenneth. "Psychic Investigators." January 11, 2007. *http://www.smh.com.au/news/tv-reviews/psychic*-investigators/2007/01/10/1168105041043.html

O'Connor, Mickey. "Put an Eye Out" http://www.ew.com/ew/article/0,,1063195,00.html

Pacatte, Rose. *"Joan of Arcadia:* An Interview with Its Catholic Producer." *St. Anthony Messenger.* http://wwww.americancatholic.org/Messenger/Mar2005/Feature1.asp

Petrone, Penny. *Native Literature in Canada: From the Oral Tradition to the Present.* Toronto: Oxford University Press, 1990.

Pomeroy, Sarah B. *Goddesses, Whores, Wives, and Slaves: Women in Classical Antiquity.* New York: Schocken Books, 1975.

"Power of *Charmed.*" http: //www.thepowerofcharmed.com.

Powers, Meredith A. *The Heroine in Western Literature: The Archetype and Her Reemergence in Modern Prose.* Jefferson: McFarland, 1991.

Purkiss, Diane. *The Witch in History: Early Modern and Twentieth-Century Representations.* London, New York: Routledge, 1996.

_____. "Women's Rewriting of Myth." In *The Feminist Companion to Mythology.* Ed. Carolyne Larrington. 441–457.

Purvis, Jennifer. "Grrrls and Women Together in the Third Wave: Embracing the Challenges of Intergenerational Feminism(s)." *NWSA Journal* 16.3 (Fall 2004): 93–123.

Rabkin, Eric S., ed. *Fantastic Worlds: Myths, Tales and Stories.* London: Oxford University Press, 1979.

Rambo, Elizabeth L. "'Queen C' in Boys' Town: Killing the Angel in Angel's House." *Slayage* 23 6.3 (Spring 2007) http://slayageonline.com/essays/slayage23/Rambo.htm

Rixon, Paul. "The Changing Face of American Television Programmes on British Screens." *Quality Popular Television: Cult TV, the Industry and Fans.* Ed. Mark Jancovitch and James Lyons. London: British Film Institute, 2003.

Ruffles, Tom. *Ghost Images: Cinema of the Afterlife.* Jefferson: McFarland, 2004.

Sancho, Jane. *Beyond Entertainment?: Research Into the Acceptability of Alternative Beliefs, Psychic and Occult Phenomena on Television.* London: Independent Television Commission, 2001.

Schofield Clark, Lynn. *From Angels to Aliens: Teenagers, the Media, and the Supernatural.* New York: Oxford University Press, 2003.

Sherman, Yael. "Tracing the Carnival Spirit in Buffy the Vampire Slayer: Feminist Reworkings of the Grotesque." *Thirdspace* 3.2 (March 2004) http://www.thirdspace.ca/articles/3_2_sherman.htm

Shugart, Helene A., Catherine Egley Waggoner, and D. Lynn O'Brien Hallstein. "Mediating Third-Wave Feminism: Appropriation as Postmodern Media Practice." *Critical Studies in Media Communication* 18.2 (June 2001): 194–210.

Smith, Barbara. "Greece." In *The Feminist Companion to Mythology.* Ed. Carolyne Larrington. London: Pandora Press, 1992.

Spence, Lewis. *Encyclopedia of Occultism and Parapsychology.* New York: Dover Publications, 2003.

Stacey, Judith. "The Making and Unmaking of Modern Families." In *Family: Critical Concepts in Sociology.* Ed. David Cheal. London/New York: Routledge, 2003.

Bibliography

Stadler, Jane. "Becoming the Other: Multiculturalism in Joss Whedon's *Angel*." http://flowtv.org?p=997

Swigart, Jane. *The Myth of the Bad Mother: Parenting Without Guilt*. New York: Doubleday, 1991.

Tasker, Yvonne, and Diane Negra. "Postfeminism and the Archive for the Future." *Camera Obscura* 62.21.2 (2006): 171–176.

Taylor, Robert B. "The Captain May Wear the Tight Pants, but It's the Gals Who Make *Serenity* Soar." In Jane Espenson, ed. *Finding Serenity: Anti-heroes, Lost Shepherds and Space Hookers in Joss Whedon's* "Firefly."

Thurer, Shari L. *The Myths of Motherhood: How Culture Reinvents the Good Mother*. Boston: Houghton Mifflin, 1994.

Tierney, Helen, ed. *Women's Studies Encyclopedia*. Westport: Greenwood Press, 1999.

Todorov, Tzvetan. *The Fantastic: A Structural Approach to a Literary Genre*. Trans. Richard Howard. Ithaca: Cornell University Press, 1973.

Twain, Mark. *Joan of Arc*. Retold by Patrice Selene. Wishbone Classics. New York: HarperCollins, 1996.

Vande Ber, Leah R. "Dramedy." *The Museum of Broadcast Communications*. http://www.museum.tv/archives/etv/D/htmlD/dramedy/dramedy.htm

Vavrus, Mary Douglas. "Opting Out Moms in the News: Selling New Traditionalism in the New Millennium." *Feminist Media Studies* 7.1 (2007): 47–63.

Volk, Stephen. "Interviews: Steve Volk — Writer of *Ghostwatch* and *Afterlife*." *Bad Psychics*. *http://badpsychics.com/thefraudfiles/modules/news/article.php?storyid=21*

W Network. *http://www.network.com/corporate/producer_info/index.asp*

Warn, Sarah. "Interview with *Wonderfalls'* Bryan Fuller." March 23, 2004. http://www.afterellen.com/People/bryanfuller-interview.html

Warner, Marina. *Joan of Arc: The Image of Female Heroism*. New York: Penguin, 1987.

"What Happens Next: Information for Kids about Separation and Divorce." Chapter Six: Blended families and extended families, foster families and guardianship. http://www.justice.gc.ca/en/ps/pad/resources/children_booklet/chap6.html

"The White Ribbon Campaign." *http://www.whiteribbon.ca/about_us/Thirdspace: A Journal of Feminist Theory and Culture*. Vancouver, B.C.

Whitedove, Michelle. http://www.safesearching.com/michellewhitedove/about/

Wilcox, Rhonda V. "God's Clothes, God's Bones: The Ethics of Representation on *Joan of Arcadia*." *Studies in Popular Culture* 28.1 (October 2005): 85–97.

_____. *Why Buffy Matters: The Art of Buffy the Vampire Slayer*. London: I.B. Tauris, 2005.

_____, and David Lavery, eds. *Fighting the Forces: What's at Stake in* Buffy the Vampire Slayer? New York: Rowman and Littlefield, 2002.

Wolfe, Susan J. "*Charm*ing the Elders: Girl Power for Second-Wave Feminists." In Beeler and Beeler, eds. *Investigating Charmed*. London: I.B. Tauris, October 2007.

Wollstonecraft, Mary. From "A Vindication of the Rights of Woman." *The Norton Anthology of Literature by Women*. 141. New York: W.W. Norton, 1985.

Wonderfalls. *TV Tome*. http://www.tvtome.com.

Wood, Julia T. *Gendered Lives: Communication, Gender and Culture*. Belmont: Wadsworth, 2005.

Wright, John C. "Just Shove Him in the Engine, or The Role of Chivalry in *Firefly*." In *Finding Serenity: Anti-heroes, Lost Shepherds and Space Hookers in Joss Whedon's* "Firefly." Ed. Jane Espenson. Dallas: BenBella Books, 2004.

Index

Index

Index

Index

Index

Index

Index

Index